Calculating Promises

Calculating Promises

THE EMERGENCE OF MODERN AMERICAN CONTRACT DOCTRINE

Roy Kreitner

STANFORD UNIVERSITY PRESS
STANFORD, CALIFORNIA
2007

Stanford University Press

Stanford, California

Library of Congress Cataloging-in-Publication Data

Kreitner, Roy.

Calculating promises : the emergence of modern American contract doctrine / Roy Kreitner.

p. cm.

Includes bibliographical references and index.

ISBN-13: 978-0-8047-5398-2 (cloth : alk. paper)

1. Contracts--United States--History. 2. Promise (Law)--United States--History. I. Title.

KF801.K74 2007
346.7302--dc22

2006025886

Typeset by Bruce Lundquist in 11/14 Adobe Garamond

For my parents

To ordain the future in advance . . . man must first have learned to distinguish necessary events from chance ones, to think causally, to see and anticipate distant eventualities as if they belonged to the present, to decide with certainty what is the goal and what the means to it, and in general be able to calculate and compute. Man himself must first of all have become *calculable, regular, necessary*, even in his own image of himself, if he is to be able to stand security for his own *future*, which is what one who promises does!

This precisely is the long story of how *responsibility* originated. The task of breeding an animal with the right to make promises evidently embraces and presupposes as a preparatory task that one first *makes* men to a certain degree necessary, uniform, like among like, regular, and consequently calculable.

—FRIEDRICH NIETZSCHE

Contents

Acknowledgments

The debts I incurred in the long process of writing this book are too numerous to list, and extend well beyond the intellectual plane. I acknowledge some of them here, however inadequately, with gladness.

This book began as a doctoral dissertation at Harvard Law School, where I had the benefit of extraordinary teaching and sensitive guidance. Were it not for Jerry Frug, who shepherded this project from before its inception, I probably would not have written a book. Bob Gordon and Duncan Kennedy were driving forces behind the research, and were it not for them it would have been a different book. Terry Fisher and Barbara Johnson were my guides into academia, and I could not have asked for better.

A number of friends and colleagues read parts of the manuscript, offering thought-provoking comments and invaluable editorial suggestions that improved the final product. While I cannot name them all, I am especially grateful to Eric Berlow, David Charny, Dick Craswell, Hanoch Dagan, Kathy Eade, Michele Graziadei, Ted Janger, Tony Kronman, Assaf Likhovski, Rick Pildes, Anne-Marie Slaughter, Chris Tomlins, and Eyal Zamir. Yishai Blank, Sharon Hannes, and Shai Lavi are direct participants in the thought processes represented in this book; their contribution goes far beyond reading the manuscript.

Conversations with Mort Horwitz, Chris Desan, and Menny Mautner had formative effects on my thinking about American legal history and contracts. I have also enjoyed unflagging support at the Law Faculty at Tel Aviv University, for which I am most grateful to my colleagues, in particular Omri Yadlin and Ariel Porat.

I presented portions of the book and received helpful comments at faculty workshops at the University of Virginia School of Law; Hebrew University; Haifa University; the Interdisciplinary Center in Herzliya; Northwestern University Law School; the Legal History Workshop at Tel Aviv University;

the Stanford Yale Junior Faculty Forum; and the Graduate Program Colloquium at Harvard Law School. Special thanks are due to Alison White, the Special Collections Librarian at the University of Virginia School of Law. The final stages of preparation of the manuscript were greatly aided by the excellent research assistance of Yael Anatot and Dan Ziv.

My deepest debt, which continues to grow daily, is to my family: parents, siblings, children, and most of all Michal. They do not always make writing easier, but their presence feeds the illusion that it might be worthwhile.

I am grateful for financial assistance from the Alon Fellowship of the Israel Council for Higher Education, the John Marshall Harlan Fellowship at New York Law School, the Mark DeWolfe Howe Fellowship Fund, the Byse Fellowship at Harvard Law School, and the TMR Network Project on "Common Principles of European Private Law."

An early version of Part One was previously published as "The Gift Beyond the Grave: Revisiting the Question of Consideration," 101 *Columbia Law Review* 1876 (2001); and a version of Part Two was published as "Speculations of Contract, or How Contract Law Stopped Worrying and Learned to Love Risk," 100 *Columbia Law Review* 1096 (2000).

Calculating Promises

Introduction

The Imagined Individual at the Borders of Contract

This book is a genealogy of the emergence of our modern conception of contract. It argues, against conventional wisdom, that our current conception of contract is not the outgrowth of gradual, piecemeal refinements of a centuries-old idea of contract. Rather, contract as we know it was shaped by a revolution in private law undertaken by classical legal scholars toward the end of the nineteenth century. Further, the revolution in contract thinking is best understood in a frame of reference wider than the rules governing the formation and enforcement of contracts. That frame of reference is a cultural negotiation over the nature of the individual subject and his role in a society undergoing transformation.

American lawyers typically see contract as the art of enforcing promises, believing that for the most part, "contract law is confined to *promises*," and that, "No question for the law of contracts arises unless the dispute is one over a promise."[1] The view that contract is essentially about enforcing

---

1. E. Allan Farnsworth, *Contracts* 4 (3d ed. 1999).

promises is not limited to those who believe that the independent moral force of promises forms the underlying basis of contract enforcement.[2] Instead, this common conception is shared by a wide range of scholars and observers of contract, including some who might prefer to see a retreat from the emphasis on promise. Thus, it is an oversimplification but not a wild exaggeration to claim that, "To a lawyer, a 'contract' is a legally enforceable promise."[3] But if, as Patrick Atiyah argues, contract was not always primarily about promise, how did the current conception of contract take root?[4] How did the definition of contract as enforceable promise become so obvious? I attempt to awaken these questions by highlighting the relatively technical process by which the promissory conception of contract became the taken for granted backdrop to almost all discussions of contract.

For anyone who has experienced the first year of law school and probably for a much wider public, it is difficult to imagine an alternative view of contract. The consensus over the general definition of contract is sometimes understood as evidence of its unchanging character. Yet such consensus is not the mark of the necessity of the conception itself, but rather a trace of a successful revolution, one whose effects are so ingrained that they appear completely natural. The very essence of contract seems tied inherently to the idea of enforceable promises, and any characterization that displaces the centrality of promise seems to miss the point. In this sense, historical claims that ancient, or medieval, or early modern sources on the law did not equate contract with promise are seen as evidence, not that contract was once different, but that contract was not well understood. If we believe that the essence of contract is the enforceable promise, the history of contract becomes a story of the refinement of the art of making, classifying, and enforcing promises.

Such a history of contract is written from the present to the past, or, as it were, backward. If contract *is* enforceable promise, then the law of contract can be understood teleologically, as the sometimes bumpy road along which the enforceability of promises progressed.[5] Such a teleological history

---

2. See, e.g., Melvin A. Eisenberg, "The Theory of Contracts," in *The Theory of Contract Law: New Essays* 206, 242–43, 259–64 (Peter Benson ed., 2001). For the view that the moral force of promise undergirds contract law generally, see Charles Fried, *Contract as Promise* (1981).

3. Thomas W. Joo, "Contract, Property, and the Role of Metaphor in Corporations Law," 35 *U.C. Davis L. Rev.* 779, 789 (2002).

4. P. S. Atiyah, *The Rise and Fall of Freedom of Contract* (1979).

5. See E. Allan Farnsworth, "The Past of Promise: An Historical Introduction to Contract," 69 *Colum. L. Rev.* 576 (1969). Farnsworth's history is teleological in the broad view: "Over the course of the fifteenth

makes it easy to underestimate the role of the changes in our conception of contract in generating the frame for the modern discourse of contract, and of private law generally. The frame supplied by the conception of contract is the private ordering paradigm. Within the frame of private ordering, individuals are preexisting entities with preexisting preferences or desires. They use contract as a means to achieve their preexisting ends by exchanging their entitlements.[6] The development of modern contract law, according to the teleological picture, goes hand in hand with the expansion of the free market. And that concurrent development is the story of individuals capturing the power to make their own decisions about production and consumption, in accordance with their own preferences and interests. This much is so widely accepted that it is nearly forgotten background; it becomes the very stage on which the play of contract law is enacted.

My principal aim in this book is to undermine the stability of the perspective of modern contract discourse. The key to such a process lies in a close reading of contract cases and theory, side by side. Late nineteenth-century contract theory was revolutionary, in that it instated systematic, theoretical neatness and order into a chaotic mass of materials. Theoretical extrapolations of doctrine proposed and refined a framework for abstracting and understanding contract problems. But the case law is richer than the theory: the cases cannot be explained in accordance with the simplicity offered by the new contract theory and doctrinal articulation. They consistently have to deal more explicitly with the contaminating effects of relationships, precisely those elements that theory attempts to abstract from its treatment. The lasting theoretical framework installed by late nineteenth-century scholars articulates the autonomous calculating subject; the case law

---

and sixteenth centuries the common law courts had succeeded in evolving a general basis for the enforceability of promises through the action of assumpsit. . . . [I]n view of the difficulty that mankind the world over has had in developing any general basis at all for enforcing promises, it is perhaps less remarkable that the common law developed a theory that is logically flawed than that it succeeded in developing any theory at all." Id. at 598–99.

6. Michael Trebilcock outlines the key features of the private ordering paradigm in distinguishing private ordering from traditional economies on the one hand, and command economies on the other:

> In the case of a market economy, production and consumption decisions are decentralized and depend on the myriad decisions of individual producers and consumers, acting in furtherance of individual preferences and incentives, thus minimizing the role played by social conventions or status in traditional societies and centralized information gathering and processing and coercion in command economies.

Michael J. Trebilcock, *The Limits of Freedom of Contract* 2 (1993).

offers the site for a more complex cultural negotiation of subjectivities, the site of conflict over the shape of individuality.

Contract, then, ought to be read as part of a wider cultural discourse, and at times, cultural conflict. In the late nineteenth century, the conception of contract was undergoing fundamental structural changes. At the same time, American culture more generally experienced a period of radical change and tumult surrounding the process of industrialization. The contest between labor and capital engendered by industrialization and the nationalization of the market formed a violent backdrop to wide-ranging cultural unease.[7] In conjunction with economic debates over the labor problem, there was an ongoing debate in various circles over the nature of subjectivity and individuality. On the one hand, there were proponents of a worldview that had faith in individual autonomy, and that argued that societal progress was dependent on the disciplined, autonomous self. Discipline and autonomy in this context were—with regard to the individual—keys to rationalization, elements of what Max Weber called "the specifically modern calculating attitude."[8] On the other hand, "the rationalization of urban culture and the decline of religion into sentimental religiosity further undermined a solid sense of self. For many, individual identities began to seem fragmented, diffuse, perhaps even unreal."[9] Modern subjectivity was, at the turn of the century, both an open question and a political issue.[10]

The conflict over the subject generated many responses, but complete avoidance of the issue was not an option. Contract discourse, in this respect, should be read alongside any number of elite cultural productions. There are various agenda on the table, but one recurring issue is the shape and role of the individual. Is the individual vulnerable, exposed, in need of protection? Is the individual responsible, in control? Does the individual choose freely, or succumb to pressures? Is the individual honest, or scheming? Generous, or calculating? And contract discourse is not unified within

7. One author describes the labor-capital contest at the end of the nineteenth century thus: "Tens of thousands of industrial disputes, work stoppages, lockouts, and strikes raged throughout the northern manufacturing belt during this period and contributed to what became one of the most tumultuous and violent labor experiences in the history of industrialization." Richard Franklin Bensel, *The Political Economy of American Industrialization, 1877–1900*, p. 13 (2000).

8. 1 Max Weber, *Economy and Society* 86, 107–9 (Guenther Roth and Claus Wittich eds., 1978).

9. T. J. Jackson Lears, *No Place of Grace: Antimodernism and the Transformation of American Culture, 1880–1920*, p. 32 (1981).

10. See James Livingston, *Pragmatism and the Political Economy of Cultural Revolution, 1850–1940*, pp. 80–81 (1994).

itself. At the most basic level, even elite contract discourse would be split into at least two parts. First, there is a body of scholarly work or contract theory, produced by a handful of academic lawyers; second, there are reported cases. The case law is more complex on questions of subjectivity than the scholarship, a difference I take into account in the ensuing chapters. But for purposes of introducing the work, a reductive claim should suffice: late nineteenth-century contract discourse should be read in the context of that period's cultural upheaval. The individual posited by contract thinking is both forward- and backward-looking, but in fact represents precisely those elements of individuality that fin de siècle culture in America was either rejecting or mourning the loss of.[11]

The late nineteenth century, then, is a border, a site of transition and emergence, in two distinct but related senses. First, contract law and private law generally were undergoing a thorough transformation. The dominant conception of contract was distinguishing itself from the law governing a set of defined relations (entry into which was voluntary, but whose terms were set primarily by law), and morphing into a law of private agreement, with its terms set by the parties' actual consent or extrapolation from such consent.[12] American law was busy reorganizing itself around the concept of *will*, a reorganization that yielded our familiar categorizations of property,

---

11. It is in this sense, contract discourse is of a piece with what Jackson Lears calls a half-conscious, self-deceptive and evasive pattern of faith in individual autonomy within dominant culture. See Lears, *No Place of Grace*, 17.

12. Roscoe Pound's generalization of the principle of relation as the mode of organization for common law thinking about private law is instructive, and worth quoting at length:

> If we must find a fundamental idea in the common law, it is relation, not will. If the Romanist sees all problems in terms of the will of an actor and of the logical implications of what he has willed and done, the common-law lawyer sees almost all problems—all those, indeed, in which he was not led to adopt the Romanist's point of view in the last century—in terms of a relation and of the incidents in the way of reciprocal rights and duties involved in or required to give effect to that relation. . . . [O]ur private law is the field where the idea of relation is most conspicuous as a staple juristic conception. On every side we think not of transactions but of relations. We say law of landlord and tenant, not of the contract of letting. We say master and servant, not *locatio operarum*. We say law of husband and wife or of parent and child or of guardian and ward, or for the whole, law of domestic relations, not family law. We say principal and agent, not contract of mandate; principal and surety, not contract of suretyship; vendor and purchaser, not contract of sale of land. We think and speak of the partnership relation and of the agency, liabilities, claims and duties which it involves—which give effect to it as a relation of good faith—not of a contract of *societas*. We think of the claims and duties involved in a fiduciary relation and of the legal incidents that give effect to trusteeship or executorship as a relation of good faith, not of the implications of the declaration of will involved in accepting or declaring a trust or qualifying as executor. We do not ask what are the logical deductions from the will of the parties involved in a sale of land. We ask what incidents attach in equity when the vendor-purchaser relation arises. We do not think of giving effect to the will of the parties

contract, tort, and unjust enrichment (or quasi contract) in private law.[13] Second, rapid industrialization, urbanization, the fragmentation of "island communities,"[14] and economic and class conflict set the stage for a cultural negotiation over a calculating individual subject. The interplay within legal discourse of these two aspects of late nineteenth-century American culture is the focus of this book.

The central theme I pursue is the intersection of the transformation in contract with shifts in the image of the individual subject. Whereas the dominant story is one in which expanding contractual freedom makes room for the preexisting individual, I argue instead that a particular view of contract (as individual-centered) and a particular view of the individual (as calculating, calculable, autonomous) are actually mutually reinforcing effects of historical processes that came to a head in the late nineteenth century. The novelty in the conception of contract advanced by late nineteenth-century theorists was the centrality and calculability of the individual. Contract, under this conception, is the private law of the parties to the contract: their obligations flow directly from their agreement, not merely in the sense that they have agreed to be bound, but also in that they have agreed on the specific terms that bind them. The parties, thus, are seen as making law for themselves. Analytically, this conception requires a strict distinction between those terms that the parties actually agree to and those that are imposed by law, a distinction difficult to maintain in practice. But the analytic coherence of the conception may not be the most important factor in the success of this conception of contract. Instead, the power of the conception to capture the imagination of academic lawyers

---

> to a contract of hypothecation. We consider what incidents are involved in the relation of mortagor and mortgagee and the reciprocal claims and duties that give effect thereto.
>
> We must remember that the analogy which was ever before the lawyers and judges of the formative period of our law, the typical social and legal institution of the time, was the relation of lord and man, still represented in our law by the relation of landlord and tenant. Continual resort to this analogy, consciously or subconsciously, has made the idea of relation the central idea in our traditional mode of juristic thought.

Roscoe Pound, *Interpretations of Legal History* 56–58 (1930).

13. See Duncan Kennedy, "Toward and Historical Understanding of Legal Consciousness: The Case of Classical Legal Thought in America, 1850–1940," 3 *Res. L. Sociology* 3, 7 (1980) ("The premise of Classicism was that the legal system consisted of a set of institutions, each of which had the traits of a legal actor. Each institution had been delegated by the sovereign people a power to carry out its will, which was absolute within but void outside its sphere"). Duncan Kennedy, "The Rise and Fall of Classical Legal Thought" (unpublished manuscript, 1975).

14. See Robert H. Wiebe, *The Search for Order, 1877–1920*, p. 44 (1967).

and eventually almost everybody else seems to rely on the appeal of installing a powerful individual at the center of the system.

The fact that today it requires great effort to imagine anything but the agreement of the parties as a source of obligation is a testament to the success of this revolution in the conception of contract. The success runs so deep that two ahistorical tendencies seem to form widely accepted background assumptions. The first tendency is to forget that just prior to the classical period, contract thinking was dominated by an understanding that contracts were divided into pre-ordered types according to specified relationships, whose obligations were set as a matter of law. The parties could alter these obligations at the margins, but the source of the obligations was the relation, the contours of which were societally defined. The second tendency is to read the entire history of contract from the perspective of the current dominant conception. In other words, rather than assuming that different periods have been governed by different conceptions of contract, the tendency is to read the history of contract as an evolutionary process, a progressive rationalization of the law of promissory obligation. On this reading, contract was always about individuals creating their own obligations, even though law and theory may have misperceived the actual role of the parties or the source of their obligations.

While my argument is that this reading of contract is ahistorical and thus in some sense a distortion, it is important not to overstate the case. Classical contract scholars of the late nineteenth century did not invent out of whole cloth the idea of contract as private law making. In fact, the idea was popular in jurisprudential writing for at least a hundred years, and resonates strongly at least as far back as the writing of Hobbes, and possibly back into Roman law. The point is that classical scholars made the crucial leap of connecting the idea of individuals creating their own obligation with a systemic derivation of contract doctrine.[15] They thus linked contract law with an interpretation of the idea of contract: that linkage, with the individual as its crux or its glue, still forms the heart of the dominant conception of contract.

This book focuses on issues that are traditionally considered marginal to contract. The argument, however, is that these marginal issues are crucial

15. James Gordley, *The Philosophical Origins of Modern Contract Doctrine* 160–64 (1991).

in shaping the conception of contract at its core. Marginal issues shape the conception of contract in two distinct senses. First, the very shape or content of the conception is defined in opposition to those elements that are not considered part of the core. To the extent that marginal elements may change their character, or expand in scope, they may change the basic conception. Second, a focus on issues perceived as marginal, and on that perception itself, allows us to examine the conception of contract as a structure of thought, without taking a position as to the content of the structure. The focus on marginality, in this sense, is a focus on the *framework* that creates a debate, rather than on the positions within that debate. Thus, the first sense of marginality is thematic, while the second sense is structural.

In the course of this book, I treat three conceptual issues within contract doctrine: wagers, gifts, and implied obligations or incomplete contracts. Each of these areas, according to traditional visions of what is central and peripheral in contract, represents an exceptional case. A recurrent argument offered here is that the seemingly exceptional is crucial to defining the seemingly central. Thematic marginality may be contrasted to a second, structural sense of marginality. The analysis throughout this book sidesteps mainstream concerns within contract scholarship, in that it withdraws from the accepted practice of evaluating the normative arguments regarding the boundaries between, say, enforceable and unenforceable promises. Instead, it points us toward a different set of questions, oriented around the possible effects of the framework that fixes our gaze on the boundaries between such promises. My analysis in this book is marginal, then, in the sense that it does not participate in the normative debate over what the rules of contract should be.

The justification for this sort of theoretical investigation is that the existing debate functions as a limitation. In order to advance solutions to problems within a framework that supplies its own rules for recognizing a problem, an analyst must do two related things: she must accept those rules as properly defining the scope of inquiry, and she must ignore the possible effects that the framework engenders. My claim throughout is that the framework of debate has important limiting effects, so that before we continue answering its questions, we should reevaluate the framework itself. Another way to put this is to suggest that before we continue providing answers, we should spend additional time and energy thinking about whether we are asking the right questions. This view does not imply that we should abandon the normative outlook on contracts, or the search for a quality normative theory of contract. It does, however, suggest that there is value in putting that project on hold temporarily in an attempt to dislocate it.

An example from the law of gifts should help clarify how the senses of marginality are related. In the nineteenth century, gifts were not a unified legal category, but rather sprang up in various areas of the law. An observer trying to understand the legal treatment of gifts would be faced with a series of problems of classification: should gifts be thought of alongside contracts or as a particular species of contracts? Are gifts actually a problem of property law, since they are often conducted through conveyances and often have land as their object? Are gifts mainly incidental to the law of wills? Or should they perhaps be a subcategory of the law of trusts? Complicating the classificatory problems, there were a host of gratuitous undertakings to be considered. These generally arose in the context of some kind of business arrangement, and it was clear that the participants did not experience them as gifts, but they were situations in which there was no directly bargained-for exchange.

Classical legal thinkers made order out of the chaos. According to these scholars, everything in contract could be conceptualized around two things: promise, coupled with consideration. Gift promises were important, because they defined the outer limit of enforceability. In theory, if a promise was met by a return, even a return promise (even a return promise of something insignificant), there was consideration, and therefore the original promise was enforceable, definable as contract. If there was no return, the promise was unenforceable, definable as gift. The simplicity of the formula was attractive, but its very economy made it rich in problems of application. In fact, the formula proved so problematic that contract scholars and judges have spent the intervening century arguing about where to draw the line between the enforceable and the unenforceable (literally, the question of the border of contract): should reliance on a gratuitous promise be protected? Should offers for unilateral contracts be enforceable? What should be done about gratuitous business promises, which the parties intend at the time they make them to be legally binding? How should the law treat promises to do something the promisor is already bound to do, either by contract or by law? These are the types of questions within the framework, and contracts scholars have tirelessly answered them and asked them again.

Over time, new justifications for answers have been proposed, and the answers most widely accepted have changed as well. In other words, it is arguable that contract law at the turn of the twenty-first century draws the line between enforceable and unenforceable promises in a different place from the law at the turn of the twentieth century. The framework, however, is lasting. Its staying power stems in part from the fact that it is commonly assumed to be the only framework for discussing contract. The important question that remains unasked is: what is the effect of using this particular framework to evaluate the social behavior under discussion? My claim is that the framework gives us, its speakers, a sense that obligation is the result of voluntary choice, based on rational, calculating decision making, exercised by an individual. It teaches us that other forms of obligation are marginal and exceptional. The road to obligation leads to the market, passing through promise and consideration, that is, contract, which can be distinguished sharply from obligation that arises elsewhere, through gift or status. Thus, the framework of the debate establishes the story of private ordering, with its particular conception of a calculating individual, as the master narrative of obligation in society.

The book is divided into three parts. Part One is about the law of gifts and consideration. The chapters of Part One focus on the way the technical building blocks of doctrine contribute to the erection of a conception of contract. Classical legal scholars installed consideration as the centerpiece of contract law. On the doctrinal plane, this required a simplification and rationalization of consideration doctrine, which until the late nineteenth century had been a congeries of doctrines with a range of functions. Classical legal scholars unified consideration around the binary question of the enforceability of promises. In the process, they set out a framework for contract thinking that distinguished contract from gifts and from status, or societally imposed obligation. An analysis of litigation surrounding gifts and gift promises shows that the scholarly framework could not comprehend the cases neatly. Nonetheless, the framework was successful in reorienting the conception of contract law, and while ensuing scholarship has challenged the concrete results propounded by classical scholars, the framework for thinking about contract has remained intact. By turning contract into the law of enforceable promises, the classical legal framework succeeded in establishing the calculating promisor as the subject of contract.

Part Two deals with the paradox raised by wagers for the concept of contract. Contract law is at pains to distinguish illegitimate speculation from legitimate risk allocation. At the turn of the last century, courts grappled with speculation in two important areas of contract litigation—commodities futures trading, and assignment of life insurance policies—just as courts today must confront their modern analogues in two fast-growing industries: trading in derivatives and viatical settlements. Part Two focuses on a transformative moment in the development of contract law when the question of gambling was eventually swallowed and internalized, as if the problem were solved. However, no analytic formula could distinguish gambling from risk allocation. Instead, the gambling question was subjected to a complex and indecisive cultural negotiation and displacement. A close reading of judicial rhetoric shows the role of legal discourse in coming to terms with the fears and uncertainties that accompanied the transition into modernity. More than straightforward prohibitions on certain types of conduct, judicial grappling with risk and uncertainty offered its audiences an image with which to identify: recognizing that an element of gambling existed in all economic activity, contract discourse made way for the emergence of an individual who could claim mastery even while acknowledging uncertainty.

Part Three considers the ongoing debate over incomplete contracts with special attention to its historical assumptions. The debate on incomplete contracts is polarized over the question of whether the completion of contracts by courts should proceed on the basis of an examination of all the circumstances up to the time of the dispute, or instead, only on the basis of the parties' putative bargain at the time of formation, had they been able to overcome the barriers to reaching explicit agreement regarding the contingency that generated the dispute. Both sides in the debate rely on a common historical narrative, asserting that the course of twentieth-century contract law has seen a gradual increase in judicial intervention into incomplete contracts, positing at one end a rigid formalistic refusal to complete contracts at the beginning of the century, and an increasing willingness since the New Deal to intervene, especially since the adoption of the Uniform Commercial Code. The participants in the debate divide over the normative evaluation of the history, with one group seeing progress where the other sees decline. An examination of cases from the turn of the century reveals, however, that the basis of the shared historical narrative is fundamentally flawed. The cases show that at the height of the classical period, courts were heavily involved in completing contracts for the parties, among other things by implying an obligation to perform in good faith. Exposing the shared historical narrative as flawed history makes the other effects of this framework more visible, revealing that the deeper work of the narrative is to establish the conception of a free-standing, preexisting individual, and his counterpart, the "free market," as limitations on the goals to be pursued through contract.

I propose to show how marginal doctrines, the borders of contract, combine to generate a particular idea of the meaning of contract. That idea is centered around an image of the contracting individual, which functions as a focal point for identification. Here, the "borders of contract" show through in their double meaning. On the one hand, the borders of contract are precisely those areas where contractual liability is uncertain, where the scope of contract thinking reaches its limit. But in a deeper sense, the borders of contract refer to the active role of the framework of discourse in creating individuals: individuality, in the sense of the calculating subject, is created through enframing, the positing of borders—the roping off, defining, delimiting—that generates *individuation.* Calculation is based on singularity, on eliminating competing impulses and undefined responsibilities to others. This type of reckoning with the meaning of contract does not engage in the standard normative debate, which always revolves around the justifications for a particular rule choice. Instead, my concern is to show how the framework of these debates over rules generates a conception of contract, one that glorifies the individual at the price of sacrificing the imagination.

PART ONE

Gifts and Promises Revisited

ONE

The Revolution in Consideration Doctrine

In the last third of the nineteenth century, English and American legal theorists revolutionized the doctrine of consideration.[1] The result of their work was that the requirement of consideration became entrenched as one of the most distinctive features of the common law, especially as a mark of its difference from continental European contract law.[2] While the common law roots of the doctrine of consideration go back at least to the fifteenth or

1. When dealing with these theorists collectively, I will at times for convenience refer to them as "classical theorists" or "classical legal scholars." What I have termed "revolutionizing" could be called "modernizing," or even "rationalizing." All these labels are apt, but I use "revolutionizing" because it mitigates a tendency to take for granted the significance of the changes brought about in the theory.

2. The significance of this distinction has since been questioned, but its standing is evinced by the opening words of a major work of comparative law:

> The landscape to be examined in this survey has been reported by many observers to include as one of its features a great gap, a chasm, that divides all legal systems derived from the English common law from those of the European continent. The gap is revealed by asking a short question: Can a fully capable person make a binding promise to another to give or do something for nothing? For countries within the sphere of influence of the English common law the standard answer would be no, almost never. For the more civilized countries of western Europe the standard answer would

sixteenth century,[3] our current understanding of the doctrine acquired its framework from the massive theorization and reformulation of the doctrine pursued by late nineteenth- and early twentieth-century legal scholars.[4] The strategy in revolutionizing consideration was two-pronged. The first aim was purification and unification, achieved by eliminating or submerging extraneous functions of consideration doctrine and replacing them with a single question that consideration was meant to answer. That question, of course, was which promises the law should enforce. The second aim was to make the question of enforceable promises (or, simply, the doctrine of consideration) into the axis around which all of contract law revolved.

Taken together, the elements of this strategy worked to submerge an underlying question, the question of the stakes in distinguishing between gifts and contracts, between gratuitous undertakings and those supported by consideration. In contract theory, these questions seem to restate one another, though in fact there are important differences. The current debate over the doctrine of consideration is no longer centered on the intricacies of doctrine that engaged late nineteenth-century writers. Instead, the focus has shifted to a more straightforward normative debate over where the line between enforceable and unenforceable promises should be drawn. That focus, however, leaves intact the framework laid over a hundred years ago,

---

> be yes, since they have never suffered from the blight that afflicts countries adhering to the English common law—the requirement of bargain consideration.

John P. Dawson, *Gifts and Promises* 1 (1980). See also Ernest G. Lorenzen, "Causa and Consideration in the Law of Contracts," 28 *Yale L.J.* 621 (1919); Arthur T. von Mehren, "Civil-Law Analogues to Consideration: An Exercise in Comparative Analysis," 72 *Harv. L. Rev.* 1009 (1959).

3. William Holdsworth explains how the term *consideration* came into the language of the law:

> Because the expression "quid pro quo" had thus acquired a technical meaning [expressing the conditions under which the action of debt would lie], some more general word was needed to express the act or other circumstances which had led up to or was the motive or reason for a given transaction. It is clear from the Year Books of the fifteenth and early sixteenth century that the word "consideration" was used for this purpose; and the way in which it was used shows that it had not then acquired a technical meaning.

8 William Holdsworth, *A History of English Law* 4 (1926) (this chapter originally published as "The Modern History of the Doctrine of Consideration," pts. 1 and 2, 2 *B.U. L. Rev.* 87, 174 [1922]); see also James Barr Ames, "The History of Assumpsit," pt. 1, 2 *Harv. L. Rev.* 1 (1888).

4. See, e.g., Oliver Wendell Holmes, Jr., *The Common Law* 267–97 (photo. reprint 1991) (Boston, Little, Brown 1881); Christopher Columbus Langdell, *Selection of Cases on the Law of Contracts, with a Summary of the Topics Covered by the Cases* 1011–39 (2d ed., Boston, Little, Brown 1879); James Barr Ames, "Two Theories of Consideration," pt. 1, 12 *Harv. L. Rev.* 515 (1899), pt. 2, 13 *Harv. L. Rev.* 29 (1899); Clarence D. Ashley, "The Doctrine of Consideration," 26 *Harv. L. Rev.* 429 (1913); Christopher Columbus Langdell, "Mutual Promises as a Consideration for Each Other," 14 *Harv. L. Rev.* 496 (1901); Samuel Williston, "Successive Promises of the Same Performance," 8 *Harv. L. Rev.* 27 (1894).

which changed the face of contract theory. Part One of this book addresses the stakes of the distinction itself, by tracing the common ground between late nineteenth-century debates over the doctrine of consideration and late twentieth-century debates over the law of gifts. Ultimately, I will claim that the stakes are the constitution of a calculating individual subject, whose actions would be open to objective economic analysis, or economic rationality. In turn, the image of the economically rational agent would justify a rhetoric of withdrawal of state power from the sphere associated with economic rationality, in other words the market. But the road to such a claim is a long one, and expressing it in a single sentence must seem especially abrupt. Mitigating that abruptness requires a restatement of the question.

What, then, are the stakes of consideration doctrine? The traditional answer has been that consideration is meant to settle a question about the legal system: which promises should the law enforce? More recently, consideration theorists have suggested that the answer to that question—in other words, the location of the line between enforceable and unenforceable promises—will determine the contours of a societal value system in distinguishing between an official or business realm and a private or family realm. But both these viewpoints concentrate only on the answer to the question of consideration, rather than on the question itself. In fact, these answers displace the *question* of consideration. This chapter posits that the placement of the question of consideration itself at the heart of contract theory has a central productive function, which is to highlight and privilege the role of promises in contract. Consideration is the technical manifestation of an underlying conceptualization of contract around promise, as opposed to a more diffuse idea of obligation arising in a number of ways, some less and some more voluntary. By placing promise at the center of contractual obligation, consideration theory privileges a conception of contracting individuals as knowing and willful, as taking on obligations in measured, calculable increments, exchanging their obligations for precise values. By establishing the calculating individual as the center and source of obligations, the theory submerges the role of the state or the courts in determining the content of parties' obligations, and subtly delegitimates state power over such obligations.

Legal classifications are, perhaps inevitably, defined in opposition to one another. Because words acquire meaning through placement in a system of differences, one important way we know anything is by knowing what it is not. As the founder of modern linguistics pointed out, "The content of a word is determined in the final analysis not by what it contains but by what exists outside it. . . . In a given language, all the words which express neighbouring ideas help define one another's meaning."[5] Contract is recognized, in large measure, by contrasting it to its "others" in the realms of obligations and transfers of property. Thus, we recognize contract only where there is a transfer free from coercion, or what in contract parlance is known as duress. Similarly, we distinguish contract from gift. The latter distinction, between contract and gift, will be a major concern here. Contract is commonly understood as the law of enforceable promises, wherein the limit of enforceability is the promise lacking consideration, or paradigmatically, the promise to make a gift. In order to grasp fully this conception of contract, it is crucial to delve into the neighboring conception of the gift.

The story that moves from classical consideration theory, to modern contract theory through the gift, and finally to the individual subject, is complicated and circuitous. It is an excavation of the not quite forgotten artifacts that shape current thinking about contract. The digging begins in the present chapter in one of the most elaborate burial sites in the history of the common law: classical debates over consideration. Buried there, we will find the gratuitous enforceable undertaking, and perhaps some remnant of the gift. Classical theorists revolutionized consideration and contract generally, primarily by redefining it as the legal category dealing with enforceable promises. Part of this redefinition and categorization entailed burying the gift. But the gift is prosopopoeial; in Chapter 2, speaking from beyond the grave, it tells us that no amount of theoretical dirt will completely fill the holes or gaps in the legal stories about who gives what to whom, in return for how much, if any, and how enforceable such giving will have turned out to be. Chapter 3 traces the early twentieth-century theoretical responses to the changes in consideration doctrine on the one hand, and the inability of those changes to govern the outcomes of cases on the other. It argues, first, that despite the advances of theory in considering justifications rather than simply elaborating the rules, the first generations of postclassical theory never challenged the basic framework of contract and consideration established by the classics. Finally, Chapter 4 speculates about where the impact of consideration theory falls, and attempts to flesh out the stakes of distinguishing between enforceable and unenforceable promises.

---

5. Ferdinand de Saussure, *Course in General Linguistics* 114 (Charles Bally et al. eds., Roy Harris trans., 1986).

Today, it may seem difficult to distinguish the doctrine of consideration from the question of which promises should be enforceable.[6] The modern understanding of contract makes this an almost unquestioned common ground for beginning to think about contract.[7] This is a testament to the success of a revolution: rather than experiencing its effects as radical, we take them for granted, believing that contract has always been (and must always be) about which promises the law should enforce. But nothing in the practice of contracting made such an exclusive focus inevitable. True, the rhetoric of agreement and enforcing promises is probably older than any surviving element of common law doctrine, and it will not be my claim here that promising was not an important part of contract law before classical theory made its contribution. Indeed, the relative importance of individual agreements and promises in economic organization was on the rise from the middle of the eighteenth century.[8] However, the conception of contract with an exclusive focus on promise is a product of classical theorists' successful work.

The task of this chapter is to elucidate the contribution of a specific doctrinal discussion, regarding the rules defining consideration, to the classical view of contract. But it is worthwhile to start with a more general account of the transformation in doctrine in order to clarify the framework for my discussion. Through the first half of the nineteenth century, most of what we know today as contract was discussed by legal scholars under a variety of headings, the most important of which described pairs of actors

---

6. An illustration of how tightly bound the questions of enforceable promises and consideration are may be seen in the title of part 1 to a widely used contracts casebook: "Part I. What Promises Should the Law Enforce?—The Doctrine of Consideration." Lon L. Fuller and Melvin Aron Eisenberg, *Basic Contract Law* 1 (6th ed. 1996). An early note attempts to clarify: "The first great question of contract law, therefore, is what kinds of promises should be enforced. The answer to that question traditionally has been subsumed under the heading 'consideration.'" Id. at 6.

7. The crucial exception is Ian Macneil's attempt to "overcome the effect on perceptions of literally hundreds of years of history . . . which have led us to equate exchange with discrete transactions and contract with promise." Ian R. Macneil, "The Many Futures of Contracts," 47 *S. Cal. L. Rev.* 691, 696 (1974); see also Ian R. Macneil, *The New Social Contract* 4–10 (1980); Ian R. Macneil, "Relational Contract: What We Do and Do Not Know," 1985 *Wis. L. Rev.* 483, 496–508, 519–22.

8. John Orth has argued that up until the mid-nineteenth century, most elements of economic and social organization typically understood today as contractual were governed by a combination of property and status regimes, and that labor law was the most important transformative field, moving from status to contract in the hundred years culminating in 1850. John V. Orth, "Contract and the Common Law," in *The State and Freedom of Contract* 44, 62 (Harry N. Scheiber ed., 1998). For the argument that status was crucial in labor law well into the twentieth century, see generally Karen Orren, *Belated Feudalism: Labor, the Law, and Liberal Development in the United States* (1991).

in standardized, statuslike relationships. But status was not the only alternative to contract; property concepts were perhaps equally central. The obligations of standardized relationships were for the most part conceived to be defined by law rather than by agreement. The transformation did not occur all at once, and there are indications of its mounting momentum throughout the nineteenth century.[9]

One of the best indications of an intermediate stage in this development is the framework offered by Theophilus Parsons in *The Law of Contracts*, first published in 1853. Whereas prior commentators (most centrally Blackstone and Kent) had relegated contract to the margins of property, Parsons reconceives contract as deserving of an entire treatise, in which major categories are subsumed into a wide-ranging field.[10] On the other hand, the content of most obligations in Parsons's schema are imposed, or at times implied, by law. The treatise went through nine editions in the half-century from its initial publication; it was, during that time, a popular work among academics and practitioners. The opening chapter on the extent and scope of the law of contracts remained nearly unaltered through the nine editions, and merits quotation at some length:

> The Law of Contracts, in its widest extent, may be regarded as including nearly all the law which regulates the relations of human life. Indeed, it may be looked upon as the basis of human society. All social life presumes it, and rests upon it; for out of contracts, express or implied, declared or understood, grow all rights, all duties, all obligations, and all law. Almost the whole procedure of human life implies, or, rather, is, the continual fulfilment of contracts. . . . It would be easy to go farther, and show that, in all the relations of social life, its good order and prosperity depend upon the due fulfilment of the contracts which bind all to all. Sometimes these contracts are deliberately expressed with all the precision of law, and are

9. Some of the relationships conceived of initially through property doctrines or status and only later as contract were conveyances, mortgages, sales of land, landlord-tenant relationships, marriage, leases, and most importantly, labor. Orth, "Contract and the Common Law," 45–49. Orth notes that "what was missing from the common law before modern times was a robust notion of contract. . . . [C]ontract thinking was rare; the exception, not the rule." Id. at 48.

10. 1 Theophilus Parsons, *The Law of Contracts* 3–4 (1st ed., Boston, Little, Brown 1853). Parsons was not the first to accord contract greater importance than Blackstone had. David Lieberman has recently pointed out that William Paley's *Principles of Moral and Political Philosophy* (1785) accorded twice as much space to contract as to property. However, despite the fact that Paley was an influential Cambridge professor, his text has been all but ignored in the histories of the rise of freedom of contract. David Lieberman, "Contract Before 'Freedom of Contract,'" in *The State and Freedom of Contract*, 89, 119–21.

> armed with all its sanctions. Far more frequently they are not expressed at all; and for their definition and extent we must look to the common principles which all are supposed to understand and acknowledge. In this sense, *contract* is coördinate and commensurate with *duty*; and it is a familiar principle of the law . . . which has a wide though not a universal application, that whatsoever it is certain a man ought to do, that the law supposes him to have promised to do. "Implied contracts," says Blackstone, "are such as reason and justice dictate, and which, therefore, the law presumes that every man undertakes to perform." These contracts form the web and woof of actual life. If they were wholly disregarded, the movement of society would be arrested.[11]

For Parsons, the field of contract was occupied largely by obligations imposed by law, according to the dictates of reason and justice. The mechanism that allowed for such imposition of duties was the concept of implication, but it is a mechanism very close to status: the standardized relationships whose elaboration make up most of Parsons's work supply the putative source for the "implied" duties imposed by law.[12] Thus, Parsons enlarges the set of fact situations and relationships that are to be conceived of as contractual. However, his conception of the meaning of "contractual" does not entail a vision of legal obligation subject to the exclusive control of the parties. Parsons's vision is not yet one in which the parties to a contract make law for themselves. Indeed, his is a world replete with contractual relations, but in it promise is just one of a number of ways to enter the contractual realm, and probably not the most important.

CLEANSING CONSIDERATION OF NONPROMISSORY ELEMENTS

The reformulation of the doctrine of consideration played a central role in redefining contract as the province of individual control, or private law making by the parties. On the doctrinal plane, the strategy for this maneuver was to marginalize elements of consideration that implicated anything other

---

11. 1 Parsons, *Law of Contracts*, 3–4.

12. Dealing with the broader topic of how classical theory rearranged the classification of private law, Duncan Kennedy analyzes these (and other) passages from Parsons, and calls their lack of persuasive effect the result of the "devastating assault" of classical legal thinkers. Duncan Kennedy, "The Rise and Fall of Classical Legal Thought" 163–75 (unpublished manuscript, 1975).

than calculated individual control. At first glance, this formulation may seem paradoxical, since the requirement of consideration is itself a limitation on individual control over the disposition of obligations. Consideration is in this sense a classic instance of a limitation of freedom of contract, since it denies state enforcement to obligations, like promises to make gifts, that do not stem from bargains. But the fact that consideration doctrine represents a limit beyond which the state will not intervene to enforce an agreement should not blind us to the positive side of the doctrine. That positive element is the enabling of parties to set the terms of their relations, and to elude state prescription regarding the content of their obligations, so long as the agreement has come about by way of exchange, or bargain. This is the sense in which contract was appealing to theorists of the time as an alternative to status: contract represented control by individual parties over the content of their obligations to one another, while status represented societal control over that content.[13]

To achieve a meaningful distinction over the source of control, however, it was not enough to rely on the word *contract* as opposed to the word *status*, since, up until the mid-nineteenth century, contract was still thought of primarily as an arrangement of the array of standardized relationships whose content, more often than not, had been established by custom. One could agree or not agree to become an agent,[14] but once one agreed, one was subject to duties imposed by law.[15] Classical theorists succeeded in rid-

13. Again, it is worth noting that the sharp distinction between status and contract is a classical development, while for preclassical thinkers, contract was an inclusive category that included societally imposed obligation with individually undertaken obligation. In other words, much of what was later pushed into the marginal category of status was seen by preclassical theorists as part of contract. On late nineteenth-century attempts to distinguish contracts from status, see Amy Dru Stanley, *From Bondage to Contract* 1–17 (1998).

14. But for many relationships, even entry was not voluntary. The obvious candidates for involuntary entry into "contractual" relationships are common carriers and innkeepers, who could not refuse particular customers the service they provided to the public. See Wyatt Paine, *Bailments: A Commentary on the Law of Custody and Possession* 199 (1901). But there were also involuntary labor relationships, at least in England, where legislation mandated wages and heavily regulated the duties of workers. See Orth, "Contract and the Common Law," 50–56; Robert J. Steinfeld, *Coercion, Contract, and Free Labor in the Nineteenth Century* 39–84 (2001).

15. Up until the early nineteenth century, agency was understood primarily as a standardized relationship, so that duties were simply state-imposed legal incidences of entering into the relationship itself; from the mid-nineteenth century onward, agency was increasingly conceived of as a contract, but one whose duties were implied by law. See 1 Parsons, *Law of Contracts*, 68–77, 79–85. For the purposes of my argument, the distinction between implied and imposed duties is only mildly significant (despite the fact that the shift makes the contractual party based vision more accessible), since the source of control is conceded to be societal in both cases. And the argument is not limited to agency; it holds

ding contract of much of the association of duties implied by law, in part by their reformulation of consideration doctrine. The technical aspect of this reformulation was a kind of cleanup project, in which extraneous functions of consideration doctrine were discarded, or at least made to seem peripheral and insignificant addenda to a doctrine of major importance. What follows, then, is a discussion of several of those extraneous functions that consideration doctrine performed before the classical revolution was brought to bear on contract theory. While the doctrinal particulars of consideration discussed below may seem arcane, they are important to show how the technical features of contract doctrine were reformulated to build a general theory centered on promise.

Until the classical theoretical revolution in consideration doctrine, consideration played some role in the following issues, none of which centered on the question of whether a *promise* was enforceable: (1) determining whether an obligation could be implied; (2) determining the duty of care in an undertaking; (3) determining the extent of liability; and (4) determining privity of contract.[16] A brief explanation of each of these is necessary here.

Implying an Obligation

The first preclassical function of consideration lay in determining whether an obligation could be implied. The problem arose when a plaintiff had performed a service or given something of value to a defendant with an expectation of receiving something in return, but without having bargained

---

for the myriad relationships that were conceived of as including duties, from bailment, to partnership, to factors and brokers, to husband and wife—the list goes on. Classical theorists tried to put agency on a wholly contractual (read: promise-based) footing, claiming that extraconsensual duties (i.e., those implied or imposed by law regardless of actual consent of the parties) were anomalous. See James Barr Ames, "Undisclosed Principal—His Rights and Liabilities," 18 *Yale L.J.* 443 (1909). For an early and influential critique of the classical position, see Warren A. Seavey, "The Rationale of Agency," 29 *Yale L.J.* 859 (1920). For a modern treatment of the issue claiming that contract theory can accommodate agency rules that appear at first glance to obviate consent, see Randy E. Barnett, "Squaring Undisclosed Agency Law with Contract Theory," 75 *Cal. L. Rev.* 1969 (1987).

16. An additional issue that generated a great deal of litigation was the question of what kinds of consideration could take an obligation of surety out of the statute of frauds. Due to the technical nature of the issue, and because it could be argued that it eventually devolves to the question of whether a promise is enforceable (as opposed to void for violation of the statute), I do not include a discussion of it here. For the key cases on the issue, see Mallory v. Gillett, 21 N.Y. 412 (1860); Leonard v. Vredenburgh, 8 Johns. 29 (N.Y. 1811). Yet another issue was determining the time when liability began. For a full discussion, see 101 *Colum. L. Rev.* 1876, 1891–93 (2001).

for anything particular in exchange.[17] Certain kinds of consideration were sufficient to raise an obligation, sometimes through the construct of an implied promise, though it was clear that such an implication was a legally imposed duty and had nothing to do with the will of the defendant. The clearest example of the construct—and the most important fact situation in which this kind of consideration raised an obligation—was the case of surety. In abstract terms, the situation is as follows: *A* purchases goods on credit from *B*, who demands some security, and accepts *C* as a surety. Typically, this is carried out by *A* giving a promissory note to *B*, and *C* indorsing the note as surety. When the note comes due, *A* does not pay; *B* demands and receives payment from *C*. *C* can then sue *A* to recover the payment. The relationship between *A* and *C* need not involve direct consideration between them (*C*'s willingness to be a surety may be gratuitous, or it may be a distinct transaction for consideration), and *C* need not prove any promise, prior or subsequent to payment, for reimbursement.[18] Where the surety was called on to pay the loan and did so, she could recover from the principal debtor, without proving either a request by the debtor to pay or a promise by the debtor to repay, since the entire structure mandating repayment would be implied by law.[19] Classical consideration theory merged this entire problematic with two promise-centered issues: the status of moral consideration, and more directly, the distinction between executed and past consideration.

The strategy taken up by classical theorists had several variations, with some common maneuvers. The first was to present cases of this sort as anomalous, and then to show that other remedies, particularly a doctrine of quasi contract, were better equipped to deal with the situation. The second was to portray the history of contract as beginning with the true rule (i.e.,

---

17. Technically, any existing debt without an explicit agreement for its repayment satisfied these conditions, and the early form of pleading in such a situation was an action of debt, where no promise to pay had to be proved.

18. The gratuitous aspect of the relationship is not central here, because it is *C*'s right to recompense that is interesting, since it arises through a legal construction implying an obligation, based on the fact that *C* has paid a debt that actually accrued to *A*, and not on the question of whether *A* promised *C* to reimburse her. For a clear example see Swift v. Bennett, 64 Mass. 436 (1852), in which the defendant was a minor who bought a suit of clothes for a whaling expedition and the plaintiff was his surety, who paid for the clothes when the note came due. The court held that the plaintiff-surety could recover from the defendant.

19. 1 Parsons, *Law of Contracts*, 391–96. That this was a genuine issue for early consideration theory is attested to by the fact of differentiation among different considerations: some were sufficient to raise liability without any request for service or any promise of payment (such as the surety situation), while others might be sufficient to raise liability only when one of the other elements was present.

that past consideration is no consideration), followed by lax interpretation of the rule, and finally a recovery of the true doctrine in the nineteenth century. The clearest example of the classical theory maneuver is the earliest, in Langdell's *Summary*:

> When the action of assumpsit was becoming the ordinary remedy for the recovery of debts by simple contract, a difficulty was experienced from the fact that a promise was indispensable to that action, while debts were often created without any actual promise. To obviate this difficulty, and to make assumpsit an available remedy in the latter class of cases, the courts invented the fiction that, wherever there was a simple contract debt, the law would imply a promise to pay it. . . . As the implied promise was a mere creature of the law, of course it was neither necessary nor possible that it should have a consideration *in the proper sense of that term*; yet it came to be the practice, in declaring upon an implied promise, to follow the analogy of a declaration upon an actual promise, by alleging that the promise was made in consideration of the indebtedness; and hence originated the notion of a past or executed consideration. As an implied promise does not constitute any part of the plaintiff's cause of action, and as an executed consideration will not support any other than an implied promise, of course it follows that a declaration on an executed consideration will never be good unless it states a good cause of action (*i.e.* a debt) independently of the promise. If this simple rule had always been understood and applied, the subject of executed consideration would have caused no trouble; but unfortunately it was not understood until within recent times. On the contrary, the opinion long prevailed that an executed consideration which had been performed at the defendant's request would support a subsequent actual promise; and hence it would follow that a declaration would never be bad because upon an executed consideration, provided a request was alleged.[20]

After explaining why such a view would create an untenable exception to the proper doctrine of consideration, Langdell concludes:

> As the fiction of a promise implied by law from an executed consideration was invented merely to render the action of assumpsit a more extensive and available remedy, it follows that such promises can have no existence in places where the action of assumpsit has been abolished, and hence in such places the phrase "executed or past consideration" has ceased to have any legal meaning.[21]

---

20. Langdell, *Selection of Cases*, 1035 (emphasis added).

21. Id. at 1039.

Together with the ensuing discussion of "Debt," Langdell's treatment of obligations created without promises has an overriding concern, which is to show that despite consistent references to the doctrine of consideration in the sources dealing with such obligations, the problems of these obligations should not be considered as truly contractual.[22] Other classical theorists offered similar analyses of the problem.[23]

Determining the Required Degree of Care

A second function of consideration unrelated to promises, and one of importance in commercial law, was determining the level of care required in an undertaking. The most important area where this function of consideration played a role was in the law of bailment. Traditionally, bailments were a category of contract that could be binding without consideration,[24] raising a problem for classical theorists interested in asserting a general rule that only promises supported by consideration could be binding. The response of classical theorists was to marginalize the law of bailments generally, by questioning the characterization of bailments as contracts, and by treating elements of bailment as exceptional or as matters proper to statu-

---

22. Langdell excludes debt from contract by shifting attention to the actual transfer of property:

> The legal mode of creating a debt is not by contract, but by grant. . . . It is clear, therefore, that it is the transfer of the property for a certain price, and not the previous executory contract, that creates the debt. . . . But what kind of contract is that in which the obligation arises not from a promise, but from the receipt of an equivalent for the obligation by the obligor from the obligee?

Id. at 1040–41; see also id. at 1027 (discussing promises to pay for services already rendered).

23. See, e.g., 8 Holdsworth, *History of English Law*, 14–17, 37–39; Holmes, *Common Law*, 285–87, 295–97; Frederick Pollock, *Principles of Contract* 181–82 (7th ed. 1902); Ames, "History of Assumpsit," 53–59. One of the most detailed examples is Williston's treatment. After stating the rule that, generally, past consideration is no consideration, he notes that "however anomalously, a past consideration has been regarded formerly by the law as sufficient consideration, and at the present time in some of these classes [of cases] at least, the early law still persists." 1 Samuel Williston, *The Law of Contracts* § 142 (1st ed. 1920). Discussing the history of such recognition, Williston says that by the end of the seventeenth century, quasi-contractual obligations were enforced "under the guise of promises implied in law," concluding that this approach obviates the need for reference to any promises: The creditor is "amply protected both as a matter of substantive law and matter of procedure, and this without imposing the strain upon the doctrine of consideration of maintaining the exception to the general definition, involved in holding that a subsequent promise to pay the debt creates a new contract." Id. § 143. Admitting that the question of promises is clumsy in this context, Williston concludes the section thus: "That the real basis of the plaintiff's right in indebitatus assumpsit in modern times has been the debt and not the alleged promise, whether that promise was in fact real or fictitious, is shown by the circumstance that though in form the defendant in the action pleaded non assumpsit, in substance that traverse put in issue the existence of the debt."

24. For a discussion of various categories of gratuitous bailments, see Paine, *Bailments*, 8–85.

tory law rather than common law contract.[25] More narrowly, consideration scholars were faced with the fact that in bailment, consideration was not a question of enforceability of promises, but rather a question of the level of care required by the bailee. The rule, as extrapolated from Roman law and reiterated in almost every common law discussion of bailment, was that a gratuitous bailee was responsible only for gross negligence, or held only to a slight duty of care, while a bailee for hire was responsible for negligence, or held to a duty of ordinary care.[26] The distinction was still current in American case law while classical theorists were writing.[27]

The classical theorists' response was to claim that the duty of care was actually unrelated to the question of reward, despite explicit judicial statements to the contrary. The tactic employed was to subject cases stating that consideration impacted on the degree of care to close reading and interpretation, and on the basis of those interpretations, to assert that the cases were actually decided on a hidden principle of a consensually adjusted degree of care. Joseph Henry Beale's discussion is a succinct example:

> The proposition that I shall consider by this method is this: that the degree of care required of an undertaker is not proportionate to the reward, and therefore that the fact that the duty was undertaken gratuitously is immaterial, except as *evidence* of the extent of care undertaken. This, as I shall try to show, is the general result of the authorities, though there has been no explicit decision to that effect.[28]

Beale was not alone in trying to rid bailment law of the Roman-law inspired determination of the duty of care in accordance with consideration, or reward.[29]

---

25. For example, Williston argued that gratuitous bailments are rarely contracts. 2 Williston, *Law of Contracts*, §§ 1038–39.

26. The structure was actually tripartite, rather than binary. In a bailment for mutual benefit of the parties, the bailee was held to ordinary care; in a bailment for the bailee's sole benefit, the bailee was responsible for even slight negligence, or was held to extraordinary care. See William Jones, *An Essay on the Law of Bailments* 4–10; 118 (photo. reprint 1998) (Philadelphia, Hogan and Thompson 1836); Paine, *Bailments*, 4; 2 Williston, *Law of Contracts*, § 1033.

27. See, e.g., Preston v. Prather, 137 U.S. 604, 608 (1891) ("The general doctrine, as stated by text writers and in judicial decisions, is that gratuitous bailees of another's property are not responsible for its loss unless guilty of gross negligence in its keeping"); Baker v. Bailey, 145 S.W. 532, 534 (Ark. 1912); Sherwood v. Home Sav. Bank, 109 N.W. 9, 12 (Iowa 1906); King v. Exch. Bank, 78 S.W. 1038, 1040 (Mo. Ct. App. 1904).

28. Joseph H. Beale, Jr., "Gratuitous Undertakings," 5 *Harv. L. Rev.* 222, 227 (1891).

29. Holmes's discussion in *The Common Law* attempts an analogous maneuver, but with a different focus. See Holmes, *Common Law*, 164–205. Holmes works through the common law on bailment to show,

Determining the Extent of Liability

A third area of preclassical contract law where consideration played a role unconnected to the enforceability of promises was in determining the extent of damages available for the breach of a contractual obligation. Parsons, writing in 1853, made the following matter-of-fact statement regarding the issue: "If an agreement be unreasonable or unconscionable, but not in such a way or to such a degree as to imply fraud, though the court will not declare the contract void, they will give only reasonable damages to a plaintiff who seeks compensation for a breach of it."[30] Through the eighteenth century and into the early nineteenth, inadequacy of consideration was deemed a good reason to reduce damages from the otherwise accepted expectation measure.[31] And while explicit acknowledgment of this function of consideration decreased over the course of the nineteenth century, it was still applied by the Supreme Court in a case in 1889.[32] The classical response was to insist that consideration was a binary variable: either consideration was present, resulting in expectation damages for breach, or consideration was absent, resulting in no damages whatsoever. Classical theorists, led by Williston, claimed that the damage measure flowed from the very nature of contract, and thus could not

---

contrary to popular opinion, that the law is of Germanic rather than Roman origin, and that originally, all bailees were treated equally: "Chief Justice Popham probably borrowed his distinction between paid and unpaid bailees from [Christopher St. German's 1523 dialogue, Doctor and Student], where common carriers are mentioned as an example of the former class. A little earlier, reward made no difference." Id. at 181–82. Critique of the three-tiered structure of liability in bailment continued after the classical period. See Shelden D. Elliott, "Degrees of Negligence," 6 *S. Cal. L. Rev.* 91, 114–15 (1933); William King Laidlaw, "Principles of Bailment," 16 *Cornell L.Q.* 286, 306–10 (1931). For a rare modern treatment, see R. H. Helmholz, "Bailment Theories and the Liability of Bailees: The Elusive Uniform Standard of Reasonable Care," 41 *U. Kan. L. Rev.* 97 (1992).

30. 1 Parsons *Law of Contracts*, 362. In later editions, Parsons added that in such cases, courts of equity would not grant specific performance. See 1 Theophilus Parsons, *The Law of Contracts* 384 (3d ed., Boston, Little, Brown 1857).

31. See Morton J. Horwitz, *The Transformation of American Law, 1780–1860*, pp. 164–67 (1977). Horwitz discusses the "substantive doctrine of consideration" that allowed juries to reduce damages where consideration was inadequate; for instance, noting that "in Massachusetts, the eighteenth century rule was that a defendant in an ordinary contract case could offer evidence of inadequacy of consideration in order to reduce his damages." Id. at 165. Williston himself, while opposing damages based on consideration, acknowledged that under the early law of assumpsit damages had been "based on the consideration given rather than on the value of the defendant's performance." 3 Williston, *Law of Contracts*, § 1339.

32. Hume v. United States, 132 U.S. 406, 413 (1889); see also Scott v. United States, 79 U.S. (1 Wall.) 443, 445 (1870) (using language reminiscent of Parsons in stating that "if a contract be unreasonable and unconscionable, but not void for fraud, a court of law will give to the party who sues for its breach damages, not according to its letter, but only such as he is equitably entitled to").

reflect the level of consideration, which would entail an examination of its adequacy.[33]

Supplying an Exception to the Rule on Privity of Contract

An additional role of consideration, unrelated to the direct question of enforceability of promises, was that it was a factor in deciding whether a plaintiff could avoid the effects of the doctrine of privity of contract. Until late in the nineteenth century, certain types of consideration afforded a plaintiff an exception to the rule that a "stranger to the consideration" (i.e., one who had not supplied the consideration) could sue to enforce rights according to the contract. This rule mandated that third-party beneficiaries of contracts could not sue on them. But there was no question of whether the obligation itself was enforceable—all the discussions assume it was. The main exception was for cases where there was a "good" or "meritorious"

33. This conflict arose in at least two settings. The first was the classical attempt to distinguish sharply between contracts and quasi contracts, which classical theorists repeatedly claimed were not contracts at all, and breaches of which were remedied by restitution damages. Williston's textbook treatment is typical and thorough:

> The expression "implied contract" has given rise to great confusion in the law. Until recently the divisions of the law customarily made coincided with the forms of action known to the common law. Consequently, all rights enforced by the contractual actions of assumpsit, covenant and debt, were regarded as based on contracts. Some of these rights, however, were created not by any promise or mutual assent of the parties but were imposed by law on the defendant irrespective of, and sometimes in violation of, his intention. Such obligations were called implied contracts. A better name is that now generally in use of "quasi-contracts." This name is better since it makes clear that *the obligations in question are not true contracts*, and also because it avoids confusion with another class of obligations which have also been called implied contracts. . . . Furthermore, the measure of damages appropriate to contractual and quasi-contractual obligations differs.

1 Williston, *Law of Contracts*, § 3 (emphasis added).

The second setting was the classical assertion that only expectation damages were appropriate for contract breach. The most famous classical statement on the singular propriety of expectation damages is Williston's contribution to the Restatement debate over remedies for breach of an obligation arising out of § 90:

> Either the promise is binding or it is not. If the promise is binding it has to be enforced as it is made. . . . I could leave this whole thing to the subject of quasi contracts so that the promisee under those circumstances shall never recover on the promise but he shall recover such an amount as will fairly compensate him for any injury incurred; but it seems to me you have to take one leg or the other. You have either to say the promise is binding or you have to go on the theory of restoring the *status quo*.

4 A.L.I. Proc. 103–4 (1926) (quoted in Melvin Aron Eisenberg, "The World of Contract and the World of Gift," 85 *Cal. L. Rev.* 821, 834–35 [1997]). For a critique of the classical monistic view on remedies, see L. L. Fuller and William R. Perdue, "The Reliance Interest in Contract Damages," pts. 1 and 2, 46 *Yale L.J.* 52, 373 (1936–37).

consideration between the promisee and the third party—in other words, a relationship of love and natural affection between the promisee and the beneficiary—which was held to extend the rights of the former to the latter.[34] The classical response to this issue was simply to call it a historical error, a misunderstanding of the true nature of consideration. Again, Langdell's discussion is indicative. He admits that *Dutton v. Poole* (1677) had at one time established an exception to the rule of privity, but says this had led to "untenable" results:

> In the case of a promise made to one person for the benefit of another, there is no doubt that the promisee can maintain an action, not only in his own name, but for his own benefit. If, therefore, the person for whose benefit the promise was made could also sue on it, the consequence would be that the promisor would be liable to two actions. In truth, a binding promise to A to pay $100 to B confers no right upon B in law or equity. . . . Of course it follows that the distinction upon which Dutton *v.* Poole was decided is untenable; and accordingly that case has been overruled.[35]

There is reason to doubt the soundness of this reasoning, but the point here is not to critique Langdell's conclusions about the truth of consideration. Instead, the question is how eliminating this additional function of consideration helped to establish the framework for a promise-centered vision of contract. For this purpose, it is worthwhile to look at how Langdell continues the discussion:

> What has been said in the preceding paragraph does not in strictness relate to the subject of "consideration;" but it was necessary to say it in this connection, because the case of Dutton *v.* Poole has given rise to the notion that the consideration of a promise need not move from the promisee, though that

---

34. See 8 Holdsworth, *History of English Law*, 12. Holdsworth discusses the leading case of Dutton v. Poole, 93 Eng. Rep. 523 (1677), linking this rule to an equitable conception of consideration: "As the law stood at the end of the seventeenth century, ideas derived from the equitable conception of consideration had introduced a considerable exception to the rule that consideration must move from the promisee, which tended to obscure the common law doctrine. It was not till the decisions of the nineteenth century that this obscurity was removed." Id. at 12–13. An additional exception arose when a debt was transferred from an original debtor to a substitute debtor on the basis of payment between them (with no additional payment to the creditor, who could nonetheless sue the new debtor, though there was seemingly no privity between them). In *Perry v. Swasey*, the defendant was a boarder of the original debtor, who agreed that he pay her debt to plaintiff rather than the rent he owed her. Chief Justice Shaw stated that "the law creates the privity, and enables the party who is to have the benefit of the promise to treat it as a consideration moving from him." 66 Mass. (12 Cush.) 36, 40 (1853). On the definition of good or meritorious consideration, see 1 Williston, *Law of Contracts*, § 110.

35. Langdell, *Selection of Cases*, 1020–21.

> case really only decided that it need not always move from the person who sues on the promise. It is clear from the definition of consideration (§ 45) that it must move from the promisee. Indeed, it is of the very essence of consideration that it be received from the promisee. What is received from one person cannot possibly be a consideration for a promise to another person.[36]

The maneuver here is clear: Langdell says that this use of "consideration" is not strictly part of consideration, as he has defined it properly.[37] His definition limits the law of consideration to the issue of supporting the enforceability of the promise; in turn, he will limit the scope of contract law generally to such enforceable promises.

Summary: Limiting Consideration to the Enforceability of Promises

Until classical theorists reformulated the doctrine of consideration, it was far from being a unified doctrine with one consistent meaning, or even one specific context for use. Although this internal differentiation or diversity of consideration seems lately to have been forgotten, as recently as 1941 Karl Llewellyn introduced a symposium on consideration with these words:

> "Consideration" is not in any meaningful sense *a* topic. The term, as roughly used in these papers, relates to no unified body of states or problems of fact.
>
> There is instead an historically collected agglomeration of states of fact—like pebbles in pudding-stone—held together by the sole tie of being allegedly covered by "the same" legal doctrine. But the legal doctrines concerned are not "the same"; they are not a single body.[38]

In each of the areas discussed above, classical theorists attempted to cleanse the doctrine of consideration of its nonpromissory elements. In each case, the doctrine was recharacterized, shifting its contribution from

36. Id. at 1021.

37. Id. at 1011 ("The consideration of a promise is the thing given or done by the promisee in exchange for the promise").

38. Karl N. Llewellyn, "On the Complexity of Consideration: A Foreword," 41 *Colum. L. Rev.* 777, 778–79 (1941). Llewellyn continues, in an argument closely analogous to the one made here:

> In learning or teaching or "applying" "the doctrine" of "consideration," we have rather successfully obscured the disunity of field of fact-problem and also of doctrine by several devices. The first has been to make out a field "of contract"; to call it a field of "promise" (while leaving out such promises as were traditionally or by neglect treated under other heads, but including such non-promissory agreements as we chose).

determining the contents of an obligation toward the question of its formation. Significantly, this was an attempt to define contract as against other forms of obligation, whether rooted in gifts, in some other version of gratuitous transaction, in an idea of status, or otherwise imposed through standardized relationships.

A quick rundown of the oppositional ideas may clarify. In purging consideration of its connection to implied obligations, classical theorists were marginalizing what they came to call quasi-contractual obligation, a type of obligation understood by all as resting on state imposition of duties. In denying the functions of consideration regarding the duty of care and the extent of liability, theorists were submerging the importance of standardized relationships, like bailor-bailee, in determining the content of obligations between contractual partners. Finally, eliminating the function of consideration that dealt with exemptions from the requirement of privity was a way to limit the importance of an existing statuslike relationship (nearly always between a father and his dependent children) from conceptions of contract enforcement.

It is worth emphasizing that my claim here is not that classical theorists invented out of thin air the important function of consideration in determining which promises the law should enforce. Rather, it has been my intention to show that consideration doctrine up until the late nineteenth century also encompassed a number of other questions and problems, and that classical theorists purged consideration theory of these "extraneous" elements in order to advance a promise-centered conception of contract. That purging was the first prong in a two-part strategy, and I now turn to the second, positive part, of generalizing the question of promise enforcement.

GENERALIZING THE QUESTION OF PROMISE ENFORCEMENT

The second half of the classical revolution of consideration theory was to present consideration as the answer to the question of which promises the law should enforce, and in turn to make that question the boundary defining the scope of contract law generally. Thus, whereas contract up until the mid-nineteenth century included an entire array of state-imposed obligations entered into wholesale by some manifestation of voluntariness, classical theorists reconceived the field as including primarily obligations undertaken by rational agents who promise, and by promising, shape the contents of their own obligations.

Classical theorists made consideration the axis around which all of contract revolved. The most effective strategy for making consideration so central was simply to accord it heightened attention, to show that it was a doctrine worth the investment of scholarly energy. Before the classical period, consideration, like offer and acceptance, was a minor issue in contract theory. Parsons, for instance, devoted less than 5 percent of his treatise to the combination of consideration and assent.[39] In contrast, in both his casebook and *Summary*, Langdell devoted close to thirty percent of the work to consideration.[40] In the decades following publication of Langdell's casebook, there was a veritable outpouring of writing on consideration, dealing with everything from general theories of consideration to the most intricate or "nice" questions regarding the time of consideration and to whom and from whom the consideration must move.[41]

To get a feel for the way a debate over consideration made the doctrine central, it is helpful to focus on what was agreed upon and what was in conflict during the debate. The underlying point of convergence in this

39. See 1 Parsons, *Law of Contracts*, 353–408. Parsons devotes approximately forty-five pages to consideration, and ten to assent. As an indication of consideration's relative importance or lack thereof, this is about one-third of the space devoted to bailments. See id. at 569–722. And Parsons devoted more attention to consideration than his peers: Addison's treatise did not even have a table of contents entry for consideration, and the discussion itself occupied less than half the space of Parsons's, in a work of similar scope. See C. G. Addison, *A Treatise on the Law of Contracts and Rights and Liabilities ex Contractu* 11–26 (4th ed., London, V. and R. Stevens and G. S. Norton 1856).

40. Langdell, *Selection of Cases*, 164–441, 1011–39.

41. See, e.g., Ames, "History of Assumpsit"; Ames, "Two Theories of Consideration"; Ashley, "The Doctrine of Consideration"; Henry Winthrop Ballantine, "Is the Doctrine of Consideration Senseless and Illogical?" 11 *Mich. L. Rev.* 423 (1913); Henry Winthrop Ballantine, "Mutuality and Consideration," 28 *Harv. L. Rev.* 121 (1914); Joseph H. Beale, Jr., "Notes on Consideration," 17 *Harv. L. Rev.* 71 (1903); Arthur L. Corbin, "Does a Pre-Existing Duty Defeat Consideration?—Recent Noteworthy Decisions," 27 *Yale L.J.* 362 (1918); Arthur L. Corbin, "The Effect of Options on Consideration," 34 *Yale L.J.* 571 (1925); Arthur L. Corbin, "Comment, Part Payment of a Debt as Consideration for a Promise," 17 *Yale L.J.* 470 (1908); W. S. Holdsworth, "Debt, Assumpsit, and Consideration," 11 *Mich. L. Rev.* 347 (1913); Holdsworth, "Modern History of Consideration"; Albert Kocourek, "A Comment on Moral Consideration and the Statute of Limitations," 18 *Ill. L. Rev.* 538 (1924); Langdell, "Mutual Promises"; Edmund M. Morgan, "Benefit to the Promisor as Consideration for a Second Promise for the Same Act," 1 *Minn. L. Rev.* 383 (1917); Frederick Pollock, "Afterthoughts on Consideration," 17 *L.Q. Rev.* 415 (1901); Roscoe Pound, "Consideration in Equity," 13 *Ill. L. Rev.* 667 (1919); Samuel Williston, "Consideration in Bilateral Contracts," 27 *Harv. L. Rev.* 503 (1914); Samuel Williston, "Contracts for the Benefit of a Third Person," 15 *Harv. L. Rev.* 767 (1902); Williston, "Successive Promises." This list does not begin to approach comprehensiveness. For additional writing on consideration during this period, see generally *Selected Readings on the Law of Contracts* 320–597 (Assoc. of Am. Law Schools ed., 1931).

debate was that consideration was the way to isolate those promises worthy of enforcement. This isolation was meant first and foremost to separate such promises from "gratuitous" ones, those promises that did not have a direct and visible partner in exchange. Classical theorists repeatedly explained the reason for the requirement of consideration in reference to the nonenforcement of gratuitous promises. One typical expression follows:

> The underlying principle of consideration would seem to be negative,—a denial that ordinarily there is sufficient reason why gratuitous promises should be enforced. From a nude pact no obligation arises. The courts have not felt impelled to extend a remedy to one who seeks to get something for nothing. English law accordingly will not usually enforce a promise unless it is given for value, or the promise of value, *i.e.*, something which the law must assume to be of some value to the promisor and which the parties make the subject of bargain or exchange.[42]

While this idea had a long history in contract cases, classical theorists made it into the cornerstone of the contractual edifice.

Classical consideration theorists take as the starting point the idea that consideration is required to render a promise enforceable. They conflict, not over this principle, but rather over the sometimes intricate question of whether particular classes of reciprocating promises are valuable enough to be counted as nongratuitous, that is, as consideration. There are many versions of this basic conflict, including debate over the preexisting duty rule, the rules on moral consideration, the questions surrounding void promises as consideration, and the commercially important issue of mutuality and illusory promises.[43] Theorists also debated the basic question of whether consideration should be conceived of as a detriment to the promisee or a benefit to the promisor, or as something else, like reciprocal conventional induce-

---

42. Ballantine, "Mutuality and Consideration," 121. Substantially similar statements can be found throughout classical consideration theory; see, e.g., Morgan, "Benefit to the Promisor as Consideration," 385; Pollock, *Principles of Contracts* (7th ed.), 169; Williston, "Bilateral Contracts," 503–4; Ames, "Two Theories of Consideration," 42.

43. On preexisting duty, compare Ames, "Two Theories of Consideration," 530–31, and Corbin, "Pre-Existing Duty," 377–81, with Williston, "Bilateral Contracts," 38, and Williston, "Successive Promises," 528–29. For commentary on the various conflicts, see generally Kevin M. Teeven, *Promises on Prior Obligations at Common Law* 11–70 (1998). On moral consideration, see Langdell, *Selection of Cases*, 1025–30; Kocourek, "A Comment on Moral Consideration," 538–39; see generally Teeven, *Promises on Prior Obligations at Common Law*, 71–123. On void promises, see W. P. Rogers, "Void, Illegal, or Unenforceable Consideration," 17 *Yale L.J.* 338 (1908); Samuel Williston, "The Effect of One Void Promise in a Bilateral Agreement," 25 *Colum. L. Rev.* 857 (1925). On mutuality, see Ballantine, "Mutuality and Consideration," 131–34.

ment.[44] The importance of these conflicts was twofold: first, by taking for granted their common starting point, they established the framework of contract theory around the question of enforceable promises; second, they extended the application of consideration to promises generally, not only in the formation of contractual relations, but also in their modification and discharge.

The conflicts over the shape of consideration doctrine defined contract theory for the coming generations, and the attempt at generalization at times brought the doctrine into disrepute, at least in critics' eyes. Even among some classical theorists, the use of consideration in fact situations related to the discharge of contractual obligations seemed problematic,[45] and modern commentators have lamented that consideration, expanded to discharge and modification, had become a "scrap-collector."[46] The reconceptualization of all contract problems in terms of promise is well illustrated by the question of discharge. Traditionally, discharge was an issue of performance, and any executed "consideration" was sufficient to discharge an obligation.[47] The theoretical problem arose when the agreement to discharge was examined independently, as a pair of mutual promises. If the substituted performance was "different," it did not raise a problem, since it could be considered a detriment to the promisee and thus a valid consideration. If, on the other hand, it was simply "less"—in other words, a smaller sum of money—it could not be perceived as a detriment, making void, for lack

44. See Ames, "Two Theories of Consideration," 29–33; Holmes, *Common Law*, 292–94; Williston, "Bilateral Contracts," 503–6.

45. Pollock complained that "the doctrine of Consideration has been extended with not very happy results beyond its proper scope, which is to govern the formation of contracts, and has been made to regulate and restrain the discharge of contracts." Pollock, *Principles of Contracts* (7th ed.), 190.

46. Dawson, *Gifts and Promises*, 207. Grant Gilmore vividly describes that process:

> The theoretical basis having thus been provided, the next step was the extension of the newly minted theory of consideration to the entire life-history of a contract, from birth to death. Consideration theory was used to explain why offers, even if they are expressed to be irrevocable, are in their nature necessarily revocable at any time before acceptance—why modifications of going contracts under which A promises to pay B more than the originally agreed contract price for doing the work are not binding on A—why agreements by creditors to discharge their debtors on payment of less than the amount due are not binding on the creditors. For the result in each of these situations there was indeed some case law precedent, past or current, but accommodation of the cases to the newfangled theory required something like major surgery on the cases themselves.

Grant Gilmore, *The Death of Contract* 23–24 (2d ed. 1995) (footnote omitted).

47. Samuel Williston, "Accord and Satisfaction," 17 *Harv. L. Rev.* 459 (1904); Arthur L. Corbin, "Discharge of Contracts," 22 *Yale L.J.* 513 (1913).

of consideration, the entire agreement to discharge.[48] To some classical theorists, this seemed an irresolvable tension, forcing them to choose between the perceived logical consistency of the rules and the embarrassing result of voiding agreements that were an obvious commercial necessity.[49]

The overall effect of the heightened attention to consideration theory was to turn promise (and especially, promise with consideration) into the axis around which contract theory revolved. As a conclusion to this part of the discussion, I will devote some attention to two texts, to show first, that the dominance of the promise-centered vision was a fresh development in the late nineteenth century, and second, that the promise-centered vision entailed a realignment of existing conceptions of private law.

INTRODUCING PROMISE

The fact that a promise-centered vision of contract was an innovation is attested to by the leading English authority writing on the topic, Sir Frederick Pollock. In the first edition of *Principles of Contract*, published in 1876, Pollock laments that "no such thing as a satisfactory definition of Contract is to be found in any of our books." He announces that not one, but a series of definitions will be required to approach "how special and complex a nature the conception really is." Pollock then begins the journey toward a satisfactory definition by noting that, although consent is often thought to be the "main thing" creating a contract, there are many noncontractual transactions that are based on consent. For consent, as "agreement in the widest

48. Merton L. Ferson, "The Rule in Foakes v. Beer," 31 *Yale L.J.* 15 (1921).

49. Compare Ferson's view that "this doctrine is not only patently absurd but is inconvenient in commercial dealings, and, accordingly, distasteful to the courts," with Williston's:

> The application of the law of consideration to attempted discharge of liquidated claims has not infrequently been criticised by courts and law writers; and in a few jurisdictions the law has been changed by decision, or statute. But the rule of the common law has at least the merit of consistency with the general rule of consideration governing the formation and discharge of contracts.

1 Williston, *Law of Contracts*, § 120 (footnote omitted). Grant Gilmore commented that the doctrine engendered "a generation or more of totally unnecessary litigation," and saw it as an example of the way "the general theory of contract wreak[ed] havoc within the commercial community." Gilmore, *Death of Contract*, 37 (citation omitted). Aside from requirements contracts discussed by Gilmore, the most important commercial areas where application of the rule was problematic were (a) modification of long-term contracts (especially building contracts or service agreements), and (b) readjustment of credit agreements, or what was known as composition with creditors. See Ames, "Two Theories of Consideration," 529–31.

possible sense," encompasses any communication of common intentions: "If people make arrangements to go out for a walk . . . that is no agreement in a legal sense." Instead, Pollock argues, there is only agreement in the legal sense when the parties express a common intention such that their rights and duties are determined.[50] Even this definition of agreement, however, is too inclusive to delineate the limited realm of contract:

> The first point that strikes us in this definition is its extreme comprehensiveness. It includes every kind of transaction which affects the rights of the parties and to which the consent of more than one of them is necessary. Not only contract, but every sort of conveyance is covered by it; even a conveyance by way of absolute and immediate gift. . . . [It] includes, of course, gratuitous obligations as well as those made upon valuable consideration. So much as to its general contents. . . . [F]urther analysis is required before we can arrive at anything applicable to the special treatment of contract.[51]

The difficulty Pollock exposes here is how to distinguish between contract and other ways of dealing with property, especially conveyancing and gift giving. Another two pages go by before Pollock reaches the distinction he is after, as he moves from the general notion of common intention mutually communicated, through the Roman Stipulation, and on to a formalization of proposal and acceptance.[52] Finally, the crucial distinction emerges: "In the case of a contract something remains to be done by one or by each of the parties, which the other has or will have a right to call upon him to do."[53] This finally leads to the conclusion that "the expression of this intention [to be bound] is accordingly nothing else than an undertaking to perform the

---

50. Frederick Pollock, *Principles of Contract at Law and in Equity* 1–2 (1st ed., London, Stevens and Sons 1876). The first American edition was published in 1881. Frederick Pollock, *Principles of Contract at Law and in Equity* (Cincinnati, Robert Clarke 1881).

51. Id. (citations omitted). The passage removed by the ellipsis is:

> (Conveyance, of course, contains something beyond agreement, namely, the transfer of property; all that is meant is that every conveyance includes an agreement.) The last item is at first sight startling, especially as there are certain ways of making a gift (otherwise than by a transfer of property) in which the assent or knowledge of the donee is immaterial. But to say that a conveyance by way of gift imports an agreement is only to say that ownership cannot be thrust on a man against his will, and in this form there is nothing strange in the proposition. And in fact there is express authority in our law to show that "it requires the assent of both minds to make a gift, as it does to make a contract" (*i.e.*, when the gift is to take effect by way of a transfer of property to the donee), although the donee's assent is readily presumed, and therefore if money is offered as a gift but not accepted as such, the subsequent agreement of the parties may make it a good loan.

52. Id. at 4–5.

53. Id. at 5.

thing he is bound to—in other words, a promise. This is the specific mark of Contract which we sought."[54]

The important point for us in Pollock's original introduction is the novelty of defining contract as promise. Assuming that his readers are comfortable with not only the everyday notion of consent, but also with legal notions like conveyance, and even the Roman Stipulation, he must still cover a great distance before he has laid the groundwork for introducing a definition of contract based on promise. By the time of the fifth edition, only thirteen years later, Pollock is quite confident that the concept of contract as promise has become familiar, even dominant, allowing him to open the treatise thus:

> The law of Contract may be described as the endeavour of the State, a more or less imperfect one by the nature of the case, to establish a positive sanction for the expectation of good faith which has grown up in the mutual dealings of men of average right-mindedness. Accordingly *the most popular description of a contract that can be given is also the most exact one, namely that it is a promise or set of promises which the law will enforce.*[55]

Whereas only a few years earlier there had been no adequate definition of contract available, and Pollock had arrived at one only through a tortuous dissection of concepts of consent and agreement, theoretical reflection has now provided a concise and most exact definition, and succeeded in popularizing it. This is not necessarily a radical change, but it should be an indication that our current conception of the link between promise and contract was not something one could take for granted before the classical revolution. While the emergence of promise in the definition of contract for Pollock's discussion is particularly dramatic, other treatises exhibit an analogous shift toward an increasingly important role for promise as the classical period extended. An additional striking example may be found in the transformation over the years in C. G. Addison's treatise on contract. The first edition, published in 1847, begins with preliminary observations on deeds and simple contracts, which mentions promises briefly in passing.[56] From there, Addison moves on

54. Id.

55. Frederick Pollock, *Principles of Contract* 1 (5th ed., London, Stevens and Sons 1889) (emphasis added). The substance of this new opening is already present in an earlier edition as a part of the introduction, published before the table of contents, that deals with Holmes's lectures on the common law, but it does not become the opening of the book until the fifth edition.

56. C. G. Addison, *A Treatise on the Law of Contracts and Rights and Liabilities ex Contractu* 1–4 (London, W. Benning 1847).

to a substantive discussion of deeds that occupies all of chapter 1 of the book, and in chapter 2 he reaches simple contracts and discusses promises, though primarily through an explanation of the suspicion toward promises and the necessity of consideration.[57] There is barely any attempt to define contracts in the first place and no effort to define them through promise; indeed, simple contracts are said not to constitute immediate obligations, but to function merely as a mode of evidence.[58] In contrast, by the eleventh edition the treatise opens with a definition of contract that centers on promise: "Every contract includes a concurrence of intention between two parties, one of whom promises something to the other, who on his part accepts such promise. . . . There must be two parties to every contract, a promisor or party making the promise, and a promisee or party to whom the promise is made."[59]

Many of the older treatises did not attempt to define contract, but when a definition was assayed, they proceeded by working out the meaning of agreement or by using the concept of an undertaking. The result of the agreement or the undertaking was an obligation. Such treatises sometimes refer to promises in passing, but typically do not concentrate on its importance.[60] Toward the end of the century, promise typically takes on a more important role, though Pollock's *definition* through promise retains a groundbreaking simplicity in the Anglo-American setting. By the third decade of the twentieth century, Pollock's definition of contract as enforceable promise had become the dominant formulation.[61]

---

57. Id. Chapter 1 runs from pages 5 through 16; the discussion of promises in chapter 2 runs from pages 17–20.

58. Id. at 1–2.

59. C. G. Addison, *A Treatise on the Law of Contracts* 1 (William E. Gordon and John Ritchie eds., 11th ed. 1911). Additional treatises evince the expanding role of promise in defining contract. Compare William R. Anson, *Principles of the English Law of Contract* (Oxford, Clarendon Press, 1st ed. 1879), with William R. Anson, *Principles of the Law of Contract with a Chapter on the Law of Agency* (Arthur L. Corbin ed., 14th Eng. ed., 3d Am. ed. 1919). Similarly, compare S. Martin Leake, *The Elements of the Law of Contracts* (1st ed., London, Stevens and Sons 1867), with S. Martin Leake, *Principles of the Law of Contracts* (A. E. Randall ed., 7th ed. 1921).

60. American treatises often analyze Chief Justice Marshall's definition according to which a "contract is an agreement, in which a party undertakes to do, or not to do, a particular thing." Sturges v. Crowninshield, 17 U.S. 122, 197 (1817). Examples of treatises that do not use promise to define contract include Theron Metcalf, *Principles of the Law of Contracts as Applied by Courts of Law* 1–3 (New York, Hurd and Houghton 1867); Francis Hilliard, *The Law of Contracts* 1–6 (Philadelphia, Kay and Brother 1872); Parsons, *Law of Contracts*, 6–7.

61. See 1 Williston, *Law of Contracts*, § 1; *Restatement of Contracts* § 1 (1932) ("A contract is a promise or a set of promises for the breach of which the law gives a remedy, or the performance of which the law in some way recognizes as a duty").

USING PROMISE TO REALIGN OBLIGATION

The attention to the fine points of consideration could be seen as an overt, though subtle, avenue for navigating promise toward its central position in contract doctrine. But there was another avenue as well: attempting to eliminate elements of what had previously been seen as contract from the domain of the "new" contract. The most important such attempt involved undertakings that relied on standardized relationships for their content rather than on promises. For the most part this was done silently, by ignoring those topics altogether, pushing them out of contract, eliminating them from treatises, or diminishing the attention devoted to them. Sometimes, such categories were reclassified: moved from contract to tort, or to the new field of quasi contract, or, as in the case of bailments, to some other newly minted field thought to be outside the scope of private law discussions.

Here and there we find traces of this process in motion. One is Beale's 1891 article "Gratuitous Undertakings." As someone at the center of a project of reclassifying private law, Beale sets out to reconsider the division of personal actions into torts and contracts, which he saw as inadequate.[62] He first defines and distinguishes contract and tort rights:

> A contract is a right which A has (*in personam*) against B, because B has consented, for a consideration, or in some formal manner, to assume the correlative duty. A tort is a violation of a right which A has (*in rem*) against B, equally with all others, because society has decreed that the corresponding duty should be laid upon every member of it.[63]

He then describes a kind of obligation that fits neither of these categories:

> Between these classes of rights exists a third; which, unlike a tort, depends upon some voluntary act by B, by which he undertakes a duty, and, unlike a contract, does not depend upon any promise of B, but only upon the mutual relations of A and B. In other words, B assumes a duty merely by voluntarily entering into a new relation towards A.[64]

It is crucial to note how Beale makes the conception of contract as promise with consideration the centerpiece of his treatment. Beale's definition of

---

62. Beale, "Gratuitous Undertakings," 222.

63. Id.

64. Id.

contract creates the entire problem he addresses, as it raises the necessity of finding some nomenclature to cover those cases that were traditionally treated as contracts, but no longer fit into the definition that he considers conclusive.[65] Beale continues:

> To create such a right and duty no consideration need be shown, since no contract is necessary. As a matter of fact, entrance into such a relationship is often the occasion of a contract, which may to some extent supersede the principles of the common law, and govern the rights and duties of the parties. . . . But even in these cases the terms of the contract seldom embrace the whole transaction. . . . There is no technical name for these rights. In the old law, action for the breach of such a right was induced by an assumpsit, or, as it should be translated in such a case, *he undertook.* Following this old use, which is by no means uncommon to-day, I shall call a right of this sort an undertaking.[66]

After delineating some of the relationships to which the common law attaches independent content, Beale comments:

> All these are cases where the relationship between the parties was voluntary; in none of them is there any contract, and in most of them the liability of B could not arise from any tort, properly so called. One of the most important classes of undertakings, however, is bailments; and for a long time it was held that every bailment included a contract. There has lately been a determined effort to controvert that doctrine, which is certainly untenable with regard to gratuitous bailments, because there is no consideration to support a contract.[67]

Ultimately, Beale's solution to this problem is to generate a new classification, undertakings of relational duties, and to make the duties conform to a model of implicit consent. The actual duties should be those that are consented to, even when there is no explicit mention of the duties, or when the parties rely on custom or common practice with regard to their content. Thus, Beale preserves the contractual idea of duties based on consent,

---

65. Another author, trying to reconcile a promise-centered conception of contract with liability for gratuitous undertakings, wrote: "Such liabilities, reasonable enough in themselves, are difficult to reconcile with a logical use of the English doctrine of consideration; and they may well be exceptions to its universal application in contract." William R. Anson, *Principles of the Law of Contract* 134–35 (Arthur L. Corbin ed., 3d Am. ed. 1919).

66. Beale, "Gratuitous Undertakings," 222–23.

67. Id. at 223–24.

but since there is no consideration, and usually no promise, he must find a noncontractual category to describe the undertaking. "In brief, the rule applicable in all cases of agency, bailment, or other undertaking, whether gratuitous or not, is this: The undertaker is held to such a degree of care and exertion in the business as in fact he undertook to bestow."[68]

Beale's effort to create a new classification is analogous to the attempts at extruding quasi contract from contract—a project that was advanced definitively in William Keener's treatise just two years after Beale's article appeared.[69] This, along with the other efforts at highlighting and advocating a promise-centered conception of contract, was aimed at banishing relational duties from contract, and particularly at isolating and marginalizing the gratuitous undertaking, which these scholars analogized to the gift and to an older regime of status. Whether or not they referred overtly to Henry Maine's claim that the movement of progressive societies is one from status to contract, classical thinkers used the evolutionary framework to reformulate contract law. Instead of dealing with contract as encompassing statuslike relational duties, classical theorists attempted to paint contract as a wholly consensual realm, where the parties themselves determined the content of their mutual duties.

While the classical attack on gratuitous undertakings was primarily aimed at business relationships, there was also a parallel attempt to make the law of personal gratuitous transactions—namely gifts—coherent with the concept of contract advanced by the classicists. The attack on gratuitous business undertakings was one arm of the establishment of the donative promise principle; the other was a rationalization of the law of gifts. In a manner of speaking, efforts like Beale's, and the reinforcement of consideration theory as the center of contract, combined to bury the gift.

---

68. Id. at 231.

69. William A. Keener, *A Treatise on the Law of Quasi-Contracts* 3–16 (New York, Baker, Voorhis 1893). The treatise was a part of a larger project. See William A. Keener, *A Selection of Cases on the Law of Quasi-Contracts* (New York, Baker, Voorhis 1888).

TWO

The Gift Beyond the Grave: Case Law

Commentators have generally assumed that the changes in legal theory at the end of the nineteenth century had a deep impact on the case law of the period.[1] It seems true that the style of justification employed by judges underwent significant changes.[2] But there is good reason to suspect that even the establishment of a particular rule does not generate the determinate results that might be expected from the formal justification.

The case law of gifts provides a crucial example that sheds light on the workings of consideration doctrine. Chapter 1 showed how classical theorists tried to ground consideration doctrine in the verifiable aspects of exchange. The analysis of gift cases, however, shows that the baseline for the application of consideration doctrine could never escape the ambiguities that the classicists were trying to avoid. Their strategy relied on isolating contract, making a sharp distinction between the contractual realm and other forms of obligation, notably quasi contract and gifts. But the cases

1. See P. S. Atiyah, *The Rise and Fall of Freedom of Contract* 681–87 (1979).

2. See Karl N. Llewellyn, *The Common Law Tradition: Deciding Appeals* 35–45 (1960).

show that the gift cannot easily be contained within its boundaries. Where even rigidly formulated and widely accepted rules cannot succeed in erecting an impenetrable border, the classical strategy of isolating contractual obligation is threatened.

A close reading of gift and gift-promise cases reveals a tension in classical contract theory. Classical theory set out to minimize the importance of duties based in relationships, in part because these were perceived to be state-imposed. Correlatively, it accorded heightened importance to individual determination of the content of contractual obligations. But what happens when these two impulses conflict, when individual intentions are rooted in incalculable relationships, as in gift cases? On the one hand, gifts and gift promises are made in the context of intimate relationships, where a calculable exchange is difficult or impossible to pin down. On the other hand, gift givers often manifest clear intentions to give. The tension between these two theoretical directives—privileging intention while playing down relationship—is reflected in the technical requirements for valid gift giving.

Before delving into the case law, however, it is worth emphasizing and justifying a shift in focus from the preceding chapter. In the discussion of the development of consideration and its marginalization of gratuitous undertakings, the context was primarily that of business agreements. Here, in contrast, the focus is on "transactions" that do not simply lack consideration, but rather are specifically intended as gifts. I do not pretend to offer an ontology of gifts or to say that a gift could never be given in the context of business; however, it is worth noting the difference in context between those cases in which a nominally gratuitous transfer is incidental to business,[3] and those in which the transfer is incidental to a relatively intimate relationship.[4]

Gratuitous business undertakings include, among other things, many cases of bailments, agency, surety, and guaranty (particularly surety for the debts of married women or others of limited contractual capacity, such as infants). These cases were the difficult ones for the new theory of contract

3. An illustrative example is the recurrent case of gratuitous bailees, such as banks, who undertake to hold securities for customers. This is gratuitous, but it is actually a collateral engagement that is parasitic on the client/service-provider relationship, which is experienced as part of business. See Preston v. Prather, 137 U.S. 604, 612–13 (1891).

4. This is not to say that gifts in intimate relationships are unimportant. As Brian Simpson reminds us in the context of rules governing the alienability of land, gifts were and remain very important in the distribution of wealth. A. W. B. Simpson, "Land Ownership and Economic Freedom," in *The State and Freedom of Contract* 13, 34–35 (Harry N. Scheiber ed., 1998).

at the level of categorization, because everyone acknowledged, on some level, the existence of a whole set of enforceable obligations without consideration, and thus the challenge was to distinguish these obligations from contract. But the second category, gifts, should have provided the easy case. As far as delineating a set of formal rules, it was easy for the theorists to say simply that gift promises were unenforceable. The real problem for the neatness of the theory, then, is to deal with "easy" cases that do not conform to the ideal image, which separates strictly enforceable from unenforceable promises. Instead, the two are liable to bleed into one another by raising the same question that was supposed to distinguish between them: why should the state intervene to enforce an obligation? In cases where some kind of fairness or justice consideration seems too weighty to be ignored, the rules begin to bend. Indeed, a close examination of the cases leaves a reader with the sense that ad hoc considerations of fairness and justice or propriety do much of the work in leading judges to decisions.

Litigation over the validity of gifts arises almost exclusively after the donor has died. It has long been accepted that in addition to donative intent, delivery of the object of the gift is necessary to effect a valid gift. Often, this requirement is spoken of as if it were an ancient feature of the common law, but in fact, the requirement was not established definitively until 1890.[5] Even after this, at which point the requirement of delivery was a part of the consolidation of the law of consideration, there were important exceptions to the rule requiring delivery.[6] The most blatant exception was the ability to establish a trust by parol. Thus, a declaration that *A* held a chattel in trust for *B* without delivery of the chattel was sufficient to pass equitable title

5. Cochrane v. Moore, 25 Q.B.D. 57 (Eng. C.A. 1890); See 7 William Holdsworth, *A History of English Law* 503–9 (1926); Jane B. Baron, "Gifts, Bargains, and Form," 64 *Ind. L.J.* 155, 161–64 (1989). In the mid-nineteenth century, some American courts ruled that gifts could be effective without delivery. See, e.g., Leddel's Ex'r v. Starr, 20 N.J. Eq. 274, 287 (Ch. 1869); Brinckerhoff v. Lawrence, 2 Sand. Ch. 400 (N.Y. Ch. 1845); Ziegler v. Eckert, 6 Pa. 13 (1847); see also C. R. McCorkle, Annotation, Gift of Debt to Debtor, 63 A.L.R. 2d 259, 282–86 (1959).

6. A note authored by Harlan Fiske Stone outlines some of the important exceptions:

> It is frequently stated in judicial opinions that in order to effect a gift of a chattel there must be a delivery of the chattel by the donor to the donee or to some third person for the donee. . . . Nevertheless there has probably been no time in the history of the law, certainly not since the time of Edward IV, when the statement . . . was literally true, or when ownership in a chattel might not under proper conditions be transferred without a deed or other instrument and without a delivery of the chattel as an essential element in the transfer of ownership.

Harlan F. Stone, "Note, Delivery in Gifts of Personal Property," 20 *Colum. L. Rev.* 196, 196–97 (1920) (footnote omitted); see also Roscoe Pound, "Consideration in Equity," 13 *Ill. L. Rev.* 667, 672–75 (1919).

to *B*, even though a declaration of gift would have no effect.[7] Such a trust could only be enforced at equity, but in effect it meant that anyone with sufficient legal sophistication (actually knowledge of one esoteric rule) could circumvent the necessity of formality for enforcement of gift promises.

While the exceptions are interesting and important, I will postpone considering them further, in order first to devote attention to the workings of the rules in the heart of their area of applicability. Litigation over gifts has undergone relatively dramatic changes in the last hundred years. Today, much gift-related litigation is either part of a tax dispute, part of a divorce settlement, or part of a will contest where the decedent had more than one spouse during his or her lifetime. Around the end of the nineteenth century, however, the context of gift litigation was markedly different. Litigation arose in two areas. The first, and probably most prevalent, was a situation sometimes called the poor man's will, where a donor, in anticipation of death, attempted to give personal property to the people closest to him or her prior to death. Very often, the attempted gift was of the donor's life savings, held in a savings bank. As we will see, these cases were especially problematic for the courts. The other scenario that generated a great deal of litigation was the attempt to forgive loans made to family or close friends. In almost all the reported cases, the litigation is between the donee and someone representing the heirs at law of the donor/decedent.

FORMALITIES AND GIFT PROMISES

My first goal here is to show that even when the legal rules of gift transfer were well settled, those rules could not ensure like outcomes in like cases. This formulation may be misleading. It is not crucial that the identical case

---

7. One early writer expressed his frustration at the inconsistency between legal and equitable standards regarding gifts:

> In reality very different standards are applied for the purpose of determining the completeness of a transfer, according as it falls on one side or other of the thin line which separates a gift from a declaration of trust. The difference amounts, in the first place, to nothing less than this,—that, if it falls one side of that line, all that is necessary for a complete transfer is to establish the intention of the donor that the transfer shall immediately take effect, while if it falls on the other side of that line, the most clearly expressed intention of the donor will not render the transfer a perfect one, unless certain formalities, laid down by the law as appropriate to such transfer, are complied with.

C. B. Labatt, "The Inconsistencies of the Laws of Gifts," 29 *Am. L. Rev.* 361, 363 (1895) (footnote omitted); see also Pound, "Consideration in Equity," 669–71.

presented twice would have been decided differently by the same court. The claim is simply that cases that could not be distinguished on the basis of their "legally relevant" facts might generate opposite results. "Legally relevant" here refers to those facts that have a direct bearing on the rules. The pliability of outcomes opens another angle in the examination of gift cases. Even where the rules are relatively clear, two related but possibly unexpected things occur: first, people still litigate the occurrences a great deal; second, people continue to behave in ways that bring them into conflict with the rules as stated. This is at least some indication that for the people who end up litigating these cases, the rules and the cases more generally have little incentive effect. But if these cases have little to do with how people will try to dispose of property, they raise the question of how legal norms might affect cultural attitudes, or more generally, how legal rules can influence society.[8]

An examination of the relationship between the legal norms and the behavior of real people, then, requires an in-depth examination of the cases. While the requirements for the validity of gifts were spelled out in various ways in different cases, there were two issues that were of major practical importance.[9] One requirement was that the donor intended to give the donee a gift; the second was that the donor "delivered" the object of the gift to the donee. While the question of intent occupied judges in many cases, it was the seemingly technical requirement of delivery that afforded decision makers wide latitude in deciding whether or not a particular gift was valid.

---

8. I hope to offer some kind of answer to this question in what follows, based on the idea that a particular framework within which the choice of rules is bounded has greater cultural significance than the specific rule choices adopted within that framework. But the first step in providing an explanation of the cultural significance of legal rules requires a skeptical attitude toward any simple theory of the incentive effects of rules. Sophisticated versions of such skepticism have been forwarded, and even made the basis of extended theoretical reflection. See David Charny, "Nonlegal Sanctions in Commercial Relationships," 104 *Harv. L. Rev.* 373 (1990). However, the literature on gifts and consideration, and on private law generally, is too often motivated by an unstated economism that translates rules directly into incentives, without considering the way people might adopt, live by, succumb to, or alternatively be ignorant of or actively ignore or rebel against rules that potentially apply to their lives.

9. Simple explanations of the requirements of a valid gift mentioned that "two things are indispensably necessary,—an intention to make the gift, and a delivery of the thing given." Newman v. Bost, 29 S.E. 848, 848 (N.C. 1898). More elaborate explanations included additional elements:

> The elements necessary to the validity of a gift inter vivos have been specifically stated as follows: (1) The donor must be competent to contract. (2) There must be freedom of will. (3) The gift must be complete, with nothing left undone. (4) The property must be delivered by the donor and accepted by the donee. (5) The gift must go into immediate and absolute effect. Reduced to simpler form, it is held that a gift must be voluntary, gratuitous, and absolute.

Fisher v. Ludwig, 91 P. 658, 660 (Cal. Ct. App. 1907) (citations omitted).

But this latitude did not arise from uncertainty in the formulation of the rule. Rather, as will be shown, the rule was well settled by the time of the cases considered. Instead, in applying the rule to the facts of the cases judges had the opportunity to decide on the validity of the gift in accordance with other considerations regarding the transfers. An examination of a few cases will clarify the factual context in which such gifts were attempted.

The relatively straightforward litigated cases on gifts are those in which the donor offers the donee a bank book or a deed or mortgage document as a gift.[10] A paradigmatic example is the much-cited case of *Ridden v. Thrall*,[11] in which the donor, a Mr. Charles Edwards, delivered to the plaintiff, his friend James Ridden with whom he lived,[12] a tin box containing sixteen bank books representing forty thousand dollars in deposits. Edwards gave the box to Ridden before entering the hospital for a hernia operation, from which he feared he might die, saying that if he should not return, the box and everything in it was to belong to Ridden. The operation was a success, but Edwards died of heart failure while still in the hospital recovering (as it were) from the operation. The court held the gift valid.[13] The delivery of the bank books in the tin box was testified to by the plaintiff's wife and corroborated by a letter that Edwards left in a bureau in the room he occupied in the plaintiff's house.[14] The court, noting the significant size of the

10. A simpler case would be the handing over of cash or a chattel, but these cases are rarely litigated. The majority of cases are those in which a symbol of indebtedness, like a bank book, is the object of the delivery.

11. 26 N.E. 627 (N.Y. 1891).

12. The fact that Edwards lived with Ridden is difficult to glean from the court of appeals opinion, but is clear in the decision of the general term. Ridden v. Thrall, 7 N.Y.S. 822, 823 (Gen. Term 1889).

13. *Ridden*, 26 N.E. at 628–29. The court explained:

> The gift was consummated by the delivery of the books, and no other formality was needed to constitute the actual delivery of the bank deposits needful to vest the possession and title in the donee. In savings banks in this state such deposit books are issued as evidence of indebtedness of the banks. . . . The decisions are not entirely harmonious as to the sufficiency of the mere delivery of such deposit books to constitute a valid gift, either *inter vivos* or *causa mortis.* But the general rule in England and in this country, and particularly in this state, is that any delivery of property which transfers to the donee either the legal or equitable title is sufficient to effectuate a gift; and hence it has been held that the mere delivery of non-negotiable notes, bonds, mortgages, or certificates of stock is sufficient to effectuate a gift.

14. Id. at 628. The letter was addressed to the plaintiff, and read:

> Friend Jim: Should I not survive from the effects of the operation about to be performed on me at St. Luke's Hospital, this is my last will and request, that you will take charge of my body, and have it placed in my family plot in Greenwood Cemetery; and also that you will take full charge of all my personal effects of every kind, and to have and hold the same unto yourself, your heirs and assigns, forever. You will find my papers and all my accounts in the box. C.H. Edwards.

deposits, said, "such a gift should be proved by very plain and satisfactory evidence, and, if the case depended upon the evidence of the wife alone, any court might well hesitate to uphold the gift." The corroboration provided by the letter was sufficient to quell any doubts about the authenticity of the delivery, leading the court to conclude that "while standing alone, it would not have been sufficient to establish the gift, it furnishes strong confirmation of the evidence of plaintiff's wife as to the gift, and leaves no reason to doubt that it was made as she testified."[15]

This seemingly straightforward case touches on several issues that require individual exploration. First, there is the question of what acts will amount to a sufficient delivery; second, the question of what evidence will be sufficient to establish the making of a gift; and finally, and closely related to the first two issues, the question of the relationship between the acts of delivery and the intention to make a gift.

What Counts as Delivery?

The question of which acts will amount to a sufficient delivery is complicated by the fact that in most of the litigated cases a gift is made of a chose in action, typically the debt of a bank to a donor, or the debt of the donee to the donor. Because these gifts are not simple chattels, and thus cannot be delivered in themselves, the question is what object will suffice to symbolize a delivery.[16] In *Ridden* and many cases like it, the gift is a deposit in a bank, and the bank book is held out as the best symbol of the asset.[17] However, while savings bank accounts were susceptible of being given through such

15. Id.

16. The question of whether symbolic delivery was ever sufficient plagued theorists and bothered some courts. Holdsworth claimed that symbolic delivery was never sufficient, but that in certain cases "constructive" delivery (for instance, by supplying the key to a safe or a warehouse) might be. 7 Holdsworth, *History of English Law*, 503–4. American courts usually did not distinguish between constructive and symbolic delivery, accepting both terms. But see *Newman*, 29 S.E. at 851, in which, after discussion of the diversity of holdings in different states requiring either symbolic or constructive delivery, the court held that "there is no such thing in this state as 'symbolical delivery' in gifts either inter vivos or donatio causa mortis in this state."

17. See, e.g., Fisher v. Ludwig, 91 P. 658, 660 (Cal. Ct. App. 1907) (holding that savings bank deposits may be transferred by delivering the pass book); McCoy's Adm'r v. McCoy, 104 S.W. 1031, 1031–32 (Ky. Ct. App. 1907) (stating that "the authorities hold, almost without exception, that the delivery of a pass or deposit book in a savings bank transfers the money on deposit to the donee," citing six cases from different jurisdictions); see also 1 Samuel Williston, *The Law of Contracts* § 439, n. 54 (1st ed. 1920) (citing additional cases).

delivery, many courts held that checking accounts or accounts in banks of general deposits could not be given through delivery of the pass book.[18] More complex cases arose when donors attempted to make a gift by forgiving a debt. Some examples should clarify the problems embedded in these questions.

Complex forms of delivery raised ambiguities for the courts. For example, sometimes donors did not deliver the bank book or note in question, but rather some means of attaining it, for instance, a key to a safe deposit box or trunk where the bank book or note was kept. Courts divided internally (majority and dissenting opinions within particular cases), and externally (among cases with similar facts), over whether the key to a trunk, a safe, or a safe deposit box in a bank could suffice as delivery.[19]

---

18. See, e.g., Jones v. Weakley, 12 So. 420, 421 (Ala. 1893) (holding that delivery of the pass book in "a bank of issue, discount, and deposit" would not validate gift, though the same delivery of a savings bank pass book would). But see *McCoy*, 104 S.W. at 1032 (rejecting the distinction between savings banks and banks of deposit, holding that delivery of the pass book in either case would perfect the gift). For a discussion of the issue and critique of the distinction, see Harold C. Havighurst, "Gifts of Bank Deposits," 14 *N.C. L. Rev.* 129, 133–35 (1936).

19. In *Phipard v. Phipard*, plaintiffs were the four sons of the deceased, who had taken out a life insurance policy and repeatedly said that the policy was for the benefit of his children. 8 N.Y.S. 728, 729 (Gen. Term 1890). The court held that in addition to a valid trust created by parol, the policy was in effect delivered to one of the plaintiffs as a gift. Id. at 729–30. The deceased had given his son Harvey, one of the plaintiffs, "the key to the box in the safe-deposit vaults in which the policy was kept, together with an order directed to the custodian of the vaults to deliver the box to his son, whom he directed to take possession of it." Id. at 730. Treating the question of whether the key to the deposit box could suffice as delivery, the court said:

> By the delivery of the key to this plaintiff, who was the eldest son of the assured, accompanied with the order for the box containing the policy, and the instrument attached to it, a constructive delivery was made, and that was sufficient for all the purposes of the law; for an actual delivery to render a gift complete is not necessary, but a symbolical delivery will be sufficient.

Id. The dissenting opinion took the opposite view of the facts:

> The mere fact that the testator, previous to his death, delivered to the plaintiff the key to his safe-deposit box, in which box these papers were, together with an order for the delivery of said box, showed no intention to deliver, by that act, these papers. It is not claimed that the plaintiff could claim any of the rest of the contents of the box because of this alleged delivery, and how is any distinction to be made? Besides, as has been already said, there is no finding that the papers in question were ever delivered, which is essential to the plaintiffs' success.

Id. at 731 (Van Brunt, P.J., dissenting). The division is instructive precisely in its lack of legalistic discussion. The judges agree that delivery is essential to the validity of the gift. It appears they also agree that, in principle, delivery of a key to a safe deposit box *may* amount to sufficient delivery. But when put to the test of deciding whether it does in fact do so, they divide, without further discussion: the majority says, "a constructive delivery was made, and that was sufficient," while the dissent says simply that no delivery was made.

Another typical case is *Reynolds v. Reynolds*, where the donor was ill and went to stay with family members, the plaintiffs, who took care of her. 45 N.Y.S. 338, 339 (Sup. Ct. 1897). On the morning before

Another form of complex delivery arose in cases where the gift was delivered to a third party, with instructions to subsequently deliver the gift to the intended donee. In *Partridge v. Kearns*, for instance, the donor made out a note for two hundred dollars with the intention of giving it to the plaintiff for the benefit of her infant sons. She gave the note to a third party, and two days before her death instructed the latter to give the note to the plaintiff. Reversing the conclusions of the trial court, the appellate division held that "there was no delivery of the thing" and that there was "none of the formality necessary to pass title."[20] On essentially the same facts, however, many courts considered delivery to a third person sufficient to pass title and to create a valid gift.[21]

---

she died, the donor said that she wanted the plaintiffs to have everything. She took some keys out from under her pillow, and gave them to the nurse, who handed them to the plaintiffs. The plaintiffs then removed a tin box from the trunk at the foot of her bed, and left the room. This was considered sufficient delivery of the bank book contained in the box, and the gift was thus upheld. Id. at 340–42. But courts were far from unanimous in accepting delivery of keys. One court explained its reluctance to find delivery in the handing over of a key to a trunk by saying that it would be a "dangerous extension" of the forms of valid gifts:

> Cogent reasons may be given for protecting the thousands of depositors in savings banks . . . in relation to the contents of safe deposit boxes and vaults of which the owners hold the key. Mrs. Kane's pass book was not the actual subject of her alleged gift, but, rather, a symbol of such gift. The key was therefore, at most, a symbol of a symbol of a gift. The delivery of the key of a trunk containing so many different articles which Mrs. Kane might desire to have taken from it for so many different purposes is an act in itself far less significant of a gift of any particular articles in the trunk than the manual delivery of the trunk itself.

Dunn v. Houghton, 51 A. 71, 76 (N.J. Ch. 1902), (holding that there was no gift causa mortis by delivery of the key, but upholding the gift on the ground that the bank accounts themselves had already been valid gifts in the life of the donor); see also Gescheidt v. Drier, 20 N.Y.S. 11, 11 (Gen. Term 1892) (holding delivery of keys to wardrobe insufficient); Pink v. Church, 14 N.Y.S. 337, 337 (Gen. Term 1891) (holding delivery of key to a safe vault sufficient).

20. 53 N.Y.S. 154, 155 (App. Div. 1898).

21. For example, in *Bump v. Pratt*, the court stated:

> To constitute a valid gift . . . there must be such an actual or constructive delivery of the possession as to place the subject of the gift beyond the possession and control of the donor, and placed in the actual possession of the donee, or of some person for the donee. Assuming, as I think we must, that the referee's findings of the question of fact upon this point are supported by the evidence, then there was a delivery of these bonds by the intestate in her lifetime to Miss Cornell for the defendant Pratt, with directions that they should at some time thereafter be delivered to the donee. That, we think, within the authorities, was such a parting with the possession by the donor, and delivery to another for the donee, as to vest the title in the donee.

32 N.Y.S. 538, 540 (Gen. Term 1895). In *Langworthy v. Crissey*, a case involving the gift of a promissory note, the court stated: "A delivery to the donee in person is not necessary. A delivery of the thing granted to another person for the use of the donee is sufficient, and the donee's subsequent demand of the property given, and his efforts to obtain possession thereof after the same has come into the hands of the donor's executor, is evidence of his acceptance of the gift." 31 N.Y.S. 85, 86–87 (Sup. Ct. 1894) (quoting the "marginal note" of Hunter v. Hunter, 19 Barb. 631, 631 [N.Y. Sup. 1855]). In *In re Essex's Estate*,

Some of the most complicated discussions of the sufficiency of delivery arose in the context of joint accounts, which were often opened with the intention of assuring the transfer of the contents of the account to the donee. Typically, a donor would open a joint account with the donor's own funds, or change an existing account from her own name into a joint account. Most often, the assumption underlying the change was that the donor would continue to have access to and control over the funds during her lifetime, but that the donee would become sole owner of the account at the donor's death. In some circumstances, courts were willing to go to great lengths, even reversing straightforward findings of fact on delivery when no contradictory evidence was presented, to rule that there was no sufficient delivery.[22] On the other hand, there were situations in which courts simply ignored problems of delivery in order to validate the gift.[23] The contrast among the cases shows that even the widely accepted formula that valid gifts require delivery and that delivery requires the surrender by the donor

---

delivery to a third party was held sufficient, with the court going further and stating, "In case of gifts *causa mortis* physical possession of the property is not necessarily parted with by the donor." 20 N.Y.S. 62, 63 (Sur. Ct. 1891). In *In re Hall's Estate*, the court stated: "It has been distinctly held in many cases that the delivery may be made to a third party for the donee, and that such delivery will be sufficient." 38 N.Y.S. 1135, 1139 (Sur. Ct. 1896).

22. An interesting example is the case of *De Puy v. Stevens*, where the plaintiff was a friend of the deceased donor, Nancy Sibbalds. 55 N.Y.S. 810, 811 (App. Div. 1899). Six weeks before her death, the donor withdrew the funds from a savings account, and redeposited them in an account "in the name of 'Mrs. Nancy Sibbalds or Miss Hattie De Puy' [the plaintiff] . . . 'Either or survivor to draw.'" Id. at 811. (The plaintiff was the donor's agent for these changes in the account.) Uncontradicted evidence showed that the donor, handing the bank book to the plaintiff, said, "'It is yours; take it, and put it away, and take good care of it;' that the plaintiff then said, 'They will talk after this,' whereupon Mrs. Sibbalds replied, 'What do you care? You are all right.'" Id. at 812–13. The trial court held that these actions were sufficient to establish the gift inter vivos, and to create a right of survivorship in the account. The appellate court reversed, saying that the evidence did not support the claim that the actions showed the deceased's intention to make a gift of the funds in the account, defeating both the gift and the claim of survivorship. Id. at 813–15. I will return to two of the issues raised in this ruling, the question of evidence and the question of intent, later in this chapter.

23. In *Kelly v. Beers*, the donor changed her savings account so that she or her daughter, the donee and plaintiff, could draw from the account, with the survivor retaining control. 86 N.E. 980, 984 (N.Y. 1909). The plaintiff and the deceased lived together, and the bank book was kept in a locked trunk in the house, to which they both had keys. The trial court held that the change in account did not amount to a valid gift or the creation of joint ownership or survivorship in the account. The court of appeals reversed, and without dwelling on the possibility of the lack of delivery, said:

> The controlling question for us has been, and is, whether [the donor] intentionally and intelligently created a condition embracing the essential elements of joint ownership and survivorship. If she did, that was sufficient, even though she did not use any particular formula in doing it. Her acts and repeated declarations indicate that she did intend to do just that which is denied, give to her daughter joint ownership in and control over this account.

of dominion over the gift was flexible in the hands of judges who saw reasons to vary their conclusions in particular cases.[24]

The Standard of Evidence

Ambiguity over the required standard of evidence to prove a gift became an important mechanism in affording judges flexibility in deciding cases on gifts.[25] While there was some conflict among courts over the proper standard of evidence required to establish a valid gift, even the most quoted formulae describing the standards were vague enough, and encompassed enough contradictory corollaries, to allow judges to decide relatively unconstrained by the legal standard. The suspicion of claims of gifts, resulting especially from the fact that deceased donors could not testify as to whether or not they actually made a donation, led judges to seek stronger evidence before validating such claims.[26] One court, dealing with what it viewed as an inherently improbable claim of a gift, said: "In many of such cases there is great danger of fraud, and all the books concede that the evidence which proves the gift should be clear and convincing, strong and satisfactory. Although

---

24. One of the most quoted formulations of the rule is as follows: "Delivery by the donor, either actual or constructive, operating to divest the donor of possession of and dominion over the thing, is a constant and essential factor in every transaction which takes effect as a complete gift." Beaver v. Beaver, 22 N.E. 940, 941 (N.Y. 1889); Compare cases where joint accounts were held to create neither gift nor survivorship, e.g., Appeal of Main, 48 A. 965 (Conn. 1901); Norway Sav. Bank v. Merriam, 33 A. 840 (Me. 1895); Whalen v. Milholland, 43 A. 45 (Md. 1899); Schippers v. Kempkes, 67 A. 74 (N.J. 1907); Cunningham v. Davenport, 41 N.E. 412 (N.Y. 1895); and Krummel v. Thomas, 25 N.Y.S. 833 (Gen. Term 1893); with cases where joint accounts were held to create valid gifts including rights of survivorship, e.g., Appeal of Buckingham, 22 A. 509 (Conn. 1891); Bangs v. Browne, 112 N.W. 1107 (Mich. 1907); Dunn, 51 A. 71 (N.J. Ch. 1902); Decker v. Union Dime Sav. Inst., 44 N.Y.S. 521 (App. Div. 1897); McElroy v. National Sav. Bank of Albany, 40 N.Y.S. 340 (App. Div. 1896); and Hannon v. Sheehan, 22 N.Y.S. 935 (C.P. N.Y. County 1893).

25. The question of the standard of evidence required to prove a gift (usually to prove delivery of the gift) should be distinguished from the question of evidence as a justification for the requirement of delivery. Judges, and then theorists, often spoke of delivery as a formality, necessary to provide evidence of the gift, and particularly as a prophylactic against fraud. The evidentiary justification of delivery, however, has no necessary relationship to the standard of evidence required to prove the delivery.

26. In fact, while the donor was silenced by death, the donee was often silenced by the rules of evidence, which in some states made it impossible for the claimant to testify that he or she had been given a gift by the donor, since testimony against the executors of an estate regarding a transaction with the deceased could not be given by a party to the transaction. See 2 N.Y. Code Civ. P. § 829 (Bliss, 4th ed., New York, Baker, Voorhis 1895) ("A party or person interested in the event . . . shall not be examined as a witness . . . against the executor, administrator or survivor of a deceased person . . . concerning a personal transaction or communication between the witness and the deceased person"); for applications, see Boyd v. Boyd, 58 N.E. 118 (N.Y. 1900); Rogers v. Maguire, 47 N.E. 452 (N.Y. 1897).

it may not be true that the law presumes against a gift, it certainly does not presume in its favor, but requires proof of it."[27]

Courts divided over what such proof consisted of. Did "clear and convincing, strong and satisfactory" evidence amount to anything more than a preponderance of the evidence, as required generally in civil cases? Some courts believed that this was precisely the question, and that it should be answered affirmatively.[28] In many cases, finding evidence that was clear and convincing, or "strong, clear, and conclusive," became a stumbling block, or an excuse, depending on one's perspective, preventing the finding of valid gifts.

The details of some of the cases merit attention. In *Podmore v. South Brooklyn Savings Institution*, the deceased gave a number of bank books to the donee, a Mrs. Reilly. The deathbed scene in which the donor, just prior to her death, gave Reilly the bank books was described by two independent witnesses. The trial court found for the defendant, validating the gift.[29] The appellate division reversed, saying that while there was independent corroboration of the event of delivering a number of pass books, there was no independent confirmation of the identity of the specific pass book in ques-

---

27. Devlin v. Greenwich Sav. Bank, 26 N.E. 744, 744 (N.Y. 1891) (citations omitted).

28. For instance, in *Tilford v. Bank for Sav.*, plaintiff claimed that the deceased, who had boarded with her for eight months prior to his death, gave her his bank book before he died, saying she should have the money for the kindness and care she showed him. 52 N.Y.S. 142, 143, 146 (App. Div. 1898). Witnesses testified to the delivery of the bank book to the plaintiff, and that the deceased did not want his son to inherit any of his money. Id. at 144, 146. There was conflicting testimony as to events after the death of the donor, regarding statements made by the plaintiff about the donor's property. Id. at 147–48. The trial court ruled in favor of the plaintiff, but the appellate division reversed, saying:

> The rule of law which governs the disposition of cases involving gifts inter vivos and causa mortis, so far as cogency of proof is concerned, is somewhat different from the strength of evidence usually found sufficient for the establishment of contracts, the rights of parties arising thereunder, and of other similar questions. The reason for this rule is found in the fact that fraud may be quite easily perpetrated, that weakness and uncertainty of will are often attendant upon the donor, and temptation to construe an act and circumstances into a gift, by reason of interest, presses strongly upon the donee. For these and other reasons the courts have uniformly hedged about the establishment of these gifts [with] somewhat unusual requirements, and have insisted that the proof in support thereof shall be strong, clear, and conclusive.

Id. at 142–43.

29. 62 N.Y.S. 961 (App. Div. 1900). The suit was brought by the donor's administrator against the bank; the donee had, prior to the suit, presented the bank book and received payment, and the administrator challenged the propriety of the payment. Suits were also brought against the other banks in which the deceased had accounts. See Mahon v. Dime Sav. Bank of Brooklyn, 87 N.Y.S. 258 (App. Div. 1904) (reversing judgment for administrator as against the weight of the evidence); Podmore v. Dime Sav. Bank of Williamsburgh, 66 N.Y.S. 1071 (App. Div. 1900) (affirming directed verdict for administrator, *invalidating* the gift, in a suit against both Dime of Williamsburgh and the Brooklyn Savings Bank); Podmore v. Seamen's Bank for Sav., 71 N.Y.S. 1026 (N.Y. City Ct. 1901) (reversing judgment for administrator of estate, on grounds that Reilly's testimony of the gift should not have been excluded).

tion.[30] The combination of a relatively straightforward account of the gift and the corroboration of two external witnesses in addition to the donee makes the response of the court puzzling. One is tempted to ask, if this evidence is not clear and convincing, what could be? The mystery deepens upon consideration of a later decision of the same court, with an almost identical panel, in a case originating from the same facts. In *Mahon v. Dime Savings Bank of Brooklyn*,[31] the appellate division reversed a finding of a jury as against the weight of the evidence, holding that the evidence of the gift, including evidence of the identity of the bank book, was sufficient.[32] The facts of the *Podmore* gift generated almost all the legal outcomes available, with the only point of contention being whether "clear and convincing" evidence existed regarding the identity of a specific pass book.[33] The search for evidence identifying a particular pass book seems even more peculiar when contrasted with cases where witnesses only saw a box, or even keys to a box, being delivered, but the identity of the pass books was never raised as an issue.[34]

Judicial language to the effect that the law presumes neither for nor against the gift has a balanced ring, but one should not be fooled. When the claimant of a gift has possession of the bank book, any demand for "clear and convincing" evidence (if the phrase has any meaning) creates a presumption

---

30. Podmore v. S. Brooklyn Sav., 62 N.Y.S. at 963–64. Proof of the identity of the bank book was supplied by Reilly herself, and though she was not a party to the suit, the court said that she practically stood in the shoes of the defendant, thus exposing her testimony to suspicion. Id. at 964.

31. 87 N.Y.S. at 258. The action was originally brought by John Podmore, as administrator, but subsequent to its commencement he died, and Mahon was substituted as *administratrix de bonis non*.

32. Id. at 259–60. The panel in *Mahon* consisted of Van Brunt, P.J. (who dissented, without opinion), McLaughlin, Patterson, O'Brien, and Laughlin, J.J., while the panel in *Podmore v. S. Brooklyn Sav.* consisted of Van Brunt, P.J., Barrett, McLaughlin, Patterson, and O'Brien, J.J. Was the replacement of Barrett by Laughlin a critical factor? Or is this simply direct "white horse case" evidence of arbitrariness in the outcome of gift cases?

33. The same maneuver, holding that evidence of delivery was sufficient, except regarding identification of specific bank books occurs in In re Wiegel's Estate, 28 N.Y.S. 95, 100 (Gen. Term 1894) (Van Brunt, P.J., concurring).

34. See, e.g., Ridden v. Thrall, 26 N.E. 627, 628 (N.Y. 1891) (validating gift of tin box containing bank books); Gibbs v. Carnahan, 25 N.Y.S. 786, 786 (Sup. Ct. 1893) (validating gift of bag allegedly containing securities and other property, without scrutiny as to contents of bag); Hannon v. Sheehan, 22 N.Y.S. 935, 936 (C.P. N.Y. County 1893) (holding that gift was valid since delivery could be inferred from possession by sister who lived with the donee); Phipard v. Phipard, 8 N.Y.S. 728, 730 (Gen. Term 1890) (holding delivery of key to deposit box sufficient without inquiry into which of its contents were part of the gift); *Reynolds*, 45 N.Y.S. at 341 (validating gift of contents of tin box made by delivery of keys). But see *Phipard*, 8 N.Y.S. at 731 (Van Brunt, P.J., dissenting) (arguing that inability to distinguish among the contents of the box should defeat gift).

against the gift. But a presumption against the gift is far from neutral: it is, in effect, a presumption of theft on the part of the claimant.[35] Some courts glossed over without comment the fact that a search for weightier evidence was tantamount to calling claimants thieves.[36] Other courts were willing to intimate that the claimants were larcenous,[37] while still others articulated their distaste at the prospect of insinuating a crime onto the claimant.[38]

It is sometimes thought that strict rules of evidence are oriented toward limiting the discretion of legal decision makers. In turn-of-the-century gift cases, however, the rules of evidence, and especially the formula requiring clear and convincing evidence, opened up wider latitude for judges, offering an additional justification with a legalistic ring, where another, more case-specific factor appears to have motivated the decision.

Intention

Perhaps the most interesting aspect of the judicial opinions on gifts is the role of intention. At a time when the objective theory of contracts was as-

---

35. At least, this is the case where the question is evidence of the delivery of the gift, where delivery is the only evidence of donative intent. This is a concrete doctrinal manifestation of the phenomenon Carol Rose has called the "gift leak[ing] into . . . theft." See Carol M. Rose, "Giving, Trading, Thieving, and Trusting: How and Why Gifts Become Exchanges, and (More Importantly) Vice Versa," 44 *Fla. L. Rev.* 295, 302–8 (1992).

36. See, e.g., Dinlay v. McCullagh, 36 N.Y.S. 1007, 1008 (Gen. Term 1895); *Gescheidt*, 20 N.Y.S. at 11; *Podmore v. S. Brooklyn Sav.*, 62 N.Y.S. at 964; *Tilford*, 52 N.Y.S. at 148.

37. See, e.g., Alsop v. Southold Sav. Bank, 21 N.Y.S. 300, 302 (Gen. Term 1892) (reversing finding in claimant's favor despite testimony to event of gift, because "the deceased is entitled to a vigilant scrutiny of the evidence, where she was in so unprotected a situation in respect to property which could be transferred by delivery"). The court in *Podmore v. Dime Sav. Bank of Williamsburgh* was even more explicit:

> The fact that the donee had possession of this particular bank book is no evidence of a gift; more especially as she and others had opportunity to take it both before and after the decedent's death. Possession of the chattels of a deceased person either before or after his death is no evidence of a gift. The law presumes nothing from it; and independent of it there must be that "clear and convincing, strong and satisfactory" proof which is required to make out a gift causa mortis, in order to prevent fraud and larceny.

60 N.Y.S. at 534.

38. For example, in *Devlin v. Farmer*, reversing a referee finding that there was insufficient evidence of delivery, the court said, "Of course, plaintiff may, when she went to the trunk at her uncle's request to get the bonds, have feloniously, and without his knowledge, abstracted the bank-books; but, as far as can be judged from the evidence . . . I should have been loath to adopt that theory." 9 N.Y.S. 530, 531–32 (C.P. N.Y. County 1890), rev'd sub nom Devlin v. Greenwich Sav. Bank, 26 N.E. 744 (N.Y. 1891). In *Gibbs v. Carnahan*, rejecting the requirement of a standard of clear, convincing, strong, and satisfactory evidence, the court pointed out the inconsistency between what amounts to a presumption of fraud or theft in the case of gifts and the presumption against such a charge in civil actions. 25 N.Y.S. at 787.

cendant, judges in gift cases seem to have been consistent in searching out the subjective intention of a deceased donor, and often with the assumption that the intention was at odds with the donor's objective behavior. But more interesting than this binary split between objective and subjective theories is the tension among the different roles that intention could play in deciding the cases. Some opinions articulate the view that the role of the court is to attempt to effectuate the intention of the donor.[39] But other courts note that the rules pertaining to gifts are a limitation on effectuating intentions.[40] One of the most quoted articulations of this view comes from *Beaver v. Beaver*:

> Anything short of [delivery] strips [the gift] of the quality of completeness which distinguishes an intention to give, which alone amounts to nothing, from the consummated act, which changes the title. The intention to give is often established by most satisfactory evidence, although the gift fails. Instruments may be even so formally executed by the donor, purporting to transfer title to the donee, or there may be the most explicit declaration of an intention to give, or of an actual present gift, yet, unless there is delivery, the intention is defeated.[41]

In some cases, formalities were viewed and employed as obstacles to effectuating the actual intention of the donor.[42] But *Beaver*'s oft-quoted formulation does not actually represent the theory of that case. *Beaver* did not present a situation where a gift was attempted without regard to the

---

39. One example is *McCoy's Adm'r v. McCoy*, where the donor had delivered the pass book to a bank account to her son prior to her death. 104 S.W. at 1032. Upholding the gift, the court said:

> The mere fact that a check might be better evidence of the intention to make the gift complete will not be allowed to defeat the purpose of the donor. In this class of cases, as well as others, the intention of the giver must be looked into. The purpose with which the delivery is made must be considered; and from the facts and circumstances surrounding the transaction the court or jury trying the case must determine whether or not the gift was designed to be and was completed. Generally the delivery must be as perfect as the nature of the property will admit; but the manifest desire of the donor will not be set aside by a narrow construction that would defeat his purpose.

40. The clearest case of the limitation on freedom of gift is that of the donor who attempts to effectuate a testamentary donation without a will.

41. 22 N.E. 940, 941–42 (N.Y. 1889).

42. The prototype for this kind of case is the widely cited case of *Young v. Young*, in which the court invalidated an attempted gift of bonds by a father to his sons because of a lack of formal delivery. 80 N.Y. 422, 430 (1880). Acknowledging that the intention to do so was clearly manifested, the opinion opens: "The intention of Joseph Young deceased to give the bonds in controversy on this appeal to his son William H. Young, reserving to himself only the interest during his life-time, was so clearly manifested, that we have examined the case with a strong disposition to effectuate that intention and sustain the gift, if possible." Id. at 422.

proper formalities, causing the gift to be defeated. In fact, just the opposite is true. The supposed donor, John Beaver, made a deposit in a bank in the name of his son. The court agreed that this was objectively consistent with an intent to make a gift.[43] But the court found that it was more likely in this case that the actual intention of the "donor" had nothing to do with making a gift to the "donee" named in the pass book. "We cannot close our eyes to the well-known practice of persons depositing in savings banks money to the credit of real or fictitious persons, with no intention of divesting themselves of ownership."[44] The court thought that validating the gift would subvert the real intention of the depositor: "We are inclined to think that to infer a gift from the form of the deposit alone would, in the great majority of cases, and especially where the deposit was of any considerable amount, impute an intention which never existed, and defeat the real purpose of the depositor."[45] Thus, while the case is often quoted as standing for the proposition that intent alone, lacking the proper formality, will not be enough to validate an attempted gift, its holding is actually based on a finding that despite fulfillment of the formal requirements, there was no intent to make a gift.[46]

The *Beaver* case provides a good introduction to the complexities of intention in gift cases. One thing it shows is that any simple opposition between formalities and intent is too reductive to explain the role of intent. The simple view might claim that a tension emerges from the inevitable generality of any rule that sets out to achieve a policy objective. Here, the policy objective implied in requiring formality in gifts (the formality being delivery) is twofold: to supply evidence (or reduce the likelihood of fraud), and to ensure deliberation on the part of the donor. The foreseeable tension arises, in theory, when donors have every intention of making a proper gift but do not succeed in delivery. Anyone advocating a rule that mandates some level of formality realizes that intention will have to be sacrificed some of the time, but that is

43. *Beaver*, 22 N.E. at 942.

44. Id. The court continued: "It is attributable to various reasons,—reasons connected with taxation, rules of the bank limiting the amount which any one individual may keep on deposit, the desire to obtain high rates of interest where there is a discrimination based on the amount of deposits, and the desire on the part of many persons to veil or conceal from others knowledge of their pecuniary condition."

45. Id.

46. See, e.g., In re Small's Will, 50 N.Y.S. 341, 346 (App. Div. 1898); Dinlay v. McCullagh, 36 N.Y.S. 1007, 1008 (Gen. Term 1895); In re Taber's Estate, 63 N.Y.S. 728, 734–35 (Sur. Ct. 1899); In re Gregg's Estate, 32 N.Y.S. 1103, 1104–5 (Sur. Ct. 1895).

seen as the price of procuring the policy objective. This view, however, misses one of the important uses of intention in the gift cases, which is to invalidate the gift *despite* the fact that the formalities have been carried out.

Importantly, the complexities of intention do not stem from a conflict over the *rules* of valid gifts. Instead, this is a conflict played out in courts' interpretations of the *facts* before them. A good example is *Kirk v. McCusker*, in which two judges offered radically different interpretations of the same facts.[47] The donor, Margaret Kirk, was ill. She delivered two bank books to her friend, Bridget McCusker, with a note saying, "If anything happens, I leave all the money I have in the bank to Bridget McCusker."[48] Kirk repeated in front of two witnesses that she wanted McCusker to have the money. (Recall the similarity of the note that evidenced the gift in *Ridden v. Thrall.*)[49] The trial court found that Kirk had made a valid gift causa mortis, that is, in apprehension of her own death. Reversing the judgment on the facts, the majority wrote:

> What, then, is the inference from these repeated expressions of Margaret Kirk? That she delivered the bank books upon the contingency of her death, or in apprehension of the threat of Thomas Kirk to burn or tear down the house? That the latter was the event, and the only event, she had in mind, and intended to provide against, is manifest, beyond the possibility of rational dispute.[50]

Finding that the delivery of the bank books was made only to guard against the actions of the donor's brother, and not against her death, the court ruled that there was no intention to make a gift causa mortis.

Two things are noteworthy in the majority opinion. First, there is the specificity of the intention the court requires: an intention to make a gift will not suffice; the donor must have an intention to make a gift under the conditions that the law recognizes. Had a general intention to give been at issue, the court need not have looked to an apprehension of death, and could have considered the gift as effective inter vivos. The question of what intent a court looks for is central to many cases. Often the question is not simply whether there was an intent to give, or even an intent to deliver, but

47. 22 N.Y.S. 780, 782–83 (C.P. N.Y. County 1893).

48. Id. at 782.

49. 26 N.E. 627, 628 (N.Y. 1891).

50. *Kirk*, 22 N.Y.S. at 783.

whether there was an intent to do particular acts that the law recognizes as adequate delivery. This problematic will resurface in other cases.

The second noteworthy element is the adamance with which the court states its conclusion, putting it "beyond the possibility of rational dispute." But dispute there is, not only with the trial court whose finding of fact contradicts the majority opinion, but also with the concurrence, which is stated just as adamantly:

> As to the original gift, all the constituents of the donatio causa mortis are found in the detailed transaction. The illness or ailment of the donor, from which she never recovered before her death, which took place within six weeks; the gift in praesenti of the bank books to the defendant, which is a delivery of the sums credited therein, the words which accompanied the gift, "There is your fortune for you," together with the whole conversation,—*make out a case beyond even a reasonable doubt*. The written paper, which at the time of the gift the deceased caused to be drawn up, and which she signed . . . confirms the gift. The contingency therein expressed referred to her death. She told them that the doctor told her that the sickness would take her off at any time.[51]

The concurrence argues that the judgment of the trial court must be reversed because of admission of improper testimony, but goes on to say that the case for the gift was sufficiently made out. Overall, the case is an economical illustration that judicial interpretation of the facts of the case, and especially the facts surrounding intention, generated wide leeway for decision makers, even without any conflict over the rules of valid gifts.

Other cases reveal additional aspects of intention that were manipulable in the hands of judges. One important recurrent question was the status of joint accounts. Depositors often turned their accounts into joint accounts, sometimes with the assurances of the bank that the added account holder would be entitled to survivorship—in other words, would become the sole owner of the account upon the depositor's death. Courts divided on whether such a change in the account could serve to create the right of survivorship, and thus be deemed a valid gift. The courts made this distinction based on an analysis of the depositor's intention.

The case of *Dunn v. Houghton*, decided by the New Jersey Court of Chancery, is a good illustration because it offers one of the fullest discus-

---

51. Id. at 784 (Daly, C.J., concurring) (emphasis added) (citations omitted).

sions of the legal questions that arise in this context.[52] The donor, Mary Kane, had accounts in several savings banks, two of which she changed in August 1894, almost six years before her death, to accounts to the credit of "Mary Kane or niece Katie Pender." The question for the court was whether this action was sufficient to establish a valid gift.[53] Noting that various courts had reached different conclusions,[54] the court critiqued other discussions of the same fact pattern for ignoring the contractual relationship among the parties.[55] The court held that by contracting with the bank to provide rights to the donee, the donor had effected a valid gift, despite the fact that the enjoyment of the gift was contingent on the donor not depleting the account prior to death.[56] By authorizing creation of a joint account as a method of making a valid gift, the court isolates the question of intent as a question of fact: did the donor, at the time of adding the donee to the account, intend for the account to be a gift to the donee?[57]

---

52. 51 A. 71, 75–82 (N.J. Ch. 1902).

53. The court dealt with three theories of how the gift might be made out: donatio causa mortis, with the crucial question being the delivery of the bank books by the donor in anticipation of her death (this theory was rejected), id. at 75–76; the effectuation of a gift by making the accounts into joint accounts (accepted), id. at 77–78; and creation of a trust (the court speculated that this would have been valid as well, but left the ruling on the footing of the valid gift), id. at 79. For the moment, I am interested only in the second theory.

54. The opinion makes mention more than once of the conflict in the case law: "The question which had given difficulty, especially in the maze of decisions in savings bank pass book cases found in our Reports, is, what is the essential form—what are the essential physical facts—which must appear in order to give effect to the donative purpose?" Id. at 76. And later: "How far the foregoing views are sustained, and how far they are controverted, by decisions of courts in other jurisdictions, which we receive with great respect, I shall not endeavor to inquire. An elaborate discussion of these decisions might be of use if it were possible to reconcile them." Id. at 80.

55. Id. at 77.

56. The court distinguished between the obligation and the monetary value of the obligation:

> In my judgment, when a man with donative purpose converts a part of his estate into an obligation of a savings bank to another person, the discharge of which obligation may, however, contingently benefit that person, and which that person can enforce in case the contingency occurs which makes such enforcement advantageous, a case is presented of a complete gift. The external form of the gift is the absolute conversion of the donor's property into a binding obligation of a third party, the performance of which according to its terms may upon certain contingencies benefit the donee. There is nothing, however, contingent about the gift. The gift is absolute. The right is vested beyond recall in the donee. It is a matter of no consequence that the right so vested may prove in the end to be of no pecuniary value.

Id. at 77–78.

57. The question of the time of the gift opens up an entire field of discussion, which I mention only briefly here. For some courts, the finality of the gift was essential, so that any retention of power over the object of the gift after the gift was made would be evidence that there was no gift at all; on the other hand, some courts acknowledged that a gift could be made, but its value affected by future actions of the

While this may seem like a commonsense construction, it does have some counterintuitive effects. For instance, while the language is that of a completed gift, the donor retains the power to make the gift valueless, since she retains functional control over the deposit in her lifetime. Other courts found that this feature could not be reconciled with the kind of intention they associated with a gift, and treated the same facts as leading to completely different conclusions about intention.[58]

The relationship between intent and the form of the deposit is complex. For some courts, it seems that it really is the thought that counts, and they concentrate on determining a conscious historical intention, that is, whether the donor intended the joint account to be a gift to the person added to the account. For other courts, the very form of the account is taken as an indication that there could not have been a donative intent, because such an intent requires that "[the gift] should go into effect, or in

---

donor. Compare Norway Sav. Bank v. Merriam, 33 A. 840, 841 (Me. 1895) (holding that "the giver must part with all present and future dominion over the property given. He cannot give it, and at the same time retain the ownership of it. . . . [T]he gift must be absolute and irrevocable, without any reference to its taking effect at some future period"); with *Dunn*, 51 A. at 78 (holding that the contingency of the pecuniary value of the gift and the donor's power to influence it does not invalidate the gift itself, which remains absolute, despite donor's continued control). Another aspect of this problematic is that some courts favored leaving the donor maximum control during her lifetime over the gift, while others tried to fix the point of making the gift as irrevocable. Compare *Cunningham*, 41 N.E. at 412 (allowing depositor who opened account in trust for his brother to revoke the trust after the brother's death, thus leaving the depositor control over the deposit despite its form implying gift); with *Kelly*, 86 N.E. at 983–84 (holding that the intent to give when the account was made into a joint account would not be revoked by any subsequent change of view regarding the gift); and Decker v. Union Dime Sav. Inst., 44 N.Y.S. 521, 522 (App. Div. 1897) (holding that a trust, once established, is beyond the power of depositor to revoke).

58. The dynamic may be seen in the following quotations:

> The deposit in the names of Miss O'Neill and Mrs. Whalen was payable to the order of either, or the survivor. Miss O'Neill, having by this form of entry retained undoubted power to draw the money out of bank [*sic*] whenever she pleased, obviously did not devest herself of dominion over it. There was nothing to prevent her from checking out every cent of the fund immediately, or at any time, after the deposit in the two names had been made. If this be true,—and it cannot be questioned,—there was no perfected gift to Mrs. Whalen, and she consequently acquired no interest in the fund by the form of the entry as it then stood.

Whalen, 43 A. at 47. This particular formulation seems to put more weight on the inherent nature of a joint deposit, while other courts often linked the issue more directly with the question of intent. This statement regarding facts similar to those in *Dunn* is typical:

> We think it is clear from the nature of the transaction that [the donor] did not intend by this transfer of her deposit to the new accounts to make at that time fully executed gifts of either the legal or equitable title to the new deposits, or to part with all control over the same . . . but rather that her intention was to make a testamentary disposition of these deposits, so that the persons named should each take, in case he or she survived her, what might be left of each sum after her death.

Norway Sav. Bank, 33 A. at 842. The court goes on to say that such a testamentary transfer is incompatible with the statute of wills, and thus void. Id.

other words, transfer the property, at once and completely; for, if it has reference to a future time when it is to operate as a transfer, it is nothing more than a promise without consideration, and cannot be enforced either in law or in equity."[59] Often, courts remained uncommitted about what the form of the deposit entailed, leaving themselves the widest possible latitude in attributing intention to the original depositor.[60]

SUMMARY

Judges' manipulations of the test of intention in gift cases reveal a deep ambivalence with regard to gifts more generally. The judges appear to be searching for sufficient reasons to enforce the gift, but this search masks a more difficult and perhaps contradictory search for reasons for giving the gift. In the search for such a cause, judges seem to rely on locating the gift within an economy of reasons. But this search, while perfectly understandable in context, undermines basic ideas about the nature of gifts. After all, if there is a gift, the donor gives it without the expectation of return and without the sense of paying off an antecedent debt. Otherwise, this giving would simply be swallowed up by the logic of exchange. The gift is, in this sense, something given for nothing, for no reason. And yet, in the context of judging, of enforcing, judges are inevitably drawn toward the reason for the gift. The test of intention, particularly, channels judicial inquiry toward a narrative in which a donor wants to give, in which a donor has her reasons. These reasons should not amount to the kinds of reasons the law can recognize as consideration, which would place the situation

---

59. *Whalen*, 43 A. at 46.

60. See, e.g., *Appeal of Main*, 48 A. at 967–68 (stating that "'the actual intention of the parties to the transaction is the main issue,'" but holding that in this case the intention was to make a "testamentary disposition of the money, [which] was void because not made in legal form") (quoting 2 James Schouler, *A Treatise on the Law of Personal Property* 87–88 [3d ed., Boston, Little, Brown 1896]); *Appeal of Buckingham*, 22 A. at 509–10 (holding that deposits in the name of donor and donees became valid gifts, despite donor's retention of sole power to draw on account in her lifetime, but reversing judgment validating the gift on grounds of admission of improper evidence); Skillman v. Wiegand, 33 A. 929, 932 (N.J. Ch. 1896) (stating that intention is paramount, and finding that the intention was not to make a gift, but rather to make transactions more convenient for original depositor); *Kelly*, 86 N.E. at 983–84 (reversing trial court's finding of fact as to intention and noting that donor's expression of desire to give gift and her inclusion of donee's name on account proved intent "with a clearness and force beyond that required by the authorities"); In re Bolin, 32 N.E. 626, 626 (N.Y. 1892) (holding joint account and delivery of pass book did not show intent); *McElroy*, 40 N.Y.S. at 341 (holding account to credit of donor and donee was perfected gift, even without delivery of pass book).

within contract, but there ought to be reasons nonetheless. But how would these reasons be articulated? What would they look like? The gift raises the specter of the subject without reason. And if the borders of the gift, and therefore of contract, are porous, the rationality of the contracting subject is threatened as well.

The close reading of gift cases yields a few tentative conclusions about the workings of doctrine. First of all, the cases show that even when a rule becomes widely accepted and courts repeat a formulaic expression of it, there is considerable leeway in decision making. One aspect of this leeway is that the rules retain significant exceptions, facts to which they simply do not apply. In the context of the rule on delivery, for instance, we saw that in certain situations, courts viewed delivery as unnecessary. But exceptions are not the main source of latitude for most rules. Instead, the greater leeway is created by the process of characterizing the facts.[61] The issue is not predominantly a question of "fact skepticism": even when there is agreement as to the objective acts carried out by the parties, courts are called upon to infuse the facts with meaning.[62] And different courts interpret identical objective acts differently.

The question arises as to whether there is any underlying regularity in the courts' interpretations of facts and their interaction with rules. A thorough investigation of the question is beyond the scope of this chapter, but it may be worth engaging in a brief speculation. Judicial rhetoric in the gift cases often reveals that judges at times extended the limitation of freedom of gift to reflect their own predilections as to who should give and, particularly, who should receive gifts. At times, this is nothing more than a reluctance to see the "natural" heirs disinherited.[63] At other times, courts were will-

---

61. Eben Moglen, "Legal Fictions and Common Law Legal Theory: Some Historical Reflections," 10 *Tel Aviv U. Stud. L.* 33, 47–48 (1990).

62. Robert Cover put the point dramatically:

> Just as the meaning of law is determined by our interpretive commitments, so also can many of our actions be understood only in relation to a norm. . . . There is a difference between sleeping late on Sunday and refusing the sacraments, between having a snack and desecrating the fast of Yom Kippur, between banking a check and refusing to pay your income tax. In each case an act signifies something new and powerful when we understand that the act is in reference to a norm.

Robert M. Cover, "The Supreme Court, 1982 Term—Foreword: *Nomos* and Narrative," 97 *Harv. L. Rev.* 4, 7–8 (1983).

63. This reluctance appears even in abstract form, when it is clear from the judgment that the court has no sympathy for the particular heirs. An example is *In re Wiegel's Estate*, where the court went to great lengths to find a way to reverse the trial court's finding of a valid gift. 28 N.Y.S. at 99. The motivation seems to appear when the court mentions that "we do not think a stranger to the blood of the intestate

ing to acknowledge that the strictness of the rules could be mitigated in cases where the gift was natural, or the donee especially worthy.[64] Courts

---

should be allowed to succeed to the entire estate upon testimony of the character which was offered to sustain his claim." Id. But the deceased was an immigrant who had lived with the plaintiff and was employed by him for twenty years, and had no known relatives in the United States. Id. at 97. The court shows no sympathy toward the deceased, and cynically says, "The intestate was not in extremis when it is asserted that he made the gift, but he had ample opportunity to express his intention by a will, executed in accordance with the laws of this state." Id. at 99. At other times, the reluctance simply translates into a propensity to uphold gifts where the donee would be the heir at law in any case. See, e.g., McMath v. O'Connor, 42 N.Y.S. 1127, 1127 (App. Div. 1896) (mentioning that the transaction claimed was "a natural and reasonable one," and saying that "it was natural that the testator, when he found his wife at the point of death, should have transferred his bank books to the plaintiff, his sister and only relative").

64. An illustration is *Dennin v. Hilton*, in which the donor was the plaintiff's seamstress, who lived with the plaintiff and his family. 50 A. 600, 601 (N.J. Ch. 1901). The court mentions that the plaintiff had been generous with her, characterizes him as her lifelong friend, and says of her, "She was very saving. She spent nothing. She got to be . . . an expert seamstress and milliner. She was a general genius." Id. at 601. Coming to a decision over whether to validate the gift, the court says:

> Now, is there any reason why this transaction should not stand? What could appeal more to a court of equity than this case? Is there anything in the law to prevent this woman's desires from being carried out? Is there anything disgraceful or disreputable in Capt. Hilton's accepting this gift from the woman for whom he held such an affection, and who held such affection for, and was so grateful to, him and his wife? I think not.

In *Rix v. Hunt*, the court ruled that in the case before it, possession by the donee of the notes in question was sufficient to create a presumption in favor of the gift, explaining its inclination thus:

> In the first place, the gift was not an unnatural act upon the part of the donor, but, upon the contrary, was just what might have been expected of a just and generous person in the same circumstances. With the exception of a brother, whose decease was in all probability but a question of a year or two at most, the plaintiff was as nearly related to Sylvester Rix as any living being. She had come to him in his old age, and had served him faithfully for nearly 10 years. There is no evidence that she ever received any compensation for the services thus rendered other than a half interest in the homestead, and the cow and notes in suit. All the other nephews and nieces of the donor were married, and living by themselves; and no reason is furnished, other than that of kinship, why they should share in the testator's bounty.

44 N.Y.S. 988, 993 (App. Div. 1897). In *Reynolds v. Reynolds*, the deceased had given a gift to a relative who took care of her in her last illness. 45 N.Y.S. at 341. The court, rejecting the strict evidence rule generally applicable to gifts, said: "When the gift is a natural one, and the evidence is reasonable and probable, and the several steps to establish the gift causa mortis are established by a fair preponderance of evidence, the donee is entitled to the decision or verdict." Id. In *Thomas v. Fuller*, the donor and donee were relatives by marriage, and the court, fighting off a slight disbelief that someone might want to give a gift, wrote:

> We are aware that gifts are not usual among the ordinary business transactions were [*sic*] valuable considerations move the parties, and that they are frequently induced by sentiment or affection. A gift must be proved like any other fact. . . . But as we have stated, there is no conflict in the evidence. . . . The contention only arises as to the inferences to be drawn therefrom. The conclusion reached by the referee appears to us to be natural and logical, such as the ordinary mind would reach upon the facts. If Baker did not intend the note as a gift, what did he intend?

22 N.Y.S. 862, 864–65 (Gen. Term 1893). In *In re Clark's Estate*, the deceased left an estate of approximately ninety thousand dollars, but in addition, his housekeeper was in possession of over sixty thousand

consistently referred to the gifts they were willing to uphold as just, probable, reasonable, and natural. For the most part, this is just a reflection of judges using their basic sense of propriety, equity, and justice when deciding whether a particular gift is valid. But this benign characterization sometimes belies a darker underside, where a sense of propriety, with that term's Victorian connotation, might collide with a vision of justice informed by a different sensibility.[65]

---

dollars, claimed by the heirs to be invalid gifts, which the court justified on the basis of her importance in his business affairs, saying:

> It appears that Mrs. Richardson had been his faithful housekeeper for almost a quarter of a century, taking charge of his elegant home, in which he was accustomed to entertain quite largely; and she was, no doubt, his confidential adviser in business matters, as she seems to be possessed of financial skill and ability scarcely less marked than that of her benefactor. It is easy to see how Dr. Clark might well have desired to reward her in a sum far exceeding simple compensation for services.

39 N.Y.S. 722, 730 (Sur. Ct. 1896).

65. *Thomas' Adm'r v. Lewis* offers an illustration. The court sets out the facts in what it calls an "unavoidably long narrative of the relations, circumstances, congruities, and situation of the parties." 15 S.E. 389, 392 (Va. 1892). Thomas never married, but lived with a woman who had been his slave, and had two daughters by her. The elder daughter died, and the younger daughter was the claimant in the case. She lived with Thomas for over twenty years, presiding over his household and taking care of him during his illness. The court's own language in the description is worth reproducing here, though the full description is much longer:

> [Thomas] never married, but cohabited with a woman of half white blood, formerly his slave . . . by whom he was the father of two daughters, Bettie, and an older sister, Fannie, who married and died, soon after the late civil war, without issue. Bettie, 35 years of age when her father died, and Fannie were always recognized and acknowledged by William A. Thomas as his children; they called him father, and he called them and cherished and lived with them as his children. The death of Fannie was a great grief to him; and, after that event, his whole and devoted affection was centered upon Bettie, as "daughter of his heart and house," whom he loved "passing well," and from whom he was never thereafter separated, except for the two years that he sent her to a boarding school.

Id. at 390. Superstitious about making a will, he gave his entire estate to his daughter Bettie (the claimant) in the final days of an extended illness that led to his death, by delivering to her deeds to property, a bank book, promissory notes and bonds, and keys to a vault at the bank, comprising his entire estate, worth over two hundred thousand dollars. Id. at 389. The trial court found for the claimant, and a divided Virginia Supreme Court affirmed. Id. at 400. The differences between the majority and dissenting opinions say a great deal about how judges' predispositions can affect the characterization of the facts. The court's language merits quotation at length:

> There is in the record very much more testimony, equally strong, explicit, unimpeached, and uncontradicted, attesting the life-long, avowed, and unwavering solicitude and purpose of this isolated old man to nourish tenderly while he lived, and to provide for amply at his death, his devoted and faithful daughter Bettie, the only light of his long life, and the only love which quickened the emotions of his introverted and self-centered soul. . . .
>
> [T]he avowed and constant object of Mr. Thomas' life, labor, and love was solicitude and provision for his daughter Bettie. . . . [T]here is not one *scintilla* of proof in the record that, through all the years of his life, and in all the references he ever made to his intended disposition of his property, he ever had in his heart or mind a purpose to provide particularly for any other than his cherished

> child, to whom he was bound by the strongest ties of nature and affection; to whom he owed the undivided obligation of a father; and whose whole tenor of life, as shown by the record in this case, from her birth to the moment of his death, was an unvarying demonstration of dutiful devotion and filial confidence and affection.

Id. at 391–92. The majority opinion relates the testimony of friends of the deceased, showing his intention to leave everything to his daughter and nothing to his estranged distant relations, and of the eyewitness to the gift, the claimant's companion, Fannie Coles. The court characterizes Coles's testimony as "clear, consistent, convincing, and uncontradicted," and "consistent throughout . . . natural, reasonable, and most probable," and mentions her "triple armor of truth" in the face of "protracted and pertinacious cross-examination." Id. at 394.

The dissenting opinion rests ostensibly on a point of law regarding the applicability of a Virginia statute on gifts to the case at hand. But the dissenting judge cannot abide the trial court's determination or the majority's characterization of the facts. Instead, he describes what almost appears to be a different set of circumstances:

> As appears from the opinion of the majority of the court, this is a suit to enforce against the administrator of a dead man's estate an alleged gift of the whole estate, amounting to over $200,000, which alleged gift is claimed to have been made by the decedent in disregard of all of his heirs and distributees,—his next of kin,—a few minutes before his death, to a colored woman living in his house, who claims to be the result of illicit intercourse with a colored slave woman.

Id. at 400 (Lacy, J., dissenting). After discussing the application of the statute to the case, the dissenting judge adds his view of the evidence, which is clearly the motivating factor in the dissent:

> I do not mean to concede that all that is testified to appears to me to be credible. It is an alleged gift of everything the donor possessed. This is the claim. Who was the donor? An infirm, sick man, advanced in years. At his bedside was the alleged donee, a colored married woman, acknowledged to be his child by the donor, no longer young. At her elbow, another colored woman, which latter is the sole witness to prove the gift of this large estate, who, with much detail, recites the circumstances of the gift.

Id. at 404 (Lacy, J., dissenting). The dissent goes on to list circumstances supposedly inconsistent with the gift, though there is no attempt to justify suspicion of the gift through the evidence detailed by the majority. Id.

Most striking here is how the racial hostility of Judge Lacy is expressed not only rhetorically but also through his recharacterization of the facts. The stark contrast between the opinions shows the obvious force of judges' predispositions influencing a decision and suggests that the same kinds of predispositions affect the decisions of jurors, trial judges, and appellate judges in more subtle ways in the plethora of cases where the relationships between donors and donees diverge from the typical. A suggestive example is *De Puy v. Stevens*, where the donor and donee were both women, and the donee told the donor, upon receiving the gift, "They will talk after this," and the donor replied, "What do you care? You are all right." 55 N.Y.S. at 813. The court, reversing the trial court's validation of the gift, noted that other cases with similar facts recognized valid gifts upon the same acts, but distinguishes those cases by noting that the gifts there were between husband and wife. Id. at 814–15.

THREE

Responding to Revolution

Moving Gifts and Consideration Through the Twentieth Century

The case law regarding gifts throws stark light onto the workings of the classical theory of consideration, and onto classical theorizing of private law more generally. While classical scholars succeeded in formulating widely accepted rules, for instance regarding the enforceability of gifts and gift promises, concrete cases with similar facts still revealed a wide range of possible solutions. This was true not only in cases lying near problematic borderlines such as gratuitous business undertakings, but also in what theoretically should have been the easy cases: promises to make gifts. The varying solutions in concrete cases, in turn, were difficult to reconcile with any single account of the justifications for the stated rules.

The revolution in consideration was conceptual. Its successes on the conceptual plane, however, did not translate into straightforward changes on the level of the outcome of the cases. Thus, as shown in the previous chapter, the theoretical proposition that gifts required delivery to be valid (viewed as an extension of the principle that gratuitous promises, without more, were unenforceable) was elevated in status. Theorists established it as the starting point for the discussion of gifts. And in the case law, the idea developed from a frequently heard but still contested proposition before the time of the classical writers into a foundational principle of the law of gifts, repeated mantralike, even in cases whose results undermined its functioning.

The generation of theorists that followed the classical writers was not oblivious to the gaps between the articulations of rules and the decisions of courts. Indeed, the acute awareness of this problem was the motivation for most private law theory in the postclassical period. The responses generally followed one of two paths, though they had important overlapping elements. One path was to attempt the reform of existing doctrine, ranging from suggestions for direct judicial variation of doctrine, to proposals for revising doctrine in the framework of the Restatement of Contracts, to ideas for legislation to correct the failures or excesses of contract doctrine. The other path was more subtle, but eventually had a deeper impact on American legal thought, reorienting the theoretical discussion of contract (and private law generally) away from its focus on the rules and their derivations from first principles, and toward a pragmatic elaboration of policy justifications for the existing rules, or alternative ones.

REFORMING CLASSICAL DOCTRINE

Attempts at reform of consideration doctrine are familiar, in that they have occupied much of twentieth-century discussion over contract. I will not attempt an exhaustive review here. Instead, it will suffice to mention a few of the leading efforts, and to highlight the aspects of classical contract thinking they leave intact. With the competing goals of variety and economy in mind, it is worth considering three attempts at reform of the rules of consideration: one a sweeping success, one an equivocal success, and the last, an apparent failure followed by incremental partial success.

The first example revolves around the rights of third party beneficiaries to a contract, or as the question was often phrased at the time, from whom must the consideration move? The classical statement of the rules received clear articulation in Langdell's *Summary*. Langdell adopted the English rule mandating that consideration must move from the promisee and would create rights only between the contracting parties. Langdell viewed the rule as a necessary, logical extension of the definition of consideration itself.[1] The

1. Christopher Columbus Langdell, *Selection of Cases on the Law of Contracts, with a Summary of the*

classical position was attacked on many grounds, and by the 1920s most American jurisdictions had rejected the English rule. The first Restatement of Contracts (1932) jettisoned the original classical position, allowing what it called the "donee beneficiary" to recover in most situations.[2] The "striking departure in American law from the English authorities" was justified both by the weight of authority in American courts, and by the commercial inconvenience caused by the alternative doctrine.[3]

A less complete success can be seen in what became one of the most famous conflicts over the rules of contractual liability, the question of promissory estoppel. The issue has been much discussed and needs little elaboration here. It is enough to note that the classical theory of consideration was a restrictive theory that attempted to limit enforceability to promises explicitly bargained for. The critique of the restrictive position has been widespread and ongoing, and received official recognition in section 90 of the Restatement. The success, however, was only partial. The language of the section does not purport to make reliance into a full-fledged alternative to bargain consideration, instead relegating promissory estoppel situations to what one writer has called "the purgatory of 'Contracts Without Consideration.'"[4] Again, the change was based on a combination of case law authority and policy argument. But even on its own terms, the section did not go as far in establishing reliance-based liability as some theorists desired.[5]

Topics Covered by the Cases 1021 (2d ed., Boston, Little, Brown 1879). ("It is clear from the definition of consideration [§ 45] that it must move from the promisee. Indeed, it is of the very essence of consideration that it be received from the promisee.")

2. *Restatement of Contracts* §§ 133–47 (1932) (chap. 6, "Contractual Rights of Persons Not Parties to the Contract").

3. Charles E. Clark, "The Restatement of the Law of Contracts," 42 *Yale L.J.* 643, 658 (1933); See Am. Law Inst., *Commentaries on Contracts: Restatement No. 3*, at 3–18 (Samuel Williston rep. 1927).

4. Melvin Aron Eisenberg, "The Principles of Consideration," 67 *Cornell L. Rev.* 640, 642 (1982). The immediate problem with this status was that it led some judges to conclude that reliance-based liability was only appropriate in noncommercial situations (such as promises within the family). See James Baird Co. v. Gimbel Bros., Inc., 64 F.2d 344, 345–46 (2d Cir. 1933). That this was not the intention of the reporters of the Restatement is clear from the comments to the section (then section 88, to become section 90 in the official version) when it was proposed, which deal with, inter alia, promises not to foreclose mortgages, licenses to use real estate, licenses between manufacturers and distributors for the exclusive right to sell a product, gratuitous bailment, and waivers in contracts for the sale of goods. Am. Law Inst., *Commentaries on Contracts: Restatement No. 2*, at 14–19 (Samuel Williston rep. 1926).

5. An example of where the section apparently stops short appears in the comments to the tentative draft. The commentators discuss reliance-based liability in a gratuitous bailment (actually a case of agency collateral to bailment), and note that the court in one case quoted Professor Parsons: "If a person makes a gratuitous promise, and then enters upon the performance of it, he is held to a full execution of all he has undertaken." A.L.I., *Commentaries No. 2*. The commentators then continue: "This quotation

An attempt at reform that did not succeed, at least in its initial stages, was the critique of the rule that a nonbinding promise could not be sufficient consideration. The rule covered several issues, ranging from the mutuality of obligation, to the validity of illusory promises, to the validity of modifications of existing contractual relations. Critics charged that the rule, while often declared by the courts, was not required by the logic of contracts, and that when it was applied it more often caused mischief than solved problems.[6] Initially, the voice of the contract establishment dug in its heels with respect to the rule on mutuality.[7] Over the course of the century, reformers managed to chip away at the rule piecemeal, though it is still nominally an accepted part of contract doctrine.[8]

These attempts at reform of consideration doctrine are representative of the dozens of reforms that have constituted the history of the doctrine in the twentieth century. The major milestones are Article 2 of the Uniform Commercial Code and the Restatement (Second) of Contracts, each of which

---

from Professor Parsons goes far beyond Section 88 [later § 90], and if literally taken goes beyond anything that can be accepted." On the turbulent career of section 90, see Randy E. Barnett and Mary E. Becker, "Beyond Reliance: Promissory Estoppel, Contract Formalities, and Misrepresentations," 15 *Hofstra L. Rev.* 443 (1987); Sidney W. DeLong, "The New Requirement of Enforcement Reliance in Commercial Promissory Estoppel: Section 90 as Catch-22," 1997 *Wis. L. Rev.* 943; Daniel A. Farber and John H. Matheson, "Beyond Promissory Estoppel: Contract Law and the 'Invisible Handshake,'" 52 *U. Chi. L. Rev.* 903 (1985); Jay M. Feinman, "Promissory Estoppel and Judicial Method," 97 *Harv. L. Rev.* 678 (1984); Robert A. Hillman, "Questioning the 'New Consensus' on Promissory Estoppel: An Empirical and Theoretical Study," 98 *Colum. L. Rev.* 580 (1998); Charles L. Knapp, "Rescuing Reliance: The Perils of Promissory Estoppel," 49 *Hastings L.J.* 1191 (1998).

6. See, e.g., Arthur L. Corbin, "Non-Binding Promises as Consideration," 26 *Colum. L. Rev.* 550 (1926); Herman Oliphant, "Mutuality of Obligation in Bilateral Contracts at Law," 25 *Colum. L. Rev.* 705 (1925); Edwin W. Patterson, "'Illusory' Promises and Promisors' Options," pt. 2, 6 *Iowa L. Bull.* 209 (1921); Clarke B. Whittier, "The Restatement of Contracts and Consideration," 18 *Cal. L. Rev.* 611 (1930).

7. The 1932 Restatement of Contracts provided that: "Except as stated in § 84(e), a promise which is neither binding nor capable of becoming binding by acceptance of its terms is insufficient consideration, unless its invalidity is caused by such illegality as does not preclude the existence of a duty on the part of the return promisor under the rules stated in §§ 599–609." *Restatement (First) of Contracts* § 80 (1932). Williston's A.L.I. Commentaries provide an explanation in context:

> One of the advisers, Professor Oliphant, questions the soundness of Section 78 [§ 80 in the official version]. He is of the opinion that there is no logical foundation for the rule there stated. He regards the decisions on voidable promises not as exceptions to the rule, Section 78, but as a contradiction of it. . . . To the other advisers the rule stated in Section 78 seems unquestionable law; and the Reporter has expressed his opinion not only to this effect but also to the point that the rule is a necessary logical consequence of the idea that value must be given in exchange for a promise—an idea which lies at the root of the whole doctrine of consideration.

A.L.I., *Commentaries No. 2*, 8.

8. See *Restatement (Second) of Contracts* § 73 (1981). For an assessment of the decline of the rule, see Eisenberg, "Principles of Consideration," 647.

contributes to a reform of consideration doctrine.[9] But just as important as the changes these reforms have brought to contract is what they have left unchallenged. With very few exceptions, the focus of the reforms has been expanding and securing *promissory* liability. Even the proponents of reliance have generally been concerned with reliance on promises, rather than, say, duties arising out of relationships. Indeed, the calls for reform of consideration doctrine, and even of contract more generally, are so often phrased in terms of the expansion of promissory liability that it becomes difficult to imagine any other source of liability in contract. In that sense, the reforms of consideration become part of the entrenchment of the most important aspect of the classical revolution, which was to center contractual liability around promise.

REORIENTING THEORY: FROM RULES TO JUSTIFICATIONS

Despite popular caricatures of Christopher Columbus Langdell, there was never a time, even at the height of classical legal theory, when theorists were concerned exclusively with the logical derivations of legal rules and completely indifferent to the social justifications of rules and their impact on the people affected by them.[10] However, the style and focus of legal analysis did change in the half-century following Langdell. Whether we adopt Felix Cohen's pejorative label of "transcendental nonsense" to describe classical legal academics' work or use Cardozo's more neutral reference to the "method

---

9. See, e.g., *UCC* § 2-205 (1999) (providing that firm offers are enforceable without consideration); § 2-209 (providing that modification agreements are enforceable without consideration); § 2-306 (providing that requirements and output contracts are enforceable, thus limiting the possibility of avoiding them for lack of consideration); *Restatement (Second) of Contracts* § 86 (1981) (providing for limited recognition of past consideration); § 87 (providing that option contracts are enforceable in some circumstances without consideration); § 89 (providing that promise of modification is enforceable if modification is fair and equitable); § 90(2) (providing that charitable subscription or marriage settlement is binding without consideration and without proof of reliance).

10. For the stereotype regarding Langdell as deaf to considerations of policy, see Melvin A. Eisenberg, "The Theory of Contracts," in *The Theory of Contract Law: New Essays* 206, 208–10 (Peter Benson ed., 2001). For recent historical research that refutes the caricature, see Bruce A. Kimball, "'Warn Students That I Entertain Heretical Opinions, Which They Are Not to Take as Law': The Inception of Case Method Teaching in the Classrooms of the Early C. C. Langdell, 1870–1883," 17 *Law and Hist. Rev.* 57 (1999); Howard Schweber, "The 'Science' of Legal Science: The Model of the Natural Sciences in Nineteenth-Century American Legal Education," 17 *Law and Hist. Rev.* 421 (1999).

of philosophy" and the "method of history" is not critical.[11] Whatever label we use to describe it, the important thing for my purposes is to note that the dominant mode of legal academic writing in the classical period concentrated heavily on detailed elaboration of the rules, and heightened attention to the problems of consistency among them. The preferred method for ensuring consistency was to erect strict boundaries between different fields, like contract, tort, and quasi contract, and to attempt to have the rules flow from a small number of first principles, which had a definitional quality.[12]

From the first decades of the twentieth century, and with increasing momentum through the 1940s, the style of legal reasoning employed in the academy shifted. Again, it makes little difference whether we adopt Cohen's "functional approach," Cardozo's "method of sociology," Pound's "sociological jurisprudence," or "legal realism" to describe the new style.[13] The important thing is to recognize that the focus of academic attention shifted from elaboration of and argumentation over the formulation of the rules themselves to the elaboration of pragmatic policy justifications, either for existing rules or for their alternatives. At certain points, there was almost no inclination to support any particular rule choice: the entire focus was on working out the underlying objectives and justifications of rules generally. The idea was that laying bare the objectives that rules could serve would allow judges to engage in more conscious and better-informed decision making, with the goal of social welfare never far from the forefront.

The most influential example of this style of work in the field of consideration theory is Lon Fuller's "Consideration and Form."[14] In that article, a contribution to a symposium on consideration, Fuller paid little attention to the host of rules that made up consideration doctrine. Instead, he concentrated on the functions of consideration as a formality (evidentiary; cautionary; and channeling), and on the substantive objectives or policies underlying the doctrine (supporting private autonomy; encouraging reasonable reliance; and preventing unjust enrichment). The functions of formality

11. Felix S. Cohen, "Transcendental Nonsense and the Functional Approach," 35 *Colum. L. Rev.* 809, 820–21 (1935); Benjamin N. Cardozo, *The Nature of the Judicial Process* 31–36, 51–58 (1921).

12. See William M. Wiecek, *The Lost World of Classical Legal Thought* 4–7 (1998); Thomas C. Grey, "Langdell's Orthodoxy," 45 *U. Pitt. L. Rev.* 1, 11–13 (1983).

13. Cohen, "Transcendental Nonsense," 821–22; Cardozo, *Nature of Judicial Process,* 65–67; Roscoe Pound, "Sociology of Law and Sociological Jurisprudence," 5 *U. Toronto L.J.* 1, 1–3 (1943). See also *American Legal Realism* (William W. Fisher, III, Morton J. Horwitz, and Thomas A. Reed eds., 1993).

14. Lon L. Fuller, "Consideration and Form," 41 *Colum. L. Rev.* 799 (1941).

and the trade-offs among them had been analyzed before, in remarkably similar terms. Fuller's real contribution was to conduct the same kind of trade-off analysis with regard to the substantive societal functions of the doctrine.[15] However, a functional analysis of the role of the formality of delivery in gifts, by Philip Mechem, had appeared fifteen years earlier.[16] Mechem's article is characterized by a combination of approaches. On the one hand, he articulates the reasons for the requirement of formality of delivery: it alerts the donor to the seriousness of the action—thus reducing the danger of nondeliberative gift giving—and it affords prima facie evidence of the transaction having occurred in fact.[17] On the other hand, Mechem devotes nearly one hundred pages of analysis to specific types of gift transfers, and to the operation of the rules of delivery regarding each one.[18]

In the same year that "Consideration and Form" appeared, Ashbel Gulliver, the dean of Yale Law School, and his research assistant Catherine Tilson, published a landmark article entitled "Classification of Gratuitous Transfers."[19] That article went beyond Mechem's functional analysis in the same way that Fuller had gone beyond the question of consideration as a formality. The conceptual starting point for Gulliver and Tilson's article is the indeterminacy of the rules regarding gifts. For instance, regarding the rules that distinguish inter vivos from testamentary transfers, they write: "In numerous cases, therefore, the validity of an attempted disposition is dependent on its being classified as inter vivos rather than testamentary. The doctrinal test supposed to determine this choice is extremely flexible and can be manipulated almost at will by the courts."[20] With the inadequacy of the

---

15. Id. at 824. For an in-depth analysis along these lines, see Duncan Kennedy, "From the Will Theory to the Principle of Private Autonomy: Lon Fuller's 'Consideration and Form,'" 100 *Colum. L. Rev.* 94, 160–67 (2000).

16. Philip Mechem, "The Requirement of Delivery in Gifts of Chattels and of Choses in Action Evidenced by Commercial Instruments," 21 *Ill. L. Rev.* 341 (pt. 1), 457 (pt. 2), 568 (pt. 3) (1926).

17. Id. at 348–49.

18. Id. at 358–74, 457–87, 568–609.

19. Ashbel G. Gulliver and Catherine J. Tilson, "Classification of Gratuitous Transfers," 51 *Yale L.J.* 1 (1941).

20. Id. at 18. They continue:

> It is stated in terms of the time at which an "interest" is intended to pass to the transferee. Following the usual philosophical description, the transfer is said to be inter vivos if an interest passes during the lifetime of the transferor, but testamentary if no interest passes until at or after his death. But the postulated "interest" is entirely abstract in character. It has no necessary relationship to the physical possession or economic enjoyment of the property, since a right to future possession and enjoyment may be, and frequently is, held to be a present interest. . . . [T]he test is not per se

rules in mind, the authors raise the level of abstraction, detailing functions the rules should perform.[21] And the functions, in turn, are to be interpreted in light of the overriding objective governing this aspect of the law:

> One fundamental proposition is that, under a legal system recognizing the individualistic institution of private property and granting to the owner the power to determine his successors in ownership, the general philosophy of the courts should favor giving effect to an intentional exercise of that power. This is commonplace enough, but it needs constant emphasis, for it may be obscured or neglected in inordinate preoccupation with detail or dialectic. A court absorbed in purely doctrinal arguments may lose sight of the important and desirable objective of sanctioning what the transferor wanted to do, even though it is convinced that he wanted to do it.[22]

The contribution of Gulliver and Tilson's article lies primarily in the way the discussion of rules is given an explicit context. By foregrounding the seemingly obvious but often unmentioned overriding goal of respecting individual intent in the disposition of property, the authors provide the background against which the rules can be developed, interpreted, and applied.

Fuller and Gulliver were part of a wave of scholarship that presented a twofold challenge to classical contract theory: First, it showed that even widely accepted rules gave judges too much latitude to afford certainty, implying that the attention lavished on the elaboration of rules by the classics was misplaced. Second, it articulated underlying reasons that would justify the rules (or alternatives to them), in the hope that such underlying justifications could better orient the interpretation and application of any rule structure. Some of the articles in this wave of scholarship challenged the classical theory of consideration at what seemed to be its heart: the bargain

---

determinative in the more marginal cases. It has achieved respectability as the verbal clothing of the result; but the compelling precedent will be the actual decision on similar facts, not judicial reiteration of this vague and abstract criterion.

21. They suggest that the requirement of formality in gratuitous transfers serves three functions: the "ritual function," geared toward impressing the transferor with the significance of the act and justifying the conclusion that the acts were deliberately intended to be operative; the "evidentiary function," geared toward ensuring the reliability of the proof of the gift; and the "protective function," safeguarding against undue influence or other forms of imposition. Id. at 3–5.

22. Id. at 2. Again, the continuation is pertinent: "If this objective is primary, the requirements of execution, which concern only the form of the transfer—what the transferor or others must do to make it legally effective—seem justifiable only as implements for its accomplishment, and should be so interpreted by the courts in these cases. They surely should not be revered as ends in themselves, enthroning formality over frustrated intent."

theory of consideration.[23] However, despite raising the recurrent theme of protecting reliance, the focus of the work was the expansion of liability based on promises, rather than an exploration of different sources of liability.[24]

Having elaborated the methodological mode of critique employed by this wave of scholarship, it makes sense to summarize the substantive positions it generated regarding consideration. When looking for the underlying justification for the doctrine, the purpose served by consideration could be viewed in a number of ways: the most influential way was as a test of when it is useful for the legal system to intervene in disputes, raising the question of whether the interaction between the parties is "productive" and therefore worthy of the effort of enforcement.[25] The critique of this view is primarily that it relies on a false intuition that gratuitous promises are unproductive, whereas in fact there is nothing to support such an intuition and much to refute it.[26]

By contrast, consideration could be conceived of as yet another tool in a repertoire of mechanisms to ensure fairness in exchange. This strain of thinking was championed by Llewellyn, and explains why he concentrated on the elements of consideration doctrine that are most directly related to preventing duress or unfair advantage, particularly in situations involving the modification of ongoing relationships.[27] The weakness (and perhaps the

---

23. See, e.g., Benjamin F. Boyer, "Promissory Estoppel: Principle from Precedents," 50 *Mich. L. Rev.* 639 (pt. 1) and 873 (pt. 2) (1952); Benjamin F. Boyer, "Promissory Estoppel: Requirements and Limitations of the Doctrine," 98 *U. Pa. L. Rev.* 459 (1950); Warren L. Shattuck, "Gratuitous Promises—A New Writ?" 35 *Mich. L. Rev.* 908 (1937); A. J. Monahan, "Note, Gratuitous Undertakings: Liability of Promisor for Nonfeasance," 9 *Cornell L.Q.* 54, 54–57 (1923).

24. Boyer's articles on promissory estoppel are illustrative. On the one hand, he draws some of his most important examples from cases of gratuitous bailment and from issues of waiver and related relinquishing of rights. Boyer, "Principle from Precedents," 644. These examples could have generated the attempt to formulate a theory of liability based on a working relationship (however that relationship comes about), rather than on what is often a fictional element in them, promise. However, the entire framework for discussion is centered on promises, and on affording enforcement to promises that are not simply bargain transactions. See also Shattuck, "Gratuitous Promises," 909–14. For hints (but little more than hints) that liability in contract may at times be based on something other than promise, see Karl N. Llewellyn, "On the Complexity of Consideration: A Foreword," 41 *Colum. L. Rev.* 777–79 (1941).

25. Fuller is often cited for this proposition and its economic resonance. The passage alluded to is his citation, in "Consideration and Form," of Bufnoir: "While an exchange of goods is a transaction which conduces to the production of wealth and the division of labor, a gift is, in Bufnoir's words, a 'sterile transmission.'" Fuller, "Consideration and Form," 815 (quoting Claude Bufnoir, *Propriété et contrat* 487 [2d ed. 1924]).

26. See Andrew Kull, "Reconsidering Gratuitous Promises," 21 *J. Legal Stud.* 39 (1992); Steven Shavell, "An Economic Analysis of Altruism and Deferred Gifts," 20 *J. Legal Stud.* 401 (1991); A. W. B. Simpson, "Land Ownership and Economic Freedom," in *The State and Freedom of Contract* 13, 34–35 (Harry N. Scheiber ed., 1998).

27. In his foreword to a symposium on consideration, Llewellyn wrote: "No man can follow either the

interesting part) of this view is that it runs counter to one of the basic components of consideration theory—the rule that adequacy of consideration is not to be evaluated. This rule seems to imply that consideration doctrine is not to be used to police the fairness of exchange, and indeed that anything that crosses the threshold of exchange is presumptively free from examination as to fairness. Consideration, then, "be it never so small," is precisely the factor that allows a particular exchange to escape scrutiny.[28] This seeming contradiction is not fatal, either to the doctrine or to the view that consideration is about ensuring fairness. It does, however, require an acknowledgment of the sort that Llewellyn made, that consideration was actually a number of doctrines that did not cohere.[29]

Both of these views, however, suggest possible purposes for a doctrine in a fixed, nonhistorical world of contract. They assume that the question for which consideration offers the answer is, which promises should the law

---

'equivalency' phases or the 'bargain' aspects down into their meaning, without tangling with the line which runs from duress through undue inequality of bargaining position on into too great inequality of what seems to have been intended as a bargain and not as a gift." Llewellyn, "Complexity of Consideration," 780; see also Karl N. Llewellyn, "Common-Law Reform of Consideration: Are There Measures?" 41 *Colum. L. Rev.* 863 (1941); Karl N. Llewellyn, "What Price Contract?—An Essay in Perspective," 40 *Yale L.J.* 704 (1941). A recent provocative account of the history of contract has taken these kinds of claims further, arguing that most of the important doctrines within the field of contract are actually means to examine the distribution of wealth among the contracting parties, and in effect to ensure an equitable distribution. See James Gordley, "Enforcing Promises," 83 *Cal. L. Rev.* 547 (1995).

28. See 1 Samuel Williston, *The Law of Contracts* § 115 (1st ed. 1920), (quoting Sturlyn v. Albany, Cro. Eliz. 67). Williston's discussion of the adequacy of consideration is telling, because it at first upholds the doctrine, but then discusses many cases where the distinction between an examination of adequacy and an examination of the very presence of a bargain is hard to uphold:

> Sometimes a consideration of one dollar or other small sum is paid or alleged to have been paid in return for a promise to give or do something of considerable value. There seems no reason to depart in such a case from the general rule that adequacy of consideration will not be regarded, though an inquiry whether the dollar was really bargained for as the consideration, will always be pertinent; for where a promise of value is stated to have been made for a small money consideration, there is often reason to doubt whether a bargain to exchange the sum mentioned for the promise was really intended by the parties.

Id. (footnotes omitted).

29. In his symposium introduction, Llewellyn wrote:

> What all this comes to, is that "the field" [of consideration] is bound, for a while, to mean different things to every man who tries to get under its surface. It is no wonder that philosophers exploring it have been unable to find any single policy-theory on which "the" doctrine rested. There is more wonder that there has not come a more adequately emphatic recognition that this is not for one reason, but for two. It is not only because "consideration" expresses a considerable number of policies, often at odds and not worked out into full harmony. It is, even more, because there is no single doctrine or body of doctrine to be found either under or near the label.

Llewellyn, "Complexity of Consideration," 779.

enforce? But when the historical view is added, we can see that one purpose of consideration, *as we know it*, is to install the question of promise (and enforceable promise) as the center of contract.

THE RESURGENCE OF THE GIFT: NEW SCHOLARSHIP

Articles like Fuller's and Gulliver's form the theoretical backdrop to the surge in writing on gifts and consideration over the past two decades.[30] The latest writing on gifts makes a significant shift from the style of writing, which reached its peak in the 1940s, that concentrated on the functional justification of the rules. The change is characterized by shifting the weight of the discussion from the relatively narrow policy justification of the requirements of formality to the broader societal implications of a particular arrangement of those requirements. Despite the inclination to consider the societal implications of the law of gifts and consideration, current debates submerge the effects of the framework of the debate itself, a framework with a limited focus on enforceable promises.

A central example of the current debate revolves around the issue of commodification. One position in this debate is that denying enforceability to gift promises underscores the law's presumption that only commodities have value and that only bargain-based exchanges of value merit the law's concern. By excluding gift promises from the realm of enforceability,

---

30. For representative articles, see Jane B. Baron, "Do We Believe in Generosity? Reflections on the Relationship Between Gifts and Exchanges," 44 *Fla. L. Rev.* 355 (1992); Jane B. Baron, "Gifts, Bargains, and Form," 64 *Ind. L.J.* 155 (1989); Melvin Aron Eisenberg, "The World of Contract and the World of Gift," 85 *Cal. L. Rev.* 821 (1997); E. Allan Farnsworth, "Promises to Make Gifts," 43 *Am. J. Comp. L.* 359 (1995); Mary Louise Fellows, "His to Give; His to Receive; Hers to Trust: A Response to Carol M. Rose," 44 *Fla. L. Rev.* 329 (1992); Robert H. Frank, "The Differences Between Gifts and Exchange: Comment on Carol Rose," 44 *Fla. L. Rev.* 319 (1992); Emily Fowler Hartigan, "Rose and Apple—Original Gifts?" 44 *Fla. L. Rev.* 347 (1992); Kull, "Reconsidering Gratuitous Promises"; Melanie B. Leslie, "Enforcing Family Promises: Reliance, Reciprocity, and Relational Contract," 77 *N.C. L. Rev.* 551 (1999); Eric A. Posner, "Altruism, Status, and Trust in the Law of Gifts and Gratuitous Promises," 1997 *Wis. L. Rev.* 567; Carol M. Rose, "Giving, Trading, Thieving, and Trusting: How and Why Gifts Become Exchanges, and (More Importantly) Vice Versa," 44 *Fla. L. Rev.* 295 (1992); Carol M. Rose, "Giving Some Back: A Reprise," 44 *Fla. L. Rev.* 365 (1992); Jeanne L. Schroeder, "Pandora's Amphora: The Ambiguity of Gifts," 46 *U.C.L.A. L. Rev.* 815 (1999); Mark B. Wessman, "Retraining the Gatekeeper: Further Reflections on the Doctrine of Consideration," 29 *Loy. L.A. L. Rev.* 713 (1996). Earlier work formed an intermediate stage in the scholarship on gifts. See Melvin Aron Eisenberg, "Donative Promises," 47 *U. Chi. L. Rev.* 1 (1979); Richard A. Posner, "Gratuitous Promises in Economics and Law," 6 *J. Legal Stud.* 411 (1977).

the law reinforces the image of gifts as marginal, rare, and economically unimportant.[31] The opposing view holds that gift promises are not denied enforcement because they lack importance, but rather because they are too important to be left exposed to legal intervention. Gifts, on this view, are an aspect of a richer social world, one that makes room for "affective values like love, friendship, affection, gratitude, and comradeship." These values would be threatened, indeed undermined, were they exposed to the alienating forces of contract law. The somewhat counterintuitive argument is that the world of gift requires shielding, and that such protection must come not by direct enforcement of its values, but rather through nonenforcement of transactions in the gift world, which can then remain pure of the alienated forces of legal intervention.[32]

Both sides in this debate are concerned about the role of law in commodifying society.[33] But their views of how commodification happens are opposed: one views the legal system as valorizing contractual wealth production at the expense of gifts, viewed by the system as nonproductive. Disparaging gifts is part of a process through which commodities come to be viewed as the only form of wealth.[34] The other views legal intervention and the threat of intervention as commodifying agents. To the extent that gifts can be protected from interaction with the mechanisms of legal enforcement, they preserve a sphere untouched by the commodified values that reign in the realm of contract.[35]

---

31. The leading expression of this view is Baron, "Gifts, Bargains, and Form." Additional discussions along these lines include Rose, "Giving, Trading," 312–17; Leslie, "Family Promises," 624–27; Hartigan, "Rose and Apple," 349–51.

32. Eisenberg, "World of Contract," 849. The roots of such a position are already present, as an undeveloped kernel, in Fuller, "Consideration and Form," 813. After discussing reasons for imposing liability and mentioning the costs of enforcement, Fuller moves on to consider a "less tangible" cost: "There is a real need for a field of human intercourse freed from legal restraints, for a field where men may without liability withdraw assurances they have once given. Every time a new type of promise is made enforceable, we reduce the area of this field." But in its current form, the insight is developed into a far-reaching positive principle. The legal enforcement of contracts has an impoverishing, alienating element, and some parts of human intercourse should remain shielded from its negative influence.

33. This concern distinguishes them from some theorists of gifts, notably those devoted to economic analysis, for whom a reduction to the commodified aspects of gift giving offers a powerful heuristic mechanism with which to evaluate legal rules. See, e.g., Posner, "Altruism, Status, and Trust," 568; Kull, "Reconsidering Gratuitous Promises," 50–51, 59–64. Much of the current literature on gifts shares some concern about commodification. See, e.g., Leslie, "Family Promises," 624–27; Rose, "Giving, Trading," 312–17; Schroeder, "Pandora's Amphora," 883–98.

34. Baron, "Gifts, Bargains, and Form," 158.

35. Eisenberg, "World of Contract," 847–49.

The most interesting thing about the debate over commodification is how much its participants, despite their adversarial positions, have in common. The debate exhibits a common goal: to reduce or at least limit the spread of commodification. Participants in the debate also agree that the crucial question for the law in this regard is where the line between enforceable and nonenforceable promises will be drawn. They disagree primarily about where to draw that line. But none of the contributions to the debate considers the possibility that framing the issue in terms of the placement of the line between enforceability and nonenforceability of promises is the debate's crucial feature. When only the limits of promising are considered, the very structure of the debate freezes its focus on the individual who decides to promise. The idea that obligation can be viewed from some perspective other than that of the individual simply disappears.

An analogous division characterizes most of the scholarly debate on gifts. While writing on the issue is diverse, it shares a basic structure with the debate over commodification. A range of normative concerns is presented as balanced on the line between enforceable and nonenforceable promises.[36] The most common normative theme recurring in the gift literature is the enhancement of autonomy that more liberal promise enforcement would afford, but other concerns range from economically measured welfare, all the way to love.[37] The common theme of the current literature on gifts is the attempt to effect changes in the social world by changing doctrine, or more specifically, by adjusting the level of enforceability of promises. This common theme should be contrasted with the earlier work on gifts and consideration. For classical thinkers, the task was simply to make doctrine out of what was perceived to be a relatively disorganized mass of often conflicting precedents. For functionalist scholars, the goal was to change doctrine by clarifying its underlying justifications, while the resulting changes in the social world were left for the most part implicit. For the current generation of gift-consideration theorists, the direct focus is the impact in the social world that changes in doctrine should have.

---

36. The debate plays itself out over various issues: regarding reciprocity, compare Leslie, "Family Promises," with Schroeder, "Pandora's Amphora"; on welfare and autonomy, compare Kull, "Reconsidering Gratuitous Promises," with Posner, "Altruism, Status, and Trust."

37. E.g., On enhancement of autonomy, see, e.g., Baron, "Gifts, Bargains, and Form," 158–61, 202; Farnsworth, "Promises to Make Gifts," 366–72; Kull, "Reconsidering Gratuitous Promises," 51. Cf. Posner, "Altruism, Status, and Trust," 608–9, with Kull, "Reconsidering Gratuitous Promises," 55–58. See also Schroeder, "Pandora's Amphora," 870–73.

The first problem with this attitude of current scholarship is that it exaggerates the potential impact of legal doctrine, and the directness of that impact. In fact, the impact of doctrine is questionable even in its purported field of application: appellate adjudication. Over the course of the century, attempts to evaluate doctrine through a close reading of case law have revealed that the rules emerge riddled with exceptions that threaten to swallow the rules themselves.[38] Moreover, even when the rules themselves are left unchallenged, they leave judges wide latitude to decide cases according to an ad hoc sense of justice and propriety.[39] Further, the specific character of gift litigation shows that the typical players, nearly all one-shot litigants, are particularly resistant to including legal rules in their incentive structure.[40] I do not mean that doctrine has no impact anywhere. I do want to suggest, however, that the impact of a particular rule is less direct than assumed in the literature. The theoretical discussion over where to draw the line between enforceable and unenforceable promises has never directly governed the decision in the cases where it was relevant. Even if it did, most of the potential litigants are not in touch with the system to the extent that the decisions would affect behavior ex ante, making concerns (about either commodification or utility) seem misplaced.

Participants in the current debate over gifts have too much in common with the boy searching for a lost coin in the light of a street lamp. When asked, the boy acknowledges that he dropped the coin a few yards away, but that it still makes sense to search under the lamp, because the light is better there. So it is with the debate over the enforceability of donative promises. The participants acknowledge the malleability of the rules, but persist in

---

38. For some of the leading examples of such analyses, see, e.g., Arthur L. Corbin, "Offer and Acceptance, and Some of the Resulting Legal Relations," 26 *Yale L.J.* 169 (1917); Roscoe Pound, "Consideration in Equity," 13 *Ill. L. Rev.* 667 (1919); George P. Costigan, Jr., "Implied-in-Fact Contracts and Mutual Assent," 33 *Harv. L. Rev.* 376 (1920); Walter Wheeler Cook, "The Present Status of the 'Lack of Mutuality' Rule," 36 *Yale L.J.* 897 (1927); L. L. Fuller and William R. Perdue, Jr., "The Reliance Interest in Contract Damages," pt. 1, 46 *Yale L.J.* 52 (1936); Karl N. Llewellyn, "On Our Case-Law of Contract: Offer and Acceptance, I," 48 *Yale L.J.* 1 (1938); Boyer, "Principle from Precedents"; Farber and Matheson, "Beyond Promissory Estoppel"; Leslie, "Family Promises." Many of the analyses in this style have proposed new groupings of the cases in order to offer alternative justifications that would rationalize the decisions. With some level of predictability, however, most of the alternative justifications would probably be just as susceptible to the kind of exposure to contradiction the analysts engaged in with regard to the initial rule structure.

39. This is the heavy-handed lesson of Chapter 2.

40. I do not mean to suggest that this is a willful position. It is simply that potential gift litigants are unlikely to consider legal rules when structuring their relationships. See Leslie, "Family Promises," 619–20.

looking for the social impact of doctrine as an extension of the rules themselves. The impact, like the coin, exists, but the theorists are looking for it too close at hand.

And yet, paradoxically, perhaps they are also looking too far away. The scholars involved in the debate focus on explicit normative prescriptions, which eventually are to be adopted or rejected by a lawmaker. The lawmaker, in turn, is supposed to evaluate the justification proposed by the theorist, and, if it is persuasive, act on it. What the theorists seem to ignore is the impact of the shape of the debate itself. In other words, by concentrating on the debate's conclusions, in the form of a set of normative prescriptions, scholars tend to efface the possible impact of the bulk of their own activity—the process of argumentation over the rules, justifications, and fact situations relevant to a particular problem. In fact, the initial characterization of the problem is one of the most significant aspects of the endeavor. In this respect, scholars whose "positions" cover the entire spectrum of current gift-consideration theory are actually united in a common project. Whether they support enforcement or reject enforcement, attempt to combat commodification or see it as the basis of rationality, they are joined by the structure of the discourse, which revolves around the question of whether donative promises should be enforced.[41]

At this point, it is worthwhile to take a slightly broader view of the gift-consideration axis in contract theory. Over the course of the century, the focus of debates over consideration seems to have shifted significantly, from the elaboration of the rules themselves, to the underlying justifications for the rules, and on to the social significance of a preference for some justifications and some rules over others. But despite these shifts, a deeper similarity persists, and in fact characterizes the entire modern discussion of consideration. That similarity lies in the retention of the central animating question of the discussion: which promises should the law enforce? In the long view, a century of discussion about consideration can be seen as the creation and maintenance of a rhetoric, one of whose effects is to shape the way lawyers envision problems of obligation among people in relationships. In the succeeding chapter, I will try to assess the impact of that frame for the debate.

---

41. More generally, this is the question of where the line between enforceable and unenforceable promises should be drawn. This is precisely the question that classical contract theorists managed to place at the center of their new conception of contract at the end of the nineteenth century, as elaborated in Chapter 1.

FOUR

Speculating on Gifts and Promises

Thus far, I have argued that the current scholarly debate over gifts and consideration is a direct outgrowth of the classical revolution in contract thinking. Classical theorists placed promise at the center of their vision of contract, replacing a conception of contract that relied heavily on patterns of typical relationships, the content of which was societally imposed. Generations of contract scholars since the classical theorists (realists and functionalists from the 1930s onward, and modern scholars over the last twenty years) successfully challenged the classical formulation of the rules, and have effected a major shift in the acceptable style of justification of those rules. However, they left the framework for the discussion intact: for the past hundred years, the question of consideration has been concerned with which promises the law should enforce, and the current debate on gifts has not challenged that. At the same time, the various answers to this question proposed by theorists do not actually determine the outcomes of many cases. My contention is that the real effects of the debate over gifts and consideration are doubly displaced: first, they stem not from the various answers different theorists have proposed, but rather from the framework of the debate itself, or, if you will, from the question; second, they are not felt on the plane of the formation of contracts, where the rules ostensibly apply.

CONTRACT AND ITS OTHERS

In order to assess the implications of contract theory centered around promise and consideration, it will be useful to expand briefly on the possible meaning of the theoretical shift for the classical scholars who pioneered it. Their vision of contract may be contrasted to several other ideas through which the obligations of relationship could be regulated or managed, which can be characterized as three parallel approaches to distinguishing contract from other forms of regulation. The first of these parallel approaches is the distinction between contract and status; the second, between a contract economy and an economy of gift exchange; and the third, between a system of regulation concentrating on the formation of obligation and one concentrating on its contents. Each of these deserves some attention.

Contract Versus Status

On one level, defining contract around promise accomplished a fundamental goal of distinguishing contract from status. As long as contract was viewed as the law governing more or less standardized relationships whose contents were implied by law or otherwise imposed by society, it was a concept perilously close to status. The connection with status was viewed as both dangerous and regressive. Indeed, for much of the nineteenth century, popular political discourse was filled with rallying cries for republican self-ownership and independence, conceptualized precisely in opposition to an imagined history of statuslike dependency. Contractarian ideology was a central motif in the cultural battle over the shape and importance of the individual.[1] Moreover, in political discourse, contract was a winning ideological figure, embraced on both sides of the intensifying divide between labor and capital.[2] However, as recent scholarship has shown, the major

---

1. See, e.g., Christopher L. Tomlins, *Law, Labor, and Ideology in the Early American Republic* 259–92 (1993); Robert J. Steinfeld, *The Invention of Free Labor* 147–56 (1991); Amy Dru Stanley, *From Bondage to Contract* 1–10 (1998).

2. See John Fabian Witt, *The Accidental Republic: Crippled Workingmen, Destitute Widows, and the Remaking of American Law* 34–36 (2004); Arthur F. McEvoy, "Freedom of Contract, Labor, and the

attempts to distinguish status from contract were most adamant precisely where they were most problematic: in the employment context and in the context of marriage. These two areas exhibited an ostensibly common structure, in which parties entered voluntarily into relationships of authority and dependence. But the similarity between marriage and employment is deceptive. It was difficult if not impossible to contract around incidences of the marriage relation, despite the efforts of legislatures to undo the doctrine of coverture.[3] In the employment context, on the other hand, employees and employers were theoretically and sometimes practically free to design their relationships according to individualized ideas of mutual benefit.[4] That very opportunity, even as an abstract potentiality, was crucial in establishing the images of free labor and republican self-ownership in their basic contours. And yet, legal regulation of the employment contract coalesced around a set of rules that granted employers hierarchical authority and control over employees. Employer control was so trenchant as to raise claims from representatives of labor that the wage bargain was indistinguishable from status, indeed close to slavery.[5]

Classical contract scholars were, like their counterparts in popular political discourse, intent on distinguishing contract from status. Their attempt to do so, however, was framed within an abstracted technical discourse, sealed off from debates over any particular sector of the economy. The preclassical doctrinal tools that at once declared freedom of contract and yet entrenched employer control, doctrines like the entire contract rule, the doctrine of enticement, and the doctrine of assumption of risk in work accidents, were all geared specifically to the employment relationship. Classical

Administrative State," in *The State and Freedom of Contract* 198, 201–11 (Harry N. Scheiber ed., 1998); Charles W. McCurdy, "The 'Liberty of Contract' Regime in American Law," in *The State and Freedom of Contract,* 161, 167–73.

3. See Reva B. Segal, "The Modernization of Marital Status Law: Adjudicating Wives' Rights to Earnings, 1860–1930," 82 *Geo. L.J.* 2127, 2127–49 (1994); Ariela R. Dubler, "Governing Through Contract: Common Law Marriage in the Nineteenth Century," 107 *Yale L.J.* 1885, 1905–19 (1998). For a rich and nuanced account, see Hendrik Hartog, *Man and Wife in America* 115–35, 287–95 (2000).

4. For a review of the recent outpouring of scholarship on the nineteenth-century employment contract including an attempt to solve the puzzle of why the parties did not often contract around formally permissive rules, see John Fabian Witt, "Rethinking the Nineteenth-Century Employment Contract, Again," 18 *L. Hist. Rev.* 627 (2000).

5. See Tomlins, *Law, Labor, and Ideology,* 291–92; Stanley, *From Bondage to Contract,* 20; Witt, *Accidental Republic,* 33. For the argument that labor relations actually exhibited the endurance of status and even feudalism well into the twentieth century, see generally Karen Orren, *Belated Feudalism: Labor, the Law, and Liberal Development in the United States* (1991).

scholars, by contrast, raised the level of abstraction and thus avoided any direct confrontation with the relations of dependence that resulted from the standardized duties imposed on parties to the contract. By shifting the emphasis of analysis to the promises that served, by definition, as the source of duties, classical scholars underscored party control over contractual obligation and portrayed promise-based contract as an evolutionary advance of individual autonomy. But classical theorists' determination to distinguish contract from status was not simply mindless submission to Henry Maine's oft-quoted aphorism that "the movement of the progressive societies has hitherto been a movement *from Status to Contract.*"[6] Importantly, the shift to promise had internal effects on the concept of contract, but also external or definitional effects: once contract was firmly centered around the axis of promise, it could more easily exclude those relations whose effects did not arise from the promise at all. Thus, the classical maneuver not only changed the internal workings of contract doctrine, allowing contract to work itself pure from status on a conceptual level; it also used the distinction in order to define its borders, to exclude its others, those relationships (like marriage) that remained too close to status to be considered contractual.

Economy of Contract Versus Economy of Gift Exchange

A second approach in the creation of a promise-based regime of contract is the distinction between a contractual economy and an economy of gift exchange. Economies based on gift exchange have been discussed extensively by anthropologists since the beginning of the twentieth century, but the concept was probably completely foreign to classical legal theorists. I therefore use the concept not to describe what classical legal theorists (or any other legal scholars) were actually thinking about the regime of contract they were creating, but to illuminate the effects of a rhetoric of promise-based exchange. The economies of gift exchange analyzed by anthropologists existed in communities where there were no state institutions. Individuals or entire social groups (tribes) would make gifts to other individuals or groups, who were obligated by custom to reciprocate with larger gifts.[7]

---

6. Henry Sumner Maine, *Ancient Law* 165 (Frederick Pollock ed., Beacon Press 1963) (1861); emphasis original.

7. For the classic analysis of gift exchange in the anthropological literature, see Marcel Mauss, *The Gift: The Form and Reason for Exchange in Archaic Societies* (W. D. Halls trans., 1990); see also Marshall Sahlins, *Stone Age Economics*, 149–275 (1972).

The economy of the United States in the late nineteenth century did not resemble such an arrangement, but there are some salient points of comparison. Many of the working relationships that governed people's lives, then as now, were relationships that implied reciprocal behavior. However, only a small part of that reciprocity was bargained over explicitly. For classical theorists, an important part of the reconceptualization of consideration consisted in purging contract of its unbargained-for elements, by denying enforcement to obligations undertaken without explicit bargaining. I will return below to the rhetorical effects of distinguishing a bargain-exchange economy from a gift economy, but for now, it is worth noting a difference on this point between classical theorists and the generations of scholars that followed them. As shown above, for classical theorists the dividing line between enforceable and nonenforceable promises "ran at the boundary between bargain promises and gratuitous promises," that is, whatever was not explicitly bargained for.[8] Modern theorists, on the other hand, draw the line at the donative promise, that is, the unrelied-upon noncommercial promise of a gift. For the classical theorist, then, the question of consideration was a question about economic organization and regulation, in a way that it is not for the modern gift theorist. But in this sense, the economic features that classical scholars were purging from contract make the comparison to the gift-exchange economy relevant.

Formation Versus Content

The third approach in the creation of the promise-centered regime of contract is the shift in attention from the content of contractual obligations to the formation of obligations. Preclassical contract theory devoted most of its energies to the content of obligations among various parties to standardized relationships, and very little attention to offer and acceptance—questions surrounding the formation of contractual obligations.[9] Classical theory radically realigned the priorities, making questions of formation absolutely central to the scheme of contract generally. Until recently, modern contract

---

8. Melvin Aron Eisenberg, "The World of Contract and the World of Gift," 85 *Cal. L. Rev.* 833 (1997).

9. Kevin Teevan points out that until the nineteenth century, "there were still no rules of offer and acceptance." In fact, "there was no concern about when a contract was formed—the parties either emerged from face-to-face negotiations with an agreement or they didn't. There was little discussion in the cases about whether a promise was revocable but rather whether a promise was actionable short of reliance." Kevin M. Teevan, *A History of the Anglo-American Common Law of Contract*, 175, 177 (1990).

theory was similarly obsessed with issues of formation, and the contemporary wave of writing on gifts extends this preoccupation.[10] Current writers' arguments that the law of formation, and specifically the demarcation of the line between enforceable and unenforceable promises, will have direct social effects, represent an elaboration and deepening of the view that formation is the central issue of contract law.

However, I would suggest that the focus is misplaced. In fact, the rhetoric of promise enforcement exerts its most significant effects elsewhere, by generating a widely agreed upon and even assumed framework for the delineation of the content of contractual obligations. The heightened attention to formation through promise, and the unquestioned assumption that the parties' obligations flow from promises that formed the contract, draw decision makers toward those promises as the sole source of the parties' obligations. Thus, it is not the location of the line between the enforceable and unenforceable that matters; instead, it is the rhetorical framework (regardless of where the line is actually drawn) that leads decision makers to accept promise as the font from which obligation flows, obscuring the role of societally imposed obligations on contractual partners. The effect of the framework created by the debate over which promises should be enforced is felt, then, in the attitude of decision makers toward the content of contractual obligation, rather than in its purported locus of application, the formation of the contract.

CONVERGENCES

In conclusion, I will venture to speculate on how these three parallel approaches of distinction, inherited from the classical revolution in consideration doctrine, in fact intersect to inflect contract thinking.[11] There are at least three areas of convergence of the differentiations outlined above. The view of contract engendered by the distinctions generates idealized

---

10. The recent flood of writing on default rules in contract is something of an antidote to this obsession. See, e.g., Symposium, "Default Rules and Contractual Consent," 3 *S. Cal. Interdisc. L.J.* 1 (1993).

11. I invoke this paradox intentionally. The different levels of distinction seem to be unrelated issues, but their overall thrust is to push the rhetoric of contract in the same direction. In that sense, they are like parallel forces whose effects intersect, and are in turn strengthened by that intersection. One way of thinking about this is through a psychoanalytical analogy, saying that the point of intersection is overdetermined. See J. Laplanche and J.-B. Pontalis, *The Language of Psycho-Analysis* 292–93 (Donald Nicholson-Smith trans., W. W. Norton 1973) (1967).

images of spheres of human activity, of the judicial role, and finally, of the individual. It matters little whether anyone is willing to defend the idealizations as an accurate depiction of society: no one may be willing to do so, and no such defense is necessary. The important thing is that the idealizations function by creating general background understandings of social life that profoundly affect how decision makers interpret situations and approach problems.

Spheres of Activity: The Market

The rejection of status and gift exchange, and the attention to formation rather than content, are part of a reimagination of the market as a distinct sphere of activity. Throughout the nineteenth century, the image of the market and the image of contract were undergoing a related transformation. The market, once understood as heavily regulated, was increasingly being imagined as "free." Contract, once understood as informed by state-mandated duties among the parties, was increasingly being understood as a realm of private lawmaking. Together, these images support the common perception about what a system of private ordering amounts to.[12] Classical theorists created the legal framework embodying such understandings out of the details of doctrine, without explicitly adopting any social theory about the market or private ordering.[13] But the rhetorical power of "freedom of contract" relies directly on the conception of contract as a realm of individual control of obligation, and that conception relies in turn on classical reformulations of doctrine. Again, the whole is larger than the sum of its parts: it is not the outcome of the conflicts regarding particular rules that is central, but rather the creation of a framework of rules that puts the focus on individual choice instead of societally imposed obligations. Rules of formation and excuses may be relaxed, promissory estoppel may be recognized as a substitute for consideration, consideration itself may withdraw from the question of enforcing commercial promises, but none of these changes alters the basic framework articulated by classical contract law. And that

12. See Robin Paul Malloy, "Framing the Market: Representations of Meaning and Value in Law, Markets, and Culture," 51 *Buff. L. Rev.* 1, 30–35 (2003).

13. Indeed, when drawn into the realm of social theory, classical scholars were likely to reject philosophical articulations about a necessary connection between the limitation of regulation and freedom. See Samuel Williston, "Freedom of Contract," 6 *Cornell L.Q.* 365, 365–72 (1921).

framework is central in supporting the image of the market as the realm of free individual action.[14]

Judicial Role

The second area of convergence of the distinctions created by classical contract theory, closely related to the reimagination of the market, is the conception of the judicial role. It is not my intention to advance any substantiated theory of the judicial role, or even of the connection between classical contract doctrine and the judicial role.[15] I have a much more modest goal at this stage, which is to point out an obvious but constantly forgotten pretension of the classical contract framework. To the extent that classical scholars succeeded in maintaining the three distinctions presented above,[16] they seemed to be making a case for the idea that judges merely facilitated, and did not regulate; that they enforced obligations freely undertaken by the parties, and did not impose obligations whose sources lay elsewhere. This at once contributes to and is informed by the vision of the market as a "free" realm, where "private lawmakers" can design their own duties.[17] The

---

14. The flip side of the articulation of the market sphere is the bounding off of a family sphere, where relations are hierarchical and not based on consent, but which is characterized by values such as love and trust. For a critique of the effects of such a division into spheres, see Frances E. Olsen, "The Family and the Market: A Study of Ideology and Legal Reform," 96 *Harv. L. Rev.* 1497 (1983). Support for the division into spheres as a safeguard against the commodification of important values is expressed by Eisenberg, who seems to argue that if the alienated world of legal enforcement is allowed to enter the bastion of trust (the family), the values that characterize it will be in jeopardy, and may not survive. Eisenberg, "World of Contract," 847–49. Critics of the position rightly maintain that rather than preserving those values by fencing them off in some purified realm, it makes sense to advocate their adoption and strengthening wherever they happen to be appropriate, including at times in the business world. See Robert W. Gordon, "Unfreezing Legal Reality: Critical Approaches to Law," 15 *Fla. St. U. L. Rev.* 194, 214–17 (1987); Carol M. Rose, "Giving Some Back: A Reprise," 44 *Fla. L. Rev.* 365, 373–75 (1992); Carol M. Rose, "Giving, Trading, Thieving, and Trusting: How and Why Gifts Become Exchanges, and (More Importantly) Vice Versa," 44 *Fla. L. Rev.* 295, 313–17 (1992).

15. Duncan Kennedy has revisited this issue repeatedly over the last quarter-century. For a recent detailed effort, see Duncan Kennedy, *A Critique of Adjudication: Fin de Siècle* 82–92, 202–12 (1997).

16. Favoring contract over status (or customary relationship), contractual economy over an economy of gift exchange, and questions of formation over those of content of obligation

17. These phrases are evocative of the private ordering paradigm, and while they resonate as if they refer to the will theory of contract, they are defensible without resort to it as well. One could easily imagine such support from libertarians, economists, or even liberals who had abandoned the will theory, including classical theorists like Williston or later theorists like Fuller. For an explanation of the connection between will theory and the various phases in American contract theory, see Duncan Kennedy, "From the Will Theory to the Principle of Private Autonomy: Lon Fuller's 'Consideration and Form,'" 100 *Colum. L. Rev.* 94, 115–17, 126–35 (2000).

conception of the judicial passivity that flows from the distinctions is not a logical necessity, but the rhetorical connection is strong.[18] Again, none of the particular rules of consideration need survive to leave intact the rhetorical image of the judge as facilitator: it is the framework that performs the labor of making this image plausible.

The Calculating Individual Subject

Finally, the third area of convergence is the creation of an ideal image of the contracting individual. The combination of distinctions outlined above is part of a rejection of the complexity of relational patterns, in which obligations were often undertaken implicitly without direct and explicit bargaining over the value of reciprocal obligations. Reciprocity was part of the pattern, but it was not necessarily strictly defined or bargained over. People continued, and continue now, to undertake such obligations, and judges have never withdrawn completely from enforcing and policing such relationships. Classical theorists, however, attempted to purge such complexity from the idealized vision of contracting. Gratuitous undertakings are the key example. Classical scholars could not deny the existence of gratuitous undertakings, usually assumed in the course of commercial dealings. They did, however, define them out of contract law because of the difficulties in ascertaining the precise elements of exchange that they entailed. Thus, part of the classical project was the advancement of an image of the economy in which participants made strictly rational choices based on bargained-for exchange. Only such transactions as fit the ideal image would be accorded the privilege of legal enforcement.[19] The denial of gratuitous undertakings is thus analogically equivalent to a denial of the image of the economy of

---

18. How many times has the maxim "judges will not make contracts for the parties" been invoked when judges refused to apply a norm of fairness? It makes no difference, from my perspective, that judges often still apply fairness norms, circumventing this rhetorical retort to their activity. The fact is that on the plane of argument, the ability to resort to such a slogan has taken on significant persuasive force. Mark Pettit, discussing the rhetorical power of certain arguments in contract discourse, has said, "The practical significance of the definitional debate is, as I have suggested earlier, the rhetorical power of the concept of freedom. Basing an argument on freedom is like playing an ace in a high-card-wins card game. Few cards in the deck can match it, and no card beats it." Mark Pettit, Jr., "Freedom, Freedom of Contract, and the 'Rise and Fall,'" 79 *B.U. L. Rev.* 263, 280 (1999).

19. It would be a mistake to assume that this idealization is limited to classical scholars. It motivates important scholarly contributions from Fuller's conception of the "Contractual Archetype" through Eisenberg's ideas of separate worlds of contract and gift. See Lon L. Fuller, "Consideration and Form," 41 *Colum. L. Rev.* 799, 815 (1941); Eisenberg, "World of Contract," 847–49.

gift exchange, where the basis of exchange was uncertain and unverifiable. Commenting on the significance of the distinction between these two images of the economy, sociologist Pierre Bourdieu offers an analysis worth quoting at some length:

> Among the consequences of the process through which the economic field was constituted as such, one of the most pernicious, from the point of view of knowledge, is the tacit acceptance of a certain number of principles of division, the emergence of which is correlative with the social construction of the economic field as a separate field (on the basis of the axiom "business is business"), as the opposition between passions and interests. . . .
>
> The gift economy, in contrast to the economy where equivalent values are exchanged, is based on a denial of the economic (in the narrow sense), a refusal of the logic of the maximization of economic profit, i.e., of the spirit of calculation and the exclusive pursuit of material (as opposed to symbolic) interest, a refusal which is inscribed in the objectivity of institutions and in dispositions. . . . The possibility that then opens up of subjecting every kind of activity to the logic of calculation ("in business there's no room for sentiment") tends to legitimate this, so to speak, official cynicism that is particularly flaunted in law (for example, with contracts providing for the most pessimistic and disreputable eventualities) and in economic theory (which, at the beginning, helped to create this economy, just as jurists' treatises on the State helped to create the State). This economy . . . leads to the legitimation of the use of calculation even in the most sacred areas (the prayer wheel) and the generalization of the *calculating disposition*, the perfect antithesis of the generous disposition, which comes hand in hand with the development of an economic and social order characterized, as Weber puts it, by calculability and predictability.[20]

---

20. Pierre Bourdieu, "Marginalia—Some Additional Notes on the Gift," in *The Logic of The Gift: Toward an Ethic of Generosity* 231, 234–35 (Alan D. Schrift ed., Richard Nice trans., 1997). Elsewhere, Bourdieu offers a more general account of what the *spirit of calculability* amounts to:

> Economism recognizes no other form of interest than that which capitalism has produced, through a kind of real operation of abstraction, by setting up a universe of relations between man and man based, as Marx says, on "callous cash payment" and more generally by favouring the creation of relatively autonomous fields, capable of establishing their own axiomatics (through the fundamental tautology "business is business", on which "the economy" is based). It can therefore find no place in its analyses, still less in its calculations, for any form of "non-economic" interest. It is as if economic calculation had been able to appropriate the territory objectively assigned to the remorseless logic of what Marx calls "naked self-interest", only by relinquishing an island of the "sacred", miraculously spared by the "icy waters of egoistic calculation", the refuge of what has no price because it has too much or too little. But, above all, it can make nothing of universes that have not performed such a dissociation and so have, as it were, an economy in itself and not for itself.

Pierre Bourdieu, *The Logic of Practice* 113 (Richard Nice trans., 1990).

Bourdieu, of course, is writing about a much earlier stage in the transformation of economic life. But the transformation is not singular: like many of a culture's formative events, its fate is to be repeated in new contexts. It should not be surprising, therefore, that Bourdieu's words sound as if they could be describing the unwitting effects of classical contract theory in turning gifts into such a problematic category. The problem with gifts for classical theory, on this view, is that they imply an individual who is not subject to a law of preservation of capital. In other words, gifts are seen as one-sided transfers of goods, within a system that can only recognize the individuals that make up the system as maximizers.[21] As such, they should not be willing to give up something for nothing. Therefore, in the absence of overwhelming evidence to the contrary, the theory would like to presume against gifts, which are seen as evidence of an irrationality of action. But such a view is based on a knowing denial: every observer of the system realizes that everyone makes gifts. Some are rationalized by describing them as part of a wider system of exchange (gifts for occasions, birthdays, weddings, etc.), and some by reference to a system of wealth preservation within a family structure (gifts, especially of real estate, to children). But the actual use of gifts is much wider, including gifts by the most rational of individuals, the "quintessential economic man," the corporation.[22] Corporations routinely make gifts to employees, to clients, to potential clients, and most significantly of late, to political candidates or parties. Gifts are the oil that keeps the property regime lubricated and running, where particularized exchange is a moving part, liable to be eroded without such lubrication. Why, then, does the system adhere to its denial regarding the place of gifts, by pushing them out of the category of enforceability? The answer, or a reformulation of the question, lies in the system's investment in the idealization of the individual, as someone whose actions are calculating and calculable.

---

21. A straightforward articulation of this idea comes from one of its enthusiastic proponents: "It is true that all individuals differ in natural endowments, in personal ambitions, in social roles, and in institutional expectations. But there is one thing that each of them wants and wants just because each is an A or a B: *more*. . . . This characteristic of wanting more is universal. It applies with equal force to both greedy and rapacious firms and self-interested individuals." Richard A. Epstein, *Simple Rules for a Complex World* 75 (1995).

22. Gregory A. Mark, "The Personification of the Business Corporation in American Law," 54 *U. Chi. L. Rev.* 1441, 1483 (1997). See Barbara Johnson, "Anthropomorphism in Lyric and Law," 10 *Yale J.L. and Human.* 549, 573 (1998) ("Theories of rationality, naturalness, and the 'good,' presumed to be grounded in the nature of 'man,' may in reality be taking their notions of human essence not from 'natural man' but from business corporations").

It may seem as if today, the calculating subject, the individual for whom there is nothing that cannot be quantified in terms of profit and loss, is in retreat even as an idealization of the human sciences.[23] The calculating disposition, however, is still with us in contract. Modern contract doctrine has reformed most of the rules that seemed extreme in their idealization of the calculating or bargaining individual. But the calculating subject is a product of the framework that supported those rules, not of the individual rules by themselves, and the framework still grounds contract discourse.

23. Indeed, even some law and economics scholars appear to be showing signs of abandoning this idealization as the basis of their analyses. See Christine Jolls, Cass R. Sunstein, and Richard Thaler, "A Behavioral Approach to Law and Economics," 50 *Stan. L. Rev.* 1471 (1998).

PART TWO

Speculations of Contract

FIVE

Distinguished Gambles

The Struggle to Separate Speculation and Insurance from Gambling

The idea of wager or even of gambling presents a paradox for contract law. A basic tenet of common law contract doctrine is that contracts to wager are unenforceable, since they are deemed contracts in contravention of public policy.[1] On the other hand, contract "is the projection of exchange into the future,"[2] and as the future is always uncertain, contracts are often acknowledged as a mechanism of allocating risk.[3] Juxtaposing these two commonplaces, the question becomes the following: how do we distinguish allocation

---

1. See 3 Samuel Williston, *The Law of Contracts* § 1664, § 1668 (1st ed. 1920). In addition to common law unenforceability, almost all states have antigambling statutes, covering particular forms of gambling, and creating exemptions for state-sponsored gambling and for activities regulated by the state that might otherwise be considered gambling (the most obvious examples are state lotteries and, where applicable, casinos; the most important example is state and federal regulation of commodities futures trading and of insurance).

2. Ian Macneil, "The Many Futures of Contracts," 47 *S. Cal. L. Rev.* 691, 712–13 (1974).

3. See Spartech Corp. v. Opper, 890 F.2d 949, 955 (7th Cir. 1989) ("A principal purpose of contracts is to allocate the risk of the unexpected in accordance with the parties' respective preference for or aversion to risk and their ability or inability to prevent the risk from materializing"). See also Anthony Kronman and Richard Posner, *The Economics of Contract Law* 4 (1979).

of risk (legitimate and central to contract) from gambling or wagering (illegitimate and outside of contract)? This question becomes particularly acute in those cases where contracts allocate risk statistically (especially insurance contracts), or where contracts seem disconnected from any underlying business logic (in speculative trading of commodities futures). The problem for contract law with transactions like these is that they look like regular, legitimate contracts, but at the same time, they look like gambling.

The chapters in this part of the book analyze that paradox by concentrating on a developmental stage of the legal treatment of transactions whose primary object is risk. The cases examined turn on the validity of commodities trading contracts and insurance contracts around the turn of the century. Like any good historical story, this is more than one tale. The history presented here offers a counternarrative to a familiar conception of contract as coming to terms with a growing uncertainty that accompanied industrial concentration.[4] It combines historical investigation into seemingly narrow doctrines of contract law with questions regarding the place of uncertainty in a changing culture, suggesting that current and popular views of the topic miss the mark. It adds to the mix questions of how policy inflects legal decision making, and looks at judicial rhetoric as part of a process of defining or constructing modern individuality. Telegraphically put, the chapters in this part make two interrelated claims: first, the problem of wager, generally considered a marginal aspect of contract, ought to be seen as central to the development of modern contract law; and second, the emergence of a thoroughly modern law of contract and the associated legal treatment of wagers are fruitfully engaged as an important part of the process of constructing our current notion of individuality, with its attendant market consciousness.

The focus on turn-of-the-century cases should not lull the reader into a false sense of security regarding the question of distinguishing between contract and gambling. While the historical view serves to concentrate attention on a period in which societal attitudes toward risk underwent a transformation, we should not assume that modern contract law is free from ambiguity on the topic. Rather, the same inability sharply to distinguish gambling from the "legitimate" and "productive" sectors of the economy is

---

4. This view is a staple of mainstream thinking about contract. Robert A. Hillman, *The Richness of Contract Law: An Analysis and Critique of Contemporary Theories of Contract Law* 173–90 (1997); Lester G. Lindley, *Contract, Economic Change, and the Search for Order in Industrializing America* 281–86 (1993); Kevin M. Teeven, *A History of the Anglo-American Common Law of Contract* 236–40 (1990).

replayed today, only at a faster pace and with larger stakes. Heated debates over the regulation of the rapidly growing market in derivatives and over the emerging industry of viatical settlements are modern examples of the same difficulties analyzed here historically.

Labeling transactions as wagers is one way to limit freedom of contract. The underlying question always revolves around the extent to which the state will support or restrict the attempts of individuals or groups to undertake obligations. Today, it is more common to frame the debate over the legitimacy of risk as one over the scope of state regulation. In contrast, around the turn of the last century, the question of wager was one of the key doctrinal areas defining the scope of freedom of contract. The parallels between these issues should emerge as the discussion proceeds. I do not set out to answer the question of how much regulation of contracting behavior is appropriate. The more modest goal here is to suggest that one basic puzzle about contract regulation, that of distinguishing legitimate from illegitimate risk, while often taken for granted as definitively settled, is actually a problem for which no satisfying solution has been offered, much less adopted.

This part comprises four chapters. The present chapter offers a brief historical sketch of the connections among gambling, speculation, and insurance, and the attempts through the nineteenth century to distinguish these practices. Chapters 6 and 7 put on display a somewhat old-fashioned exercise in reading cases, providing a detailed analysis of the development of the law surrounding commodities futures trading and life insurance contracts, with heightened attention to the policy analysis carried out by judges adjudicating disputes that arose in these areas.[5] The point of the analysis is not only to unravel the legal doctrine, but more importantly, to examine the rhetorical maneuvers through which judges justified their decisions. Through this analysis, I explore judicial rhetoric as the site of a cultural conflict whose intensity reached a peak around the turn of the century. Finally, Chapter 8

5. The reading of the cases proceeds on the basis of legal realist insights, comparing similar cases with different outcomes whose results cannot be reconciled on the basis of legal argumentation. Oliver Wendell Holmes, Jr., and the realists who followed his example believed that these decisions were based on "policy," or what they sometimes called legislative considerations. Critical legal scholars have noted that "policy" is a vehicle for ideology. This book employs a yet more expansive notion of policy, including a cultural politics. The founding instance of this mode of critique is Oliver Wendell Holmes, Jr., "Privilege, Malice, and Intent," 8 *Harv. L. Rev.* 1 (1894); an example of its developed realist form is Walter Wheeler Cook, "The Present Status of the "Lack of Mutuality Rule," 36 *Yale L.J.* 897 (1927). The strategy, and the role of the critical legal studies movement in explaining policy as ideology, is described in Duncan Kennedy, *A Critique of Adjudication: Fin de Siècle* 82–100 (1997).

is an interpretation of turn-of-the-century policy bases of the decisions, and a comment on the place of uncertainty in legal rhetoric around the turn of the century. It argues that rather than neutralizing objective uncertainty by developing doctrinal tools,[6] contract law is part of a richer and more complex story of Americans' love/hate relationship with risk.

Until the early nineteenth century, insurance, on the one hand, and stock and commodities trading, on the other, were viewed as indistinguishable from or at least very difficult to distinguish from gambling. Establishing a distinction was more than a legal question, in that it was crucially intertwined with a vision of society, and with a vision of what the individuals must be in order to make up society, or to be fit for society. In other words, the distinction between gambling and its cousins in the realm of legitimate speculation is part of a process of socializing individuals in two senses: on the one hand, it is a process that acts on concrete individuals, by imposing a view of normative behavior; but on the other hand, it is a process of creating individuals, where initially a concept of individuality may have been far less important.[7] The example of insurance is illuminating here: whereas in a more localized economic and social environment, loss was dealt with communally—for example, by extended family or neighbors caring for the families of the deceased or disabled—the rise in urbanization and mobility makes individually procured insurance the key mechanism in providing for loss, breaking the ties that cement communal feeling. Insurance thus substitutes a faceless collective for a familiar communal collective.[8]

Historians have told the story of gambling and antigambling in the nineteenth century along several lines, some of them including important race and class distinctions in the treatment of gambling. The insight I want to emphasize here, however, is that an important element of the antigambling movements, and even of incidental antigambling rhetoric, was an attempt to legitimate a certain view of human activity that foregrounded gain. In other words, part of the function of antigambling discourse was to construct acquisitive individuality (including the possibility of speculation) as

6. See Walter F. Pratt, Jr., "American Contract Law at the Turn of the Century," 39 *S.C. L. Rev.* 415 (1988).

7. Ian Hacking terms this process "making up people." See generally Ian Hacking, *The Taming of Chance* (1990).

8. Reuven Brenner and Gabrielle A. Brenner, *Gambling and Speculation: A Theory, a History, and a Future of Some Human Decisions* 106 (1990).

the normative form of human subjectivity. This may sound paradoxical at first, since who, after all, is more interested in gain than the gambler? This should become clearer as we proceed.

To begin to understand the opposition to insurance and to speculation, one must look to the reigning morality and especially the religious worldview that was dominant in the United States until late in the nineteenth century. Describing the change that occurred through the nineteenth century, Ian Hacking has written, "In 1800 the world was deemed to be governed by stern necessity and universal laws. Shortly after 1930 it became virtually certain that at bottom our world is run at best by laws of chance."[9] From its inception in the seventeenth century and well beyond, the notion of probability was linked with gambling devices like dice and lotteries, and the mathematicians who developed probability theory initially did so at the behest of professional gamblers.[9] What eventually developed into the actuarial conception of risk was a notion of probability explicitly linked with gambling, and this, in part, explains why "insurance and gambling were at first classified under the same heading."[10] An additional reason insurance was seen as gambling was that early insurance schemes were, in fact, "outright bets on human lives."[11] In England, the link between insurance and gambling was especially strong, and it was common for people to "insure" against the death of public personalities such as the king or members of the cabinet, with whom they had no personal relationship.[12]

One example of a type of insurance betting is the tontine policy, or what in American insurance parlance was known as the deferred dividend policy: this was a type of annuity shared by subscribers to a loan, with the shares increasing as subscribers died, till the last subscriber got all that was left. In other words, a number of individuals would invest money into a pool, adding to its size in the first years by paying premiums; after five (or in some cases ten) years, dividends begin to be awarded, which grow larger as

9. Tom Baker, "On the Genealogy of Moral Hazard," 75 *Texas L. Rev.* 237, 246 (1996); Ian Hacking, *The Emergence of Probability* (1975).

10. Brenner and Brenner, *Gambling and Speculation*, 104.

11. Viviana A. Rotman Zelizer, *Morals and Markets: The Development of Life Insurance in the United States* 69 (1979).

12. Lorraine J. Daston, "The Domestication of Risk: Mathematical Probability and Insurance, 1650–1830," in 1 *The Probabilistic Revolution*, 237, 244.

members of the group die off; each participant, then, is betting on the short life of his fellows, or at least on his own life being the longest.[13]

Insurance was a suspicious concept. It was widely claimed and accepted, for instance, that insurance was an attempt to interfere with divine providence. As sociologist Viviana Zelizer has recounted in detail, life insurance was viewed as immoral and sacrilegious, its benefits derided as dirty money. Critics objected that an agreement whereby one party profited from the death of a loved one was "a speculation repugnant to the law of God and man." Religion was the most prominent source of cultural opposition to life insurance, and early nineteenth-century religious leaders portrayed insuring against death a bet against God as well as a usurpation of the functions of divine providence.[14]

Even more intensely than insurance, various types of financial speculation, whether regarding the value of land, stocks, or agricultural commodities, were often associated with gambling. Critics of speculation railed against the prevalence of commercial gambling:

> If, instead of betting on something so small as falling dice, one bets on the rise and fall of stocks or on the price which wheat will reach some months hence, and if by such betting one corners the community in an article essential to its welfare, throwing a continent into confusion, the law will pay not the slightest attention. A gambling house for these larger purposes may be built conspicuously in any city, the sign "Stock Exchange" be set over its door, influential men appointed its officers, and the law will protect it and them as it does the churches.[15]

Populist movements in the agricultural states agitated for legislation to eliminate speculation in futures, using metaphors of diabolical gambling to describe speculators.[16] Speculators countered, in books, popular publications,

---

13. See Morton Keller, *The Life Insurance Enterprise, 1885–1910*, pp. 56–58 (1963); Brenner and Brenner, *Gambling and Speculation*, 104. Interestingly, despite their analytic similarity to gambling, tontine policies were not initially targeted as wager contracts in the United States, where insurable interest doctrine ignored, to some extent, the form of the policy itself: "There is no doubt that a man may effect an insurance on his own life for the benefit of a relative or friend; or two or more persons, on their joint lives, for the benefit of the survivor or survivors. The old tontines were based substantially on this principle, and their validity has never been called into question." Connecticut Mutual Life Insurance Co. v. Schaefer, 94 U.S. 457, 460 (1876).

14. Zelizer, *Markets and Morals*, 45–46, 73.

15. Unattributed, quoted in Charles A. Conant, "The Function of the Stock and Produce Exchanges," in *The Functions of the Legitimate Exchanges* 15 (1910)

16. Ann Fabian, *Card Sharps, Dream Books, and Bucket Shops: Gambling in 19th Century America* 154–62

and arguments before legislators, emphasizing that the critics had failed to appreciate the distinction between speculation and gambling: speculators were assuming economic risks that others wanted to shift; gamblers, on the other hand, were creating new and unproductive risks.[17]

Throughout the nineteenth century, however, whatever the possibilities of shifting valence for insurance or speculation might have been, it was clear to everyone that gambling was on the negative pole of human behavior: it was evil and immoral, as were the people who gambled. In order to legitimate endeavors that had been associated with gambling, one had to distinguish them from gambling, and in the process, it did not hurt to add your voice to those condemning gambling in the first place. As historian Ann Fabian has shown, gambling emerged as a "negative analogue," a form of gain that made other efforts to acquire wealth seem normal and natural. Whereas speculative profits had once seemed dangerous and possibly destructive, they were surely less problematic than the unearned and illusory profits of gambling. Condemning wagers while embracing a speculative economy, the bourgeoisie "constructed an image of themselves as virtuous and productive citizens by banishing their gambling doubles."[18] Speculation was crucial for the economy, but "for the speculation to stay, the gambling had to go."[19]

Like the attempt to legitimize speculation, the legitimation of insurance also involved the condemnation of gambling. Proponents of insurance, who included not only insurance salesmen and apologists for insurance companies, but also social reformers, attempted to overcome resistance to life insurance by portraying it as a moral building block in a complex society, where people ought not rely on the charity of the community, but rather should employ self-help and self-reliance in the form of provision for the future through insurance. One strategy for legitimizing insurance was the development of the doctrine of moral hazard. By claiming that the insurance industry itself would refuse to insure "moral hazards" the industry dissociated itself from those who would try to use insurance for gambling purposes. Gambling and insurance would be separated institutionally, in part through

---

(1990).

17. See, e.g., James E. Boyle, *Speculation and the Chicago Board of Trade* 117 (1920); Conant, "Functions of the Exchanges," 15; New York Cotton Exchange, *Dealings in "Options" and "Futures": Protests, Memorials, and Arguments Against Bills Introduced in the 52d Congress* (1892).

18. Fabian, *Card Sharps*, 4–5.

19. Id. at 61.

the attention to moral hazard. Tom Baker described the two-pronged uses of the concept: moral hazard would help the industry weed out the undesirable uses of insurance, and at the same time would allow insurers "to claim innocence by association: Gambling is immoral; people who gamble are immoral; we and people we permit to buy insurance are moral (because we exclude the immoral); therefore, insurance is not gambling."[20]

A late nineteenth-century critic summed up the opposition to various forms of gambling this way: "To deal with property on the principle of chance, which is non-moral, must be immoral because it involves the false proposition that property itself is non-moral."[21] This statement crystallizes a deep-seated view of how the distribution of wealth and power was justified before the transition to a world run by "laws of chance."

---

20. Baker, "Genealogy of Moral Hazard," 258–59.

21. W. D. MacKenzie, *The Ethics of Gambling* 43 (1895), quoted in David Dixon, *From Prohibition to Regulation: Bookmaking, Anti-Gambling, and the Law* 50 (1991). This outlook suggests a crucial point, which is that nineteenth-century morality, and especially the ideology of self-reliance, was based on a rejection of chance, and instead on an espousal of a doctrine of desert.

SIX

"Contracts" for "Futures"

Commercial Speculation and the Gambling Stigma

Part of the transition to a world run by laws of chance was a shift in attitudes toward speculation, one of the important aspects of which was commodities trading. Commodities futures trading has an intimate relationship with contract law, both historically and linguistically. The development of expectation damages for breach of contract, and of the way to measure expectation (as the difference between contract price and market price at time of delivery) are closely tied to cases of speculative trading.[1] And when commodities traders discuss their work, they talk of buying and selling not wheat, cotton, or corn, but "contracts." Commodities futures trading serves as a good model of what abstract contracting is about, its description falling clearly in line with mainstream modern contract theory. Transactions are bilateral executory promises to buy and sell a given amount of any commodity (gold, wheat, cotton, foreign currency) at a given price, on a given date in the future.

The development of organized exchanges, like the Chicago Board of Trade, allowed the nationalization of supply and demand in agricultural

1. See Morton J. Horwitz, *The Transformation of American Law, 1780–1860*, p. 177 (1977).

commodities, conforming to what economists today would call a sophisticated market supplying an efficient pricing mechanism.[2] But organized exchanges also provide for speculative transactions: people can, and frequently do, buy or sell with no intention of making or taking delivery of the product, but merely with the intention of liquidating their position before the date of delivery, hopefully at a profit. People conducting speculative trades can be specialists, whose vocation is trading on the exchanges, or simply outside investors who see particular trades as good investments. Or, people can use the exchanges to hedge. In other words, someone with an actual or expected holding of a commodity may make a futures transaction in order to prevent losses resulting from swings in the price of the commodity.[3] Today, such transactions, regardless of whether their motivation be physical sales, hedging, or pure speculation, are a completely integral and commonplace part of the market (as they are in the stock market). It is rarely considered that they could be outlawed as wagering contracts.[4] However, in the last quarter of the nineteenth century and, actually, until definitive federal regulation in the 1930s, the status of such speculative transactions was hotly contested. Indeed, at common law it was accepted that transactions for future delivery of property, including stocks and commodities in which the parties did not intend actual delivery but rather only settlement according to price differences, were unenforceable because they were mere wagers.[5] In most states, statutes (most of which are still on the books today) were passed expanding the common law position, sometimes criminalizing

---

2. See generally Henry Crosby Emery, *Speculation on the Stock and Produce Exchanges of the United States* 54–74, 113–43 (Faculty of Political Science of Columbia Univ. ed., 1896); Jonathan Lurie, "Commodities Exchanges as Self-Regulating Organizations in the Late 19th Century: Some Perimeters in the History of American Administrative Law," 28 *Rutgers L. Rev.* 1107 (1975).

3. See 7 *Report of the Federal Trade Commission on the Grain Trade* 33–68 (1926). The most intuitive illustration of a hedging transaction involves the farmer (despite the fact that most hedgers are apparently dealers and not farmers): In January, the farmer expects to have grain for sale in July. By selling the July future in January, the farmer guarantees the price for the wheat, thus protecting against the possibility that the price of wheat will fall, leaving the farmer with a smaller return on what are already sunk costs. It should be noted that the farmer also gives up the possibility of gains in the event that the price of wheat rises in the intervening period.

4. The ease with which we conceive of such transactions is, however, completely based on the existence of the organized exchanges: private individuals cannot create enforceable contracts with one another for futures, unless they actually intend delivery.

5. See 3 Samuel Williston, *The Law of Contracts* §§ 1664a–1670 (1st ed. 1920). A wager is defined as a contract performable only upon the happening of a condition which is a fortuitous event. In commodities speculation cases, the fortuitous event was the rise or fall in prices.

the transactions and sometimes granting the losers the right to recover their losses from the winners.[6]

But how is it that such transactions become susceptible to the charge that they involve gambling? Theoretically, it is difficult if not impossible to distinguish trades on the exchanges from other contracts of sale. A contract to sell goods for delivery in the future, which the seller does not own at the time, is not only legal but common. The fact that transactions are entered into "on margin" also does not brand them as wagers.[7] And the fact that the trades are often settled according to price differences rather than actual delivery of commodities simply signifies that contracting parties resolved a "breach" of the contract without recourse to the legal system, yet in accord with the legal remedy of expectation damages for breach of contract.[8] In other words, settling according to price differences is an instance of anticipatory breach, accompanied by payment of the difference between the contract price and the market price of the commodity at the time of breach.

The analogy to a simple contract of sale is illuminating here: a defaulting seller's attempt to defend against a suit, by claiming the contract is void as a wager because delivery was not contemplated, would be ridiculed.[9] But this situation is a perfect analogue to commodities trading from a pure analytic perspective. The important difference, of course, is the context. A host of factors combine to act as a prophylactic against the occurrence of the anticipatory breach, the most important being (an assumed) lack of price volatility. Where, as in commodities contracts, the time between contracting and performance is significant, price volatility is an ingrained feature of the market, and day-to-day price differences can be turned into profits, the incentive to speculate on the rise and fall of prices takes on an importance that it does

---

6. See, e.g., Ala. Code 8-1-121(a) (1993); Ark. Code Ann. 23-44-105 (Michie 1994); Cal. Corp. Code 29008, 29100 (West 1977); Mass. Ann. Laws chap. 271, 35–36 (Law. Co-op. 1992); Mich. Comp. Laws Ann. 750.126, 750.127, 750.128 (West 1991); N.Y. Gen. Bus. Law 351 (McKinney 1988).

7. See 3 Williston, *Law of Contracts*, §§ 1667–1669.

8. Indeed, the analogy of market contracts to betting is a staple of economic thinking on contract: "The contract is then essentially a bet against the future course of the market." John H. Barton, "The Economic Basis of Damages for Breach of Contract," 1 *J. Leg. Stud.* 277, 278 (1972).

9. *B* contracts to buy a quantity of widgets from *A* on January 1, to be delivered on April 1, for 100. On March 1, when the market price of widgets is 120, *A* announces that she cannot fulfill the contract, and pays *B* expectation damages of 20 (plus whatever down payment *B* initially made). To make the analogy even more obvious, assume that *A* is a wholesaler (i.e., a middleman), selling to a retailer; she is not concerned with the costs of production, but merely believes that between January and the end of March, she will be able to procure the widgets for less than 100.

not have in contracts for widgets. Thus, the tendency of classical theorists to develop a general law of contract runs into an obstacle in the shape of the specific character of the market in question.[10] The pressure to decide commodities trading cases under the general rubric of contracts brings into sharp focus the problem of distinguishing these transactions from other contracts where speculation always lurks as a spectral possibility.

The facts of a typical case help set the stage for the discussion of the legal mechanism developed to distinguish between legitimate transactions and wagers. A miller comes to a broker and arranges for a purchase of grain. The broker explains that the purchase will be made on the Chicago Board of Trade, according to the rules of the exchange, which formally require that every transaction include a commitment to make or take delivery by the specified date. The miller goes ahead with his order, the broker makes the trade on the exchange, in his own name, as is customary. Time goes by, and the price of grain goes down, at which time the miller decides to sell, taking a loss on the purchase and sale (paying the difference in prices), and paying commission to the broker for both trades. So far, not a very remarkable story. But then, the miller regrets his loss, and sues to recover on the basis of Illinois' antigaming statute, which voids trades made without the intention of taking delivery. He says that he never intended to take delivery of the grain,[11] and that if he nominally agreed to the terms imposed by the Board of Trade, he was not sincere in this part of the obligation, knowing in advance that he would liquidate his trade before the time of delivery. The broker answers that he was completely sincere in his intentions, regardless of those of his client, and that he engaged in legitimate transactions on the exchange. Further, he claims that the actual losses were paid to the opposing sides in the transactions, and if there was no delivery, it was because there was a set-off of trades, and thus, that the lost money (was not lost to him and) is not in his hands. The Supreme Court of Illinois, sitting in 1916, however, rules against the supposed sincerity of the broker, and allows the miller to recover. The aptly named case is *Miller v. Sincere.*[12]

---

10. On the tendency to generality and abstraction, see Lawrence M. Friedman, *Contract Law in America* 20-24 (1965); Christopher T. Wonnell, "The Abstract Character of Contract Law," 22 *Conn. L. Rev.* 437 (1990).

11. Maybe he even offers evidence that his mill can only handle a small percentage of the grain contracted for, thus tending to show that the transaction was a speculation on prices. See Pope v. Hanke, 40 N.E. 839, 841 (Ill. 1894).

12. 112 N.E. 664 (Ill. 1916). Further, in the actual case at hand, the broker claimed that a 1913 amend-

In dozens, if not hundreds of like cases, turn-of-the-century transactors refused to pay debts to brokers, claiming that the transactions were illegal wagers. The actions divide into two groups: (a) clients who sued brokers to recover payments already made, relying on antigaming statutes that provided for recovery of money lost in gambling; or (b) brokers who brought actions to secure payment of accounts, or of notes given in satisfaction of debts for similar trading activity, with the clients claiming they could avoid paying the notes because they were given as consideration for illegal wagering contracts.[13] Either way, the effective use of the antigaming statutes probably made the courts instrumental in reaching unintended consequences.[14]

The test of validity of transactions in commodities was the intention of the parties to perform under the terms of the contract, rather than to

---

ment to the antigaming statute exempted trades made on the Chicago Board of Trade according to its rules. The court, however, held the amendment unconstitutional, saying that there was no reasonable basis for differentiating between transactions made on the Board of Trade and those made elsewhere (112 N.E., at 666):

> There is no reason why the Chicago Board of Trade, or stock exchange, or any other similar institution anywhere in the state, should be made a sanctuary for those who commit the crime of gambling on futures in grain or stocks. If it could lawfully be done, then it would be lawful to provide that persons could gamble at cards or with dice, or at other well-known gambling devices, in a board of trade or stock exchange building, but nowhere else. Conceding that there is ample reason for the enactment of criminal statutes against gaming and betting of all kinds, then a bet or wager which is made upon any uncertain event, whether it be the future price of grain, or the result of a race, or the turn of a card, or the cast of a die, would be no different in principle than other kinds of gambling. The test is always: Is the wager or bet upon any uncertain event or contingency?

13. This defense, supported in many states by statute, often succeeded. See, e.g., Kuhl v. M. Gally Universal Press Co., 26 So. 535 (Ala. 1898); Gardner v. Meeker, 48 N.E. 307 (Ill. 1897); Swinney v. Edwards, 55 P. 306 (Wyo. 1898). See also 3 Williston, *Law of Contracts*, §§ 1675–77.

This raises one of the important doctrinal issues involved in speculative trading cases. While functionalist histories of contract have maintained that the financial interests of the merchant class demanded and achieved full negotiability of standard financial instruments, we see that in this paradigmatically commercial context, negotiability was thwarted when it could be associated with gambling. Thus, the financial interest in speculation was not strong enough to overcome the stigma of gambling, undermining the functionalist narrative of the development of commercial law. For a sophisticated version of the functionalist narrative, see Horwitz, *Transformation of American Law*, 211–26.

14. In both types of cases, it should be kept in mind what an effective use of an antigambling statute involves on the part of the person making the trades. When she wins, she collects her winnings, since the brokers are interested in generating business, and the members of the exchange are making trades, and paying out profits when people make them. When she loses, she still wins, because she comes back to the broker and claims the transactions were void wagers. The courts then, rather than effectively eliminating the practice of wagering, are actually giving people a license to gamble, and a guarantee against losses. But of course, this is just an amusing curiosity or a mild absurdity on the level of unintended incentives.

settle according to price differences.[15] The test acknowledges that the form of legitimate and illegitimate contracts can be identical.[16] The distinction relies on the ability of the courts to determine whether the legitimate form was a ruse to cover an illegitimate transaction. In this light, the test of validity seems to be the same as that for any contract with an illegal purpose.[17] However, the application of this test in the commodities context turns out to be anything but simple.

Two related issues present themselves for analysis: first, the relatively theoretical question of whether the search for intent implies that we are in the realm of the subjective theory of contract; and second, the question of how intent will be determined by the court. While it may appear that the former issue should provide a conclusive answer to the latter, in fact, both the subjective view and the objective view allow for significant latitude in determining what kinds of arguments or evidence will convince a court of the legitimacy or illegitimacy of a particular transaction.

WAGERS AND THE OBJECTIVE THEORY OF CONTRACT: A PRELUDE TO THE QUESTION OF INTENT

The contest between objective and subjective theories of contract takes on a puzzling aspect in the context of commodities trading. On the one hand, given that the form of commodities transactions was identical in cases where the transaction was sometimes held valid and sometimes invalid, and given that the form of the contract was in essence identical to other contracts for

---

15. Summing up the common law position on such transactions in 1920, Williston writes:

> The test adopted in the absence of statute distinguishes between agreements to buy and sell in which an actual delivery of the property is contemplated, and similar agreements in which it is contemplated merely that a settlement shall be made between the parties based on fluctuations in the market price. An agreement of the former kind is legal; one of the latter kind involves wagering and is illegal.

3 Williston, *Law of Contracts*, § 1670 (The heading for this section is: "Test of validity is intent to make actual delivery").

16. By "form" here I mean the conduct or outward manifestations or expressions of intent deemed the essential element of contract by the objective theory of contract.

17. For instance, if *A* contracts to deliver "a package" to *B*, where both *A* and *B* know that the "package" is stolen goods or a code word for a murder, the contract is clearly illegal and unenforceable. Freedom of contract runs out where the purpose of the contract is criminal.

the sale of goods, a strictly objective test of the contract would seem to imply that the contracts would always be valid.[18]

According to this standard, if contracts for the sale of commodities were ever allowed, none would be singled out for disqualification unless the parties made an overt provision for the fact that no delivery would be made, and that the transaction would be settled according to price differences. Most commentators agree that the objective theory of contracts does in fact hold sway, and that its victory over subjective theory was complete by the beginning of the twentieth century.[19] But in fact, the cases on commodities trading show that issues of subjective intent were still important well into the twentieth century.

The consideration of intent in this context throws some doubt on the traditional narrative regarding the ascendance of the objective theory. That narrative acknowledges that in some marginal cases, especially those cases that raise problems of fraud and duress, intent can be a relevant category. But the centrality of intent in cases where agreements are completely voluntary and the context is purely commercial, conditions that are routine in the commodities context, shows that the narrative of the marginality of policing agreements through the mechanism of intent is overstated. The ascendance of objective theory is often presented either as part of the progress of rationality in contracts, or as part of a progressive dominance of business interests and their desire for stability in contract law, but such progress narratives should be viewed with suspicion.[20]

A look at some case law fleshes out the puzzling quality of the conflict over subjective and objective theories. Courts were generally in agreement that contracts would only be valid where the parties "*really intend* and agree that the goods are to be delivered by the seller, and the price to be paid

---

18. The most famous expression of the strict objective view is Judge Learned Hand's statement:

> A contract has, strictly speaking, nothing to do with the personal, or individual, intent of the parties. A contract is an obligation attached by the mere force of law to certain acts of the parties, usually words, which ordinarily accompany and represent a known intent. If, however, it were proved by twenty bishops that either party when he used the words intended something else than the usual meaning which the law imposes on them, he would still be held, unless there were mutual mistake or something else of the sort.

Hotchkiss v. National City Bank, 200 F. 287, 293 (S.D.N.Y. 1911), aff'd, 201 F. 664 (2d Cir. 1912), aff'd, 231 U.S. 50 (1913). For theoretical defense of the objective theory see, Samuel Williston, "Mutual Assent in the Formation of Contracts," 14 *Ill. L. Rev.* 85 (1919).

19. See E. Allan Farnsworth, *Contracts* 117–18 (3d ed. 1999).

20. See Friedman, *Contract Law in America*, 86–87; Lon Fuller, "Consideration and Form," 41 *Colum. L. Rev.* 799, 808 (1941); Horwitz, *Transformation of American Law*, 201.

by the buyer."[21] The repeated phrase betrays the central sticking point: the elusive quality called "real intent." The language employed in an Iowa Supreme Court case from just before the turn of the century is suggestive here. The defendant refused to pay debts to a broker on orders to buy grain, claiming that the transactions were wagering contracts, and void. The court, in deciding whether the trial court was justified in admitting "the uncommunicated motive or intention of the defendant" into evidence, wrote:

> It is not enough, to render a contract void, that the buyer intends it as a gambling contract, unless the seller participates in that intention; that is, if, in the case at bar, the defendant, in ordering the purchase of the oats, only intended a speculation upon margins, without delivery of grain, and the plaintiff purchased the grain for actual delivery, it would not be a gambling contract. To make the contract void as between these parties, the intention to make a gambling contract must have been mutual.[22]

As far as the objective theory of contracts is concerned, this passage highlights the ambiguity of the courts' treatment of wager contracts. On the one hand, the normal situation is to expect mutual intention even where none really exists, so long as there are manifestations of intent. The manifestations of intent are taken as a proxy for real intent, deemed unnecessary. Williston's exposition of the objective theory is clear on this point: "The words and acts of the parties are themselves the basis of contractual liability, and not merely evidence of a mental attitude required by the law. In other words . . . an expression of mutual assent, and not the assent itself, is the essential element of contractual liability."[23] Here, however, real mutual intent is not only unnecessary to the contract, it is fatal. In other words, there is one kind of contract that cannot suffice with objective manifestations of intent: the gambling contract. But when you succeed in making the gambling contract, you undermine the commodities contract. The emphasis on "real intent" seems to suggest a clinging to subjective theory, but perhaps this is a case of objective theory at the extreme: the contract exists as valid

21. Embrey v. Jemison, 131 U.S. 336, 344–45 (1889); emphasis added. The court continues:

> If, under guise of such a contract, the real intent be merely to speculate in the rise or fall of prices . . . then the whole transaction constitutes nothing more than a wager, and is null and void. . . . [I]n this country, all such contracts are held to be illegal and void as against public policy. . . . Gambling is none the less such because it is carried on in the form or guise of legitimate trade.

22. Counselman v. Reichart, 72 N.W. 490, 491 (Iowa 1897).

23. Williston, "Mutual Assent," 87.

only where there is no mutual intention.[24] However, despite theoretical basis for the proposition, it presents a more coherent polemic for the objective theory than the cases will support.[25] In fact, the courts shy away from fixed determinations on the question of whether they adhere to an objective or subjective theory, allowing juries to divine the "real intent" of the parties that is supposed to determine the outcome of the cases.

DETERMINING THE INTENT OF THE PARTIES

Beyond the theoretical question of subjective or objective accounts of contract, the central problem in the commodities trading cases, viewed as a group, is how to determine intent. An influential Supreme Court decision, *Irwin v. Williar*, laid down an oft-quoted formulation for the task.[26] In that case, plaintiffs were brokers who sued for a debt incurred by a partnership, the surviving partner of which was the defendant. The defendant raised two defenses: first, that the deceased partner exceeded the scope of his authority by making speculative trades in grain, far beyond the needs of the grain business in which the partnership was legitimately engaged; second, that the transactions were wagers and thus void, and that therefore the debt was also void.[27] On this point, the Court accepted the jury instructions, mandating

---

24. Williston's treatment of the issue relies precisely on this logic:

> The importance of observing that objection to recovery is not so much the character of the contracts as the guilt of the plaintiff is illustrated in wagering contracts of this sort; for if either of the parties contracts in good faith, intending that the goods shall be actually delivered, he is entitled to the benefit of his contract, no matter what may have been the secret purpose or intention of the other party; while the party guilty of an intent to gamble cannot recover.

3 Williston, *Law of Contracts*, § 1671 (footnotes omitted).

25. See, e.g., Miller v. Sincere, 112 N.E. 664 (Ill. 1916); Counselman v. Reichart, 72 N.W. 490 (Iowa 1897); Soby v. People, 25 N.E. 109 (Ill. 1890); Waite v. Frank, 86 N.W. 645 (S.D. 1901); Mackey v. Rausch, 15 N.Y.S. 4 (Sup. Ct. 1st Dep't, 1891); Embrey v. Jemison, 131 U.S. 336 (1889). In many of the cases, where there was no direct evidence of an intent to wager, courts upheld verdicts of juries who concluded that the mutual intent was to wager.

26. 110 U.S. 499 (1884).

27. To make a claim for implied authority of the deceased partner, the plaintiffs showed that the partnership was involved in "dealing in grain" and that it took or made deliveries on some of its orders, while making countertransactions before the date of delivery on others. The trial court ruled that the partnership's legitimate "dealing in grain" made all the transactions facially authorized. The Supreme Court reversed this holding, saying, "Dealing in grain is not a technical phrase from which a court can properly infer as a matter of law authority to bind the firm in every case irrespective of its circumstances." 110 U.S. at 507. The interesting thing about the reversal is the court's willingness to complicate the factual determination on the basis of a distinction between grain for the milling business and grain

that a "transaction which on its face is legitimate cannot be held void as a wagering contract by showing that one party only so understood and meant it to be. The proof must go further, and show that this understanding was mutual—that both parties so understood the transaction."[28] Further, the Court elaborated the point that all the circumstances of the transactions could be relevant in determining intent:

> We do not doubt that the question whether the transactions came within the definition of wagers is one that may be determined upon the circumstances, the jury drawing all proper inferences as to the real intent and meaning of the parties; for, as was properly said in the charge, "it makes no difference that a bet or wager is made to assume the form of a contract. Gambling is none the less such because it is carried on in the form or guise of legitimate trade." It might therefore be the case that a series of transactions, such as that described in the present record, might present a succession of contracts, perfectly valid in form, but which, on the face of the whole, taken together, and in connection with all the attending circumstances, might disclose indubitable evidences that they were mere wagers. The jury would be justified in such a case, without other evidence than that of the nature and circumstances of the transactions, in reaching and declaring such a conclusion.[29]

At first glance, this formulation seems to adopt a stance advocating full disclosure of any relevant circumstances. But the balanced rhetoric of the passage is misleading. Plaintiffs in this case attempted to show that they had no intention of gambling by proving that the defendant had made or taken delivery on some of their orders, and that the custom of traders on the exchange of which they were members required delivery, either of actual grain or by set-off. While the trial court admitted evidence of such custom, the Supreme Court reversed, saying that since there was no evidence that the defendants had knowledge of such custom, it did not bind them.[30] In effect, then, the Court was willing to consider all relevant circumstances that might tend to show an intent to gamble, but unwilling to consider circumstances that could have shown intent to make delivery. This imbalance is just one instance that exhibits how much latitude the courts retain in determining the

---

for speculation, without taking into account the possibility of hedging. This determination is part of the Court's overall negative orientation toward speculative trading.

28. Id. at 507–8.

29. Id. at 510–11.

30. Id. at 513–16.

meaning of the circumstances, even when they declare that they are searching for the real intent of the parties.

The interpretation of circumstances surrounding a particular transaction often depends on a series of presumptions regarding commodities trading generally, or particular features of commodities trading, through which the court can impose economic sympathies or antagonisms. For instance, in *Counselman v. Reichart*, the court announced that for a transaction to be invalidated as a wager, the intention to gamble must be mutual. However, it did not require that intention be communicated between the parties, and it was undisturbed by a lack of direct evidence as to a gambling intent, because of a presumption regarding the commodities exchanges themselves: "In view of the generally known fact that business on the board of trade is conducted on a plan of nondelivery of produce, but as a speculation in margins or differences, it may well be stated that the fact of whether there was to be a delivery of the grain in question was one of understanding between the parties, independent of the orders for purchases."[31]

In other words, the court was willing to presume that trades carried out on the organized exchange are gambling contracts, and this despite the fact that in the case at hand, some of the defendant's orders were settled by actual delivery of grain.[32] On the other hand, some courts, even while sharing the assumption that many or most trades on the exchanges are a form of gambling, work out the opposite legal presumption, relying on the fact that the trades were carried out on organized exchanges as evidence of their legitimacy.[33] Brokers routinely included boilerplate language on their letterheads that all transactions contemplated actual delivery, and courts alternatively credited or ignored them, again exposing both the courts' latitude in determining intention and the relatively tenuous hold that objective theory had on the outcome of the cases.

The relationship of clients to brokers was another area of discord among

---

31. 72 N.W. 490, 491 (Iowa 1897).

32. A similar presumption seems to motivate the court in another case (*Pope*, 40 N.E.), where some orders had been settled by actual delivery.

33. See, e.g., Bank of Ettrick v. Emberson, 196 N.W. 861, 866 (Wis. 1924):

> It is undoubtedly true that the great majority of contracts made through the agency of boards of trade are gambling contracts. . . . On the other hand, a vast amount of important and legitimate business is carried on every day through the agency of boards of trade. Speculation is not necessarily gambling, and contracts to be consummated on boards of trade, if intended to be carried out in good faith, are as legitimate as the innumerable other contracts made in the business world in which gains or losses may depend on changes in market values.

various courts. As Williston points out, "If a transaction is carried out on an Exchange . . . it seems difficult to see why an agreement between the broker and customer that the latter should only be required to settle differences, should make the transaction any more objectionable."[34] However, courts sometimes denied brokers recovery, even when they acknowledged that they had made legitimate trades on the exchanges. "In Illinois, Massachusetts, and doubtless most other States, the agreement between the customer and broker may be held invalid though the transactions contemplated on the Exchange were valid."[35] In the latter type of cases, a stark injustice arises: the courts recognize that the brokers have made good on their commitments to the other members on the exchange with whom they traded; nonetheless, the courts void agreements between the brokers and the client, leaving the broker to bear the loss, while the client is never required to return any gains that may have resulted from previous trading.[36]

On the other hand, some courts were willing to grant brokers a certain type of privilege, by assuming that "reputable brokers" would not make agreements that amounted to gambling contracts. One such case was *Cohen v. Rothschild*, in which the court was faced with contradictory testimony as to the agreement between broker and client.[37] The client testified that there was an understanding between the parties that no contract should ever be retained until delivery, and thus that all transactions would be settled according to price differences. The broker denied any such understanding. The trial court appointed a referee, who found that a mutual understanding existed, but the appellate division reversed, saying simply, "It is improbable, I think, that the defendants, who so far as appears are reputable brokers, would have made such an agreement."[38] In this case, then, an appellate court was willing to overrule a finding of fact, merely on the presumption that reputable brokers would not open themselves up to charges of gambling. At the very least, a ruling based on such a presumption is a clear indication that the search for intention was influenced by courts' more general orientation toward commodities trading and even more generally, specula-

34. Williston, *Law of Contracts*, § 1672.

35. Id. (footnotes omitted).

36. Examples of cases where courts found that brokers made legitimate trades on exchanges and yet allowed clients to void their contracts with brokers as wagers include *Waite*, 86 N.W. 645, and *Counselman*, 72 N.W. 490.

37. 169 N.Y.S. 659, 660–62 (App. Div. 1918).

38. Id. at 662.

tion. More pointedly, it can be read as evidence for the proposition that the intent of the parties was not much more than a fig leaf for the courts' policy determinations regarding the legitimacy of commodities trading.

A similar conclusion was reached by Edwin Patterson in his 1931 article "Hedging and Wagering on Produce Exchanges."[39] Patterson sets out to unravel the "compromise with the devil" necessary to distinguish hedging from wagering. He notes that while judges and text writers rarely mention the issue overtly, the basis for their opposition to wagers has two sources: "the moral sentiments of the community," which he identifies as puritanical, and the antisocial consequences of encouraging nonproductive activity. Patterson's article is a protest against a legal test "too narrow to satisfy the requirements of social and economic policy," and an attempt to encourage legislative modification of the law.[40] He distinguishes among three variants of the test of intentions,[41] with a persistent theme that the tests allow courts considerable latitude in interpreting evidence: "A court which is hostile to speculation in futures will draw the introspective inference that *B* was aware, when he made the agreement, of *A*'s intent to gamble; while a court friendly to the produce exchanges will, on facts scarcely distinguishable, decline to draw such an inference. *This is not the first time that introspective terminology has been used as camouflage for unarticulated theories of policy.*"[42]

Convinced that courts cover their policy determinations with the test of intentions, Patterson is at pains to offer a practical solution that will allow the legitimate mechanism of hedging to survive but will not grant unlimited license to gambling. In this quest, however, he does not view his detailed analysis as completely successful, and just before concluding with some unanswered questions and a few limited suggestions, he writes: "In endeavoring to distinguish hedging from wagering, the courts are between the devil and the deep sea."[43] It is precisely this sense of being between two perilous options that I will focus on in examining the policy discussions that arise in judicial rhetoric.

---

39. Edwin W. Patterson, "Hedging and Wagering on Produce Exchanges," 40 *Yale L.J.* 843 (1931).

40. Id. at 862.

41. Id. at 856–63. He identifies "Undisclosed Intention of One Party," "Disclosed Intention of One Party," and "Bilateral or Mutual Intention Not to Deliver" as the three varieties of intentions test.

42. Id. at 860 (emphasis added).

43. Id. at 878.

SPECULATION IN EVERYDAY BUSINESS

Before going on to the policy analysis, it is worthwhile to point out that there is another, more general way to expose the gap that policy must fill in making the decisions that distinguish between gambling and legitimate commodities trading. At about the same time the Supreme Court of Illinois was deciding dozens of commodities speculation cases based on trades conducted on the Chicago Board of Trade, it decided the case of *Schlee v. Guckenheimer.*[44] In that case, plaintiff was the owner of a brewery, and contracted with defendant for the purchase of barley for his brewery. The terms of the contract provided for delivery of four thousand bushels of barley at fifty-seven cents a bushel on October 15, 1887, and an option to purchase up to twenty thousand additional bushels at the same price any time up to December 31. The plaintiff ordered the additional twenty thousand bushels in mid-November, but, the price of barley having risen, the defendant refused to make delivery, claiming that the contract was a wagering contract under the statute forbidding gaming, and thus void. The trial court and the appellate court ruled in defendant's favor, but the Illinois Supreme Court reversed, saying,

> This proposition or offer is similar to everyday business transactions among the people of this state with reference to every character of commodities purchased for use. The offer to sell such a commodity at a specified price, if accepted by a specified time, does not constitute a violation of the statute. Its acceptance within that time is not prohibited or made a criminal offense, but is an everyday transaction, necessary in carrying on business.[45]

To the modern view, it seems clear that the Illinois Supreme Court got it right, that the transaction was not a gambling contract, and that the lower courts simply erred. But is this so obvious? As far as the language of the gaming prohibition was concerned, the lower courts were applying a clearly worded statute.[46] In fact, in a case with almost identical pertinent facts, but dealing with an option to buy stock rather than barley, the same court

44. 54 N.E. 302 (Ill. 1899).

45. Id. at 304.

46. The code provision in question held, "Whoever contracts to have or give to himself or another the option to sell or buy at a future time any grain or other commodity, stock of any railroad or other company . . . shall be fined . . . and all contracts made in violation of this section shall be considered gambling contracts, and shall be void." Id. at 303; Schlee v. Guckenheimer, 76 Ill. App. 681 (Ill. App. Ct. 1898).

reached the opposite conclusion.[47] In these cases, then, the courts are not dealing with the question of intent, but rather trying to distinguish more broadly between regular business contracts and speculative contracts. The problem is that there is no formalistic or analytical distinction between these types of contracts.[48] True, a case such as this represents only an instance of statutory interpretation that avoids what many would consider an absurd result. In that sense, it can almost be explained away, dismissing the tension that links gambling and legitimate contracting. But how is one to distinguish between the "everyday business" of a sale of barley that includes an option from the everyday business of options in stocks? While the answers that legal decision making provides, even in the case at hand, may be more convincing intuitively than in the cases where a test for intention to make delivery is at stake, the distinction is still ultimately "a proposition of policy of rather a delicate nature."[49] At this point, we can proceed to an exploration of some of the policy considerations articulated and suggested by the case law.

POLICY IN THE CASES

Sometimes courts express their policy inclinations in the clearest language possible. One example is the oft cited case of *Cothran v. Ellis,* where a client refused to pay notes he had drawn to pay a debt on futures transactions. After discussing the statutory and common law treatment of wagers, the court vents its hostility to speculation, exhibiting both the puritanical strain and the concern for antisocial consequences identified by Patterson. The opinion speaks for itself, and merits quotation at some length:

> We are clearly of opinion that dealing in "futures" or "options" as they are commonly called, to be settled according to the fluctuations of the market, is void by the common law; for, among other reasons, it is contrary to public policy. It is not only contrary to public policy, but it is a crime,—a crime against the state, a crime against the general welfare and happiness of

47. See Schneider v. Turner, 22 N.E. 497, 499 (Ill. 1889). In that case, the court noted that the contract "could have been made the disguise for gambling on the future price of stock." And, commenting on the fact that the statute may have been a case of legislative overreaching, the court said, "The treatment is heroic, but the evil [gambling on fluctuations in stock and commodity prices] was most malignant."

48. For the same problematic as it arises in the context of requirements contracts, see National Publishing Co. v. International Paper Co., 269 F. 903 (2d Cir. 1920).

49. Oliver Wendell Holmes, Jr., "Privilege, Malice, and Intent," 8 *Harv. L. Rev.* 1, 8 (1894).

> the people, a crime against religion and morality, and a crime against all legitimate trade and business. This species of gambling has become emphatically and pre-eminently the national sin. In its proportions and extent it is immeasurable. In its pernicious and ruinous consequences it is simply appalling. Clothed with respectability, and entrenched behind wealth and power, it submits to no restraint, and defies alike the laws of God and man. With despotic power it levies tribute upon all trades and professions. Its votaries and patrons are recruited from every class of society. Through its instrumentality the laws of supply and demand have been reversed, and the market is ruled by the amount of money its manipulators can bring to bear upon it. These considerations imperatively demand at the hands of the courts of the country a faithful and rigid enforcement of the laws which have been ordained for the suppression of this gigantic evil and blighting curse.[50]

The rhetoric of the passage is self-consciously startling. A modern sensibility is likely to discount the religious elements, but it would be a mistake to overlook the sense of danger expressed in the imagery. Legitimate trade and business and even the laws of supply and demand are threatened, waging what appears to be a losing battle against a despotic, gigantic, evil, blighting curse. "Clothed with respectability, and entrenched behind wealth and power," we find, not a policy of industrialization that drives the working poor into inhuman living conditions, but rather the "national sin," the curse and crime of gambling in futures. It is precisely rhetoric like this to which Ann Fabian refers when she says that "the bourgeoisie . . . constructed an image of themselves as virtuous and productive citizens by banishing their gambling doubles."[51]

Not all courts were so evangelical or so willing to make their policy inclinations plain or overt. Often, policy considerations can be seen in the courts' presentation of facts or conclusions of law. The following pair of contrasting cases, separated by nearly fifty years, offers some indication. In *Jamieson v. Wallace*, the court made a "careful examination of the evidence" in order to decide whether in fact the parties intended to wager, and especially whether the brokers knew that the client had no intention to take delivery.[52] In ruling against the brokers, the court noted that the appellee was

---

50. Cothran v. Ellis, 16 N.E. 646, 648 (Ill. 1888).

51. Ann Fabian, *Card Sharp, Dream Books, and Bucket Shops: Gambling in 19th Century America* 5 (1990).

52. 47 N.E. 762, 765 (Ill. 1897).

a woman of limited means with no business experience whose trades were well beyond her holdings, throwing doubt on whether she understood the obligations entailed in the transactions.[53]

In *Salzman v. Boeing*, on the other hand, the court dealt with similar facts, where plaintiff said that "she had never before been to a broker's office or had an account with a broker's business," and claimed that "her inability to pay for the large amount of wheat purchased by her shows conclusively that the intention was not to take delivery."[54] The court, however, ruled that "the conclusive answer to this contention seems to be that . . . she was able to take delivery and took it, although it seems to have wiped out her account."[55] The court concludes thus: "It is to be regretted plaintiff sustained a loss she could illy afford to bear. She was, however, responsible for her own misfortune notwithstanding the observance of every restriction provided by law for her protection. The law has emancipated women."[56]

Two cases with like facts, separated by half a century. In the first, clearly articulated, is a policy of paternalism. Speculating brokers are on the prowl, looking for unsuspecting dupes (ideally women), ready and waiting to take advantage of them by luring them into gambling transactions sure to be their ruin. In the second, women, like everybody else, are expected to live up to a standard of responsibility for their economic endeavors, and the antigambling statutes will not be a stand-in for failed paternalism. "The law has emancipated women."

The question of paternalism, however, is not the central policy issue for cases that turn on distinguishing gambling from speculative but legitimate business. The more central policy discussion can be seen in an opinion written by Justice Holmes in 1905. In *Board of Trade of the City of Chicago v.*

---

53. See id. at 765:

> The appellee was a woman who had little or no experience in business. . . . She was a woman of very limited means. . . . From her relations to the appellants, and from all the circumstances disclosed by the proof, it is impossible to believe that they were not well acquainted with the limited extent of her means. A woman who was not active in business and had only $7,500 in money, could not have been expected to take and pay for stocks amounting in value to $17,500. Appellants never made any inquiry of her as to her financial ability. . . . She swears that she did not understand that the stocks proposed to be purchased were to be paid for by her.

54. 35 N.E.2d 536, 538–39 (Ill. App. Ct. 1941).

55. Id. at 538, 539. It should be noted that delivery in this case was by set-off and payment; by this standard, appellee in *Jamieson* also "took delivery."

56. Id. at 540.

Christie Grain and Stock Co.,[57] the Board of Trade prayed for an injunction against a bucket shop that was using price quotations from the exchange for its speculative trading business.[58] The bucket shop defended by claiming that the Chicago Board of Trade was "the greatest of bucket shops," in the sense that it was a place that permitted "the pretended buying and selling of grain, etc., without any intention of receiving and paying for the property so bought, or of delivering the property so sold." Being a bucket shop itself, the Board of Trade could not claim property for its price quotations. Justice Holmes dismisses the defense, saying that even if the activities are illegal, the price quotations could still be property. But before declaring this bottom line, he analyzes the underlying reasons for allowing trading on the exchange. In so doing, he begins to spell out the economic policy behind speculative trading, calling speculation "the self-adjustment of society to the probable," and saying that its value is "well known as a means of avoiding or mitigating catastrophes, equalizing prices, and providing for periods of want."[59]

Holmes goes on to cite the importance of hedging for dealers in grain and for farmers themselves, noting that trades on the exchange are consistent with the good faith of the parties and their "serious business purposes." Extending the point, he notes that "the quotations of prices from the market are of the utmost importance to the business world, and not least to the farmers."[60] Holmes concedes that the exchange may be used for pretended

57. 198 U.S. 236 (1905).

58. Bucket shops were establishments where prices of commodities were posted, and people made "trades" with small sums of money (e.g., five dollars), as "margin," gaining "profits" if the prices went their way. In effect, these were substitutes for lotteries or horse racing as modes of gambling with small sums.

59. 198 U.S., at 247–48. For the flavor of the passage, it is worth quoting in full:

> As has appeared, the plaintiff's chamber of commerce is, in the first place, a great market, where, through its eighteen hundred members, is transacted a large part of the grain and provision business of the world. Of course, in a modern market, contracts are not confined to sales for immediate delivery. People will endeavor to forecast the future, and to make agreements according to their prophecy. Speculation of this kind by competent men is the self-adjustment of society to the probable. Its value is well known as a means of avoiding or mitigating catastrophes, equalizing prices, and providing for periods of want. It is true that the success of the strong induces imitation by the weak, and that incompetent persons bring themselves to ruin by undertaking to speculate in their turn. But legislatures and courts generally have recognized that the natural evolutions of a complex society are to be touched only with a very cautious hand, and that such coarse attempts at a remedy for the waste incident to every social function as a simple prohibition and laws to stop its being are harmful and vain.

60. Id. at 249.

trades or gambling purposes, but sees that as an unfortunate side effect that must be tolerated for the sake of a modern economic order. Holmes's position then, is relatively clear: despite dressing up his discussion with a reference to the good faith of the parties and their serious business purposes, he acknowledges that the mechanism of the Board of Trade can be and is used for speculation or gambling. He acknowledges, also, that a formal legal theory will not be able to articulate a rule that distinguishes between the speculative or gambling contract and the legitimate business contract. And, at the same time, he shows that even the speculative element is part of the modern business world, because it helps to set prices in accordance with supply and demand, eventually creating efficient markets.[61]

Thirty-seven years later, the Supreme Court of Illinois, faced again with a defense to a debt based on the claim that commodities transactions were wagering contracts, could take up Holmes's policy discussion in an even more striking and generalizing manner, at this point relying also on congressional regulation of the commodities exchanges:

> The titles to the various acts of Congress make it clear that our public policy now recognizes the desirability and necessity of maintaining open markets, even if they sometimes be used for gambling, in order to stabilize values in commodities and securities. As briefly mentioned in the Monroe case, every human transaction is a gamble, which all must take whether they wish to or not. From the time he plants his seed until he sells his crop, every farmer is gambling. From the time he makes a contract of sale until he delivers the flour, every miller is gambling. The public policy has been declared to be that these contracts for future delivery are necessary to the commerce of the people of the United States in their domestic interstate economy, and since no one can tell with what intent they are entered into, it is impossible to pick and choose among them.[62]

---

61. Of course, I am putting current economic terminology into Holmes's pen here, but the argument does emerge, more or less, from his opinion in the case. To recall just how radical Holmes's policy statement was at the time, we have only to look at the rhetoric of a prior Supreme Court opinion dealing the same issues. In one such case, the court held:

> The plea makes a case of money advanced . . . solely for the purpose of carrying "cotton futures" . . . when neither party contemplated the purchase or delivery in fact of cotton, and when it was understood that any settlement in respect to such purchases should be exclusively upon the basis of . . . the difference between the contract price and the market price. . . . If this be not a wagering contract, under the guise of a contract of sale, it would be difficult to imagine one that would be of that character. The mere form of the transaction is of little consequence. If it were, the statute against wagers could easily be evaded.

Embrey, 131 U.S. at 343–44.

62. Albers v. Lamson, 42 N.E.2d 627, 630 (Ill. 1942).

This is the articulation of a modern consciousness. It sounds like simple, familiar, and sound economic policy. But in summing up a new vision of the law's relationship to speculation, it highlights the fact that more was at stake than the debt of an unlucky speculator. A tension emerges in the judicial treatment of wagers. Judges articulate a distinction between a permitted and a prohibited contractual form, but face a difficulty in applying the distinction to formally identical transactions. In response, they shifted the locus of inquiry to the question of intent, only to find that determinations of intent yielded to the same cultural and political conflict that necessitated the original distinction.

The judges, if not the speculators, of the late nineteenth century lived in a different normative universe. Their attempt to limit gambling was tightly bound up with a vision of what the community could tolerate while still remaining a community. And the shift to an idea of a community that must tolerate gambling, a community in which speculation is necessary ("these contracts for future delivery are necessary to the commerce of the people of the United States"),[63] is one made up of different components from the community that preceded it. In part, the decline of the rhetoric of moral opposition toward gambling and the rise of a rhetoric that accepts the necessity of speculation, judging the legitimacy of action by its economic consequences, marks a shift that allows people to recognize themselves in statistics. People become subjects of the law of large numbers, more than subjects of a culturally specific and recognized moral authority.

Regulation as opposed to prohibition of gambling raises an analogy to analyses of the dual role played by administrative organization in modernization. On the one hand, state activities like cadastral mapping and imposition of a simplified property regime enable the state to organize the populace, and especially to tax efficiently. On the other hand, however, the state's activity also plays a more active role, eventually transforming the individuals under its control. In our context, the state (in the form of the courts) becomes less interested in the moral intentions of the actors in question, content instead to address the overall economic consequences of their aggregate activity (here, speculative investment that creates and supports an efficient pricing mechanism). While the regulation of gambling is far from the grandiose administrative action accompanying modernization, a similar dynamic plays itself out, at least for the limited sector of the popu-

63. Id.

lace exposed to the courts' treatment of such cases. Exposed to an official narrative that judges actions by their place in an overall economic system, people begin to envision themselves, or at least to recognize themselves, as (interchangeable) parts of that system, subject to its (economic) laws.[64] The law of large numbers plays an even more central and overt role in the next topic to be addressed, the law of life insurance.

64. See James C. Scott, *Seeing Like a State: How Certain Schemes to Improve the Human Condition Have Failed* 37–52, 90–93 (1998).

SEVEN

Wagering in Lives

The Life Insurance Speculators

> Paradoxical as it may appear, there is a class of gambling which is not only considered harmless, but beneficial, and even necessary—I mean Insurance. Theoretically, it is gambling proper. You bet 2s. 6d. to £100 with your Fire Insurance; you equally bet on a Marine Insurance for the safe arrival of your ships or merchandise; and it is also gambling when you insure your life.
>
> —JOHN ASHTON (1898)[1]

How is it that Ashton is so confident that "theoretically," insurance is "gambling proper"? And what of the phrase "gambling proper" itself? Does it refer to gambling, *strictu sensu,* or possibly to gambling, reined in by propriety?

Ashton's chapter on insurance, based primarily on the records of specific policies issued by Lloyd's and on tales of some spectacular insurance frauds, can serve as a reminder of two kinds of connections between gambling and insurance. First, and most directly, Ashton details cases where underwriters actually serve as bookmakers, "insuring" against events regarding which the policy holders have no direct stake and with which they have no direct contact. Colorful examples of this sort include the outcome of an election, the "dissolution of the present Parliament"; "two of the first Peers in Britain losing their heads"; the death or capture of Napoleon Bonaparte; and the life of the queen during the months preceding the Queen's Jubilee. Ashton considers wager policies such as these, including one on the "declaration of

---

1. John Ashton, *The History of Gambling in England* 275 (1898). He continues: "Yet a man would be considered culpable, or at the very least, negligent and indiscreet did he not insure."

war with France or Spain," as "innocent" for the most part, though he does call for administrative interference in those policies with sinister political undertones, like those on the dissolution of parliament or on the lives of English peers, when the policies are underwritten by Scotsmen.[2] What is clear is that Ashton's conception of "innocence" does not distance insurance from the taint of gambling, but merely puts it into a class of gambling that has no further negative effects. Ashton, it will be remembered, is a historian of gambling, not of insurance. However, proponents of insurance could not rest with the characterization of insurance as innocent gambling; they needed to distinguish insurance from gambling more starkly.

The second connection between gambling and insurance raised by Ashton is the tendency of gambling to be exploited by organized fraud, and especially by what Karen Halttunen calls "confidence men."[3] The danger identified by Ashton and explored by Halttunen goes far beyond the individual who is cheated out of money in a particular gamble: to the extent that gambling becomes a vocation, it presents an alternative to productive industry, making the slow rewards of industrious exertion seem insipid and unattractive. Ashton's innocent wager policies and those policies tainted by fraud, like naked speculation on stocks or commodities, raise the specter of unproductive gain, of the man interested in getting something for nothing. Nineteenth-century moralists linked fraud and capitalist speculation as forces that undermined the social fabric and mutual confidence that tied the community together.[4]

Advocates of insurance, therefore, viewed distinguishing insurance from gambling as a crucial stage in the legitimation and popularization of insurance, especially life insurance. While modern histories of insurance sometimes date the success of the distinction to the early nineteenth century, Ashton, writing in 1898, assumed that insurance and gambling could not be distinguished, at least theoretically.[5] And advocates of insurance, including

---

2. Id. at 277–81.

3. Karen Halttunen, *Confidence Men and Painted Women: A Study of Middle-Class Culture in America, 1830–1870*, pp. 1–32 (1982).

4. Id. at 17–22. See generally Herman Melville, *The Confidence-Man: His Masquerade* (Harrison Hayford et al. eds., Northwestern Univ. Press 1984) (1857).

5. "By the second decade of the nineteenth century, the divorce between insurance and gambling was almost complete." Lorraine J. Daston, *The Domestication of Risk: Mathematical Probability and Insurance, 1650–1830*, in 1 *The Probabilistic Revolution* 237, 253 (Lorenz Kruger et al. eds., 1987). "By the third decade of the nineteenth century, the divorce between insurance and gambling seemed final. Gambling was, to a large extent, outlawed, whereas insurance became a pillar of social order." Reuven Brenner

the companies themselves, spent a great deal of energy on substantiating the distinction well into the twentieth century.[6] A telling example of such efforts is the history of the New York Life Insurance Company, commissioned by the company and published in 1930.[7] Early in the first chapter, the author describes the wagering policies prevalent in England in the eighteenth century and with them, the first life policy, issued on the life of one William Gibbons. He calls the Gibbons policy a "bald wager,"[8] distinguishing it from modern life insurance in that the laws of probability were scarcely taken into account, while conceding that the "mutual" or cooperative aspect of insurance did exist in the early policies. The author's advocacy of contemporary insurance practice takes the form of distinguishing insurance from betting by relying on the expertise and special knowledge employed by modern insurance companies. He elaborates:

> Life insurance has ceased to be a mere bet as it was in the Gibbons case, and has become a scientific method of estimating the duration of life by a study and application of the law of probabilities and the laws of hygiene, sanitation and therapeutics. It is for this reason that in any successful and well regulated insurance company the Actuarial Department and the Medical Department are of very great importance. Both of these departments deal with what is known as the law of probability, a law which is the very essence of life insurance.[9]

In order to emphasize the scientific basis of insurance, the author then goes on to cite several encyclopedia articles on probability, assuring the reader that the entries are "the most terrifying and unintelligible exhibit of abstruse reasoning that perhaps can be found in popular literature," comparing their calculations to hieroglyphics, and noting that "it would be impossible to quote them here without overtaxing the resources of the printer and the eyesight of the reader."[10] But the point of the mild intimidation is actually to assure the reader that the equations too complex

---

and Gabrielle A. Brenner, *Gambling and Speculation: A Theory, a History, and a Future of Some Human Decisions* 106 (1990).

6. Viviana A. Rotman Zelizer, *Morals and Markets: The Development of Life Insurance in the United States* 68–71 (1979).

7. Lawrence F. Abbot, *The Story of NYLIC: A History of the Origin and Development of the New York Life Insurance Company from 1845 to 1929* (1930).

8. Id. at 7–8.

9. Id. at 9–10.

10. Id. at 11.

for her understanding are working for her benefit, under the professional, expert supervision of the company. After quoting a "simpler" article from a "popular encyclopedia," the author, with a touch of wit, offers the definitive distinction between gambling and insurance: "Delightful reading! But without such reasoning, meaningless as it must be to the average layman, life insurance would be a mere Monte Carlo in which the roulette wheel would take the place of the actuary; with it, life insurance has become an exact science in which predictions can be made with all the certainty of mathematical calculations."[11]

However, while insurance companies expended significant energy in distinguishing insurance from gambling in popular consciousness, they were also partially instrumental in keeping the connection between the two realms alive, at least as far as legal discourse was concerned, by claiming wager as a defense against payment on certain claims.[12] In other words, while the connection between gambling and insurance had at one time threatened the insurance industry directly by contaminating insurance, labeling it an illegitimate and destructive social force,[13] by the late nineteenth century, insurance companies regularly claimed that policies were in fact mere wagers in order to avoid payment. The legal doctrine that localized the discussion of gambling was the doctrine of insurable interest.

THE DOCTRINE OF INSURABLE INTEREST

The doctrine of insurable interest is not an ancient common law doctrine, and in England wager contracts were valid until well into the nineteenth century.[14] A leading textbook on insurance law, treating the insurable interest

---

11. Id. at 12.

12. This has been a common claim by insurance companies since the popularization of life insurance in the mid-nineteenth century, but the defense was not limited to life insurance, nor has it ceased to be a usable defense up to today. See, e.g., Connecticut Mutual Life Insurance Co. v. Schaefer, 94 U.S. 457 (1876) (insurance company claimed that divorced spouse had no insurable interest in the life of the insured, her former husband); New York Life Insurance Co. v. Baum, 700 F.2d 928 (5th Cir. 1983) (insurance company claimed that beneficiaries had no insurable interest in the life of the insured, and thus should not recover); Fidelity Union Fire Insurance Co. v. Hicks, 250 S.W. 1084 (Tex. App. 1923) (insurance company claimed hail insurance was void as wagering contract due to lack of insurable interest).

13. Zelizer, *Morals and Markets*, 88.

14. See 3 Samuel Williston, *The Law of Contracts* § 1667, § 1668 (1st ed. 1920) (footnotes omitted): "The mere fact that an agreement was a wager did not make it unenforceable or opposed to public policy according to the English common law. Statutes, however, restricted various forms of betting, and apart

doctrine alongside the principle of indemnity, defines the doctrine as "the concept that there must be some significant relationship between the insured and the person, the object, or the activity that is subject to the risks covered by the insurance arrangement."[15] Without such a relationship or interest, any policy which may be issued would be void.[16] In his textbook treatment, Widiss acknowledges that the origins of the insurable interest doctrine are linked to the attempt to combat gambling, but by linking the doctrine closely to the indemnity principle, and especially by treating the doctrine's origins in property insurance as identical to those in life insurance, he limits the importance of the hostility to gambling in the development of the doctrine. He writes: "It now seems evident that the principle of indemnity and the insurable interest doctrine rest—and undoubtedly have, in reality, always been at least partially predicated—on societal interests other than opposition to gambling."[17]

In fact, however, while insurable interest doctrine is conceptually related in property insurance and life insurance, historically the doctrines developed separately. In property insurance, the indemnity principle and the insurable interest doctrine serve the same purposes, and are primarily directed toward combating moral hazard in the form of temptation to crime, or the tendency of the policy holder to destroy property in order to collect insurance.[18] Life insurance, on the other hand, is not an indemnity contract, and while the temptation to murder is a potential problem, the authorities in England who developed insurable interest doctrine were more concerned with the kind of wagering in lives and events that Ashton documented.[19] This type of insurance was pure wagering, and the authorities did not consider the danger of murder to be grave, because the bettors, common people, generally did not have any connection with or access to

---

from such statutes wagers were held against public policy as matter of common law if the subject-matter of the bet was deemed to be obnoxious to the public welfare."

15. Alan I. Widiss, *Insurance* 123 (1989).

16. Franklin L. Best, Jr., "Defining Insurable Interests in Lives," 22 *Tort and Ins. L.J.* 104 (1986).

17. Widiss, *Insurance*, 124.

18. This rationale relies on nineteenth-century terminology; from a current economic perspective, moral hazard is described as the inefficient limiting of precautions against the occurrence of the insured event, which amounts to the same thing, the difference being one of degree. On the shifting meaning of "moral hazard" see Tom Baker, "On the Genealogy of Moral Hazard," 75 *Texas L. Rev.* 237, 239–40 (1996).

19. Ashton, *History of Gambling*, 279–81; see also Zelizer, *Morals and Market*, 71: "The concept of insurable interest developed to guarantee the legitimate contractual motivation of life insurance. It was first introduced in England in 1774 as a legal weapon against the widespread wagering in lives."

the people, generally heads of state or other public figures, whose lives they "insured" or rather bet upon. The wagering aspect of insurance had given the English courts the most trouble, and it was primarily this problem that the Statute of George III, which founded insurable interest in life insurance, set out to remedy.[20]

INSURABLE INTEREST OF ASSIGNEES OF LIFE POLICIES

It is an oft-heard and long-standing charge that insurable interest doctrine is insufficiently clear. One insurance industry lawyer has complained that while "the insurer needs a single definition of 'insurable interest' that clearly distinguishes between those who have it and those who do not . . . the various states give insurers definitions that are contradictory and vague."[21] Traditional difficulties in defining insurable interest include the question of whether the interest must be pecuniary, and the question of what kinds of family ties will be sufficient to raise a presumption of insurable interest. While it is generally conceded that everyone has an insurable interest in his or her own life, "The public policy against using life insurance policies as contracts of wager is so deeply ingrained into the fabric of insurance law that some courts have expressed a willingness to ignore the rule that one has an unlimited insurable interest in one's own life."[22] But the most significant complication in insurable interest doctrine arises in those cases where the insured assigns a policy to another.

The discussion of assignability of life insurance policies brings together two technically distinct legal questions. The first question is whether the assignee must have an insurable interest; and the second, what are the requirements of insurable interest, or what constitutes insurable interest. While these questions are technically distinct, the answers to them converge,

---

20. Edwin W. Patterson, "Insurable Interest in Life," 18 *Colum. L. Rev.* 381, 392–93 (1918); Widiss, *Insurance,* 125 ("The preamble to this statute stated that the legislation addressed 'a mischievous kind of gaming' in relation to 'the making of insurances on lives, or other events, wherein the assured shall have no interest.' Nothing was said of the destruction of the subject matter of insurance . . .").

21. Best, "Defining Insurable Interest in Lives," 106 (at the time of the article's publication, Best was an Associate General Counsel of Penn Mutual Life Insurance Company in Philadelphia, Pennsylvania).

22. Johnny C. Parker, "Does Lack of an Insurable Interest Preclude an Insurance Agent from Taking an Absolute Assignment of his Client's Life Policy?" 31 *U. Rich. L. Rev.* 71, 79 (1997).

since the underlying factual problem they address is the same. In order to understand the convergence of the legal questions, it is helpful to set out the factual context in which most assignments of insurance policies occur, and to keep in mind the dual purpose of insurable interest doctrine in life insurance: first, to limit the ability to use insurance as a means of wagering; and second, to limit moral hazard, or the temptation to murder the insured.

For a range of reasons, holders of life insurance policies often sought to assign the policies. This was especially so before 1880, because up until then the insurance companies would not buy back their policies, so any policy holder who could not continue paying the premiums faced an entire loss of equity. Faced with the injustice of "investors" losing everything they had paid in premiums, regulators pressured insurance companies to make arrangements to grant some surrender value for policies, especially if several years of premiums had been paid. However, even after 1880, when nonforfeiture laws were passed in several jurisdictions, surrender values were quite low, and policy holders often had a better chance of selling their policies for value, either to strangers or to acquaintances at varying levels of familiarity. In some cases, especially in England, the sale of policies resurrected old fears of widespread wagering in lives; weekly insurance auctions where buyers in effect bet on the speedy death of the insured functioned as perhaps the most glaring reminder.[23]

The case law of the period yields an array of fact situations, which can be arranged along a spectrum, from those in which legitimacy of the transaction was widely assumed, to those in which it was widely rejected. While it was early accepted that a person had an insurable interest in his or her own life, the question of whether a person could name a beneficiary who had no insurable interest generated a fair amount of litigation. The next stage of complication involved a situation in which the insured procured the policy and named a beneficiary who had no insurable interest, but when the insured became unable to pay the premiums, the beneficiary paid the premiums to keep the policy in force. Closely related to this scenario were cases where the insured assigned the policy to one having no insurable interest but who paid the premiums, with the major difference being that in this case, the assignee would then have control of the policy, including the

---

23. See Zelizer, *Morals and Market*, 69–70. Zelizer adds: "Another form of gambling with life, known as 'graveyard insurance,' briefly flourished in the United States in the early 1880's with speculators insuring the lives of old people, preferably paupers who were likely to die soon."

power to sell it to a third party. Particularly difficult cases, including the influential case of *Warnock v. Davis*,[24] arose when a potential insured agreed before procuring the policy that the policy would be assigned immediately upon purchase. Finally, there were cases where a person without insurable interest initiated the insurance, attempting to take out a policy on another without having the necessary connection to the potential insured. Thus, the spectrum of cases includes five basic fact situations, which for the sake of clarity may be presented schematically:

1. *A* procures policy and names *B*, who has no insurable interest, the beneficiary.
2. *A* procures a policy and *B*, who is the beneficiary, pays the premiums thereon.
3. *A* procures a policy, eventually assigning it to *B*.
4. *A* procures the policy with the prior intention of assigning it to *B*.
5. *B* procures the policy on *A*'s life.[25]

At the extremes of this spectrum, the law was able to generate relatively clear (though not unanimous) solutions to the problem of wagering in lives.[26] As far as the first situation was concerned, since the insured procured the policy and continued to make the premium payments, there was little danger that the transaction was a cover for wagering, because the party who stood to gain was completely passive. The insured was in effect investing money to be given to the beneficiary after the former's death. While insured people often felt moral obligation toward those they named beneficiaries, there was normally nothing required by law on this point to validate the policies. Thus, in almost all cases,[27] an insured could make a party with no

24. 104 U.S. 775 (1881).

25. In these examples, it is always the life of *A* that is insured; thus, *A* is the Cestui Que Vie, and *B* always lacks an insurable interest in the life of *A*. In addition, it was not always the insurance company that raised the issue of insurable interest; often, the representatives of the estate of the insured raised the claim. Insurers often admitted liability, deposited the proceeds with the court, and filed bills of interpleader, so that the court would only have to decide between parties claiming rights to the policy.

26. I will for the most part disregard the other half of the purpose of insurable interest doctrine, i.e., the prevention of the temptation to murder the insured. For an interesting treatment of that issue, see Baker, "Genealogy of Moral Hazard."

27. An apparent exception to this rule exists in Texas, where the courts have stated that "in order to make a valid contract upon the life of one person for the benefit of another the beneficiary must have an interest in the life insured." Goldbaum v. Blum, 15 S.W. 564, 565 (Tex. 1891). However, in that case, and others cited for the same proposition, the beneficiaries paid all the premiums, and were instrumental in initiating the policy, so the statement was actually not controlling. For a recent case, see Stillwagoner v.

insurable interest a beneficiary, just as she could give that party a gift.[28] The final situation of the five described above—where the buyer of a policy has no connection with the insured—raises the specter of gambling in the most direct way, so the requirement of insurable interest has been applied in its most straightforward form. In other words, where a policy is procured by a party other than the insured, the moving party must have an insurable interest for the policy to be valid.[29]

In the three intermediate categories, the law vacillated between two conflicting policy objectives, with different jurisdictions reaching varying results. A look at some typical cases helps view the problem, and the courts' attempts to impose a solution based on sound policy, more concretely.

In *Rylander v. Allen*, the administratrix of Allen's estate brought an action against the Travelers' Insurance Company and Mrs. Rylander to recover the amount of an insurance policy issued by the company on Allen's life.[30] Allen, eight years before his death, procured an insurance policy on his life, payable to his estate. Four months later, he assigned the policy to Rylander, who had no interest in the continuance of his life, and who thereafter paid the premiums. The administratrix sued, claiming that Rylander had intentionally entered into a speculation on Allen's life. While the details of the transaction are not fully elaborated in the case, it appears that Rylander paid Allen "a valuable consideration" for the assignment of the policy. After summarily disposing of the moral hazard problem,[31] the court goes on to compare the beneficiary with no insurable interest to an assignee, summing up its position:

> If, where one who has in good faith procured a policy of insurance upon his own life and kept it in force for a time, and thereafter has had a new

---

Travelers Insurance Co., 979 S.W.2d 354 (Tex. App. 1998) (unbeknownst to employee, employer purchased life insurance policy on employee's life, naming employer beneficiary).

28. "If the cestui also pays the premiums, the transaction is an investment-gift—that is, a gift to the beneficiary of the investment made by the cestui. While gifts do not perform any useful function in trade or commerce, the courts recognize the validity of such policies as incidental to freedom of gift." Patterson, "Insurable Interest in Life," 397 (citation omitted).

29. Parker, "Lack of Insurable Interest," 76.

30. 53 S.E. 1032 (Ga. 1906). Faced with conflicting interests in payment, the company deposited payment with the court, leaving the only conflict between the assignee of the policy and the estate.

31. The court deals with this problem simply, by relying on the rule that a beneficiary of a policy on which the insured pays the premiums is entitled to recover. Comparing the beneficiary who doesn't pay the premiums to one who does, the court says that the temptation to hasten the demise of the insured is equal in both cases, and since it does not invalidate the policy in the first case, it should not do so in the second. Id. at 1034.

> policy issued in lieu thereof, payable to one who has no insurable interest in the life insured, the policy is not void as a wagering policy, although such beneficiary thereafter keeps the policy alive by paying the premiums or assessments falling due thereon, it must necessarily follow, we think, that if one in good faith procures a policy of insurance upon his own life, an assignment of the policy made by him will be valid, if not done by way of cover for a wager policy, though the assignee has no insurable interest in the life of the insured.[32]

The rest of the opinion is devoted to an attempt to divine what, if any, actions would amount to an indication that the policy was in fact a cover for a wager policy, with the court eventually speculating that evidence of preconceived intent to assign the policy would tend to invalidate the policy. In the absence of such evidence, or even of direct allegations to that effect, the court concludes:

> The assignment is said to be a gambling transaction, a mere bet or wager upon the chances of human life. But the wager was made when the policy was effected, and has the sanction of the law. The assignment simply transfers the policy, as any other legal chose in action may be transferred, from the holder to a bona fide purchaser. It is true, there is an element of chance and uncertainty in the transaction, but so is there when a man takes a transfer of an annuity, or buys a life estate, or an estate in remainder after a life estate. There is in all these cases a speculation upon the chances of human life. But the transaction has never been held to be void on that account.[33]

There are several noteworthy elements to the opinion. The first may be gleaned from the tone of this particular passage, which is indicative of the tone of the opinion as a whole. There is a marked air of resignation, as if the court feels compelled, with at least a hint of reluctance if not sadness, to approve transactions of insurance. Thus, the wagering element of the particular transaction, that is, the assignment, is generalized and projected onto the insurance arrangement itself: "But the wager was made when the policy was effected, and has the sanction of the law." The force of the argument that the assignment is a wager is diffused, since an initial wager, that of the insurance policy itself, has (always) already been sanctioned by law. Insurance, on this view, is still a wager, but a wager that the law sanctions.

---

32. Id.

33. Id. at 1037 (quoting Clark v. Allen, 11 R.I. 439, 443–44 [1877]).

In addition, the law's approval of the insurance wager does not occur in a vacuum, but rather in the context of other transactions involving "chance and uncertainty," and even "speculation upon the chances of human life" such as annuities and life estates.

On the one hand, then, the court will not condone and validate a transaction that is a mere cover for a wager contract. And yet, on the other hand, the court admits that an insurance policy, like other widely accepted contracts, such as transfers of annuities or life estates, are on some quite basic level wagers of a particular sort: speculations on human life. What might appear as a contradiction within the court's reasoning is actually a two-pronged strategy of containment: of wagering on the one hand, and of the legal argumentation regarding transfers of property on the other.

The practice of wagering is controlled by the court's reserving its power to invalidate contracts made with the express intention of circumventing the prohibition on gambling. But this power is no longer exercised by applying a simple label of wager; instead, the court shows itself willing to delve deep into the facts in order to distinguish the good wager from the bad. By the same token, the court limits the power of a legal argument based simply on labeling a particular transaction a wager. Where the plaintiff attempts to rely on the characterization of the assignment of the policy as a wager, the court pokes through this characterization by taking it a step further, showing that the argument is applicable to insurance generally, as well as to transfers of other property, none of which are traditionally susceptible to the claim that they are illegal wagers. The court thus recognizes the difficulty of upholding an analytical distinction between transactions that can be characterized as wagers and those that cannot, and abandoning that distinction (without saying so overtly), takes the affirmative step and responsibility of distinguishing between legitimate and illegitimate transactions. The court's new distinction is not based on the label of wager, but rather on the question of whether the practice underlying the transaction has antisocial effects.

What, then, of the underlying practice? Why does the court see a need to protect the transaction in question, this assignment of an insurance policy? Again, the key can be seen in the court's use, on its own initiative, of an expanded analogy. "The assignment simply transfers the policy, *as any other legal chose in action may be transferred*, from the holder to a bone fide purchaser."[34] The court here sees itself on the pivot of a certain moment

34. Id. at 1037 (emphasis added).

in the history of contract doctrine, and it opts to leave the past behind by adopting "the more modern and rational rule that any person has a right to procure an insurance on his own life, and to assign it to another, provided it be not done by way of cover for a wager policy."[35] Positioning itself on the progressive side of its own historical narrative, the court recalls that "a life policy is a chose in action, a species of property, which the holder may have perfectly good and innocent reasons for wishing to dispose of. He should be allowed to do so unless the law clearly forbids it."[36] This particular historical narrative is one of the expansion of contract by making the rights defined by the contract transferable, or in other words, making contractual rights into a form of property.[37] The question of what is at stake in such an expansion of contract will arise again.

Not all courts at this time, however, positioned themselves similarly regarding assignment of insurance policies, nor did they feel resigned to sanctioning some form of gambling. One example is *Manhattan Life Insurance Co. v. Cohen.*[38] In that case, Jacob Cohen took out $7,500 (in two policies) of life insurance in Texas in 1893. Before his death in October 1907, Cohen made two uses of the policy for commercial purposes. First, he obtained a loan of $1,750 from the insurance company, using the policy as collateral, and in fact with the understanding that payment would be taken from the value of the policy payment. Second, a few months before his death, Cohen assigned the policy to J. H. Hilsman, with whom he was engaged in (of all things) speculative transactions in cotton futures, which the court characterizes as gaming contracts in which the parties did not contemplate that there would be actual delivery.[39] The court notes that Hilsman, the assignee, paid Cohen $460 for his equity in the policies, but significantly, it attributes greater importance to the nature of their business relations than to the specifics of the transaction of assignment. Because Hilsman and the insurance company claimed

---

35. Id. at 1036.

36. Id. at 1037.

37. This is a narrative of "expansion" because at early common law, choses in action were not assignable. Assignability grew with the rise in importance of negotiable paper, and is in some ways a mirror image in this aspect of the rise of a commercial law of contract. See 1 Williston *Law of Contracts*, §§ 404–6, 410, 414. See also Tony Freyer, "Antebellum Commercial Law: Common Law Approaches to Secured Transactions," 70 *Ky. L.J.* 593, 595 (1981); Morton J. Horwitz, *The Transformation of American Law, 1780–1860*, pp. 212–26 (1977).

38. 139 S.W. 51 (Tex. Civ. App. 1911).

39. Id. at 52.

that Georgia, rather than Texas law, governed the transaction, the court was forced to deal with the issue of validity of assignment comparatively:

> Where the policy is taken out by the insured himself for his own benefit, there is an irreconcilable conflict in the authorities upon the question as to whether he may make a valid assignment of it to one who has no insurable interest in the life of the assured. This conflict grows out of the general rule above stated. In some jurisdictions it is held that the same principle of public policy which inhibits one from insuring the life of a person in whom he has no insurable interest forbids him from taking an assignment of a policy taken out by the insured for his own benefit. In others it is held that such an assignment is not affected by public policy, and that it is of the same validity as the assignment of any other chattel.[40]

This presentation of the conflict of authorities is helpful in delineating the central point of uncertainty in the law, but it relies, in its final sentence, on a subtle distortion. By claiming that the jurisdictions allowing assignment ignore public policy, the court implies that the opposing rule is an unthinking or even irrational attachment to a technical rule by which choses in action are assignable.[41] In fact, as will later be shown, both sides in the conflict over assignability rely primarily on public policy to justify the rule they adopt.

There were two closely related reasons for the reliance on public policy in this context. First, as briefly mentioned above, the doctrine of assignability of choses in action, while often referred to in these cases, was not an ancient doctrine, and its validity and especially its borders were far from well established. Writing on the difficulty of establishing negotiability for commercial paper, Morton Horwitz comments that "it ran completely contrary to the ancient common law hostility to assignment."[42] Full negotiability of promis-

---

40. Id. at 55. Regarding which jurisdictions fall into which camp, the court continues: "The courts of Alabama, Kansas, Kentucky, Missouri, Pennsylvania, and Virginia hold with Texas that such assignments are invalid, on the ground that they are opposed to public policy." Id. at 56.

41. In technical terms, the court overstates the case made by those jurisdictions that allow assignment, in that they all view the insurance policy as a chose in action, and not as a chattel. Although this is a minor and technical distinction (which the court in a later paragraph abandons), in this passage it serves to expand the opposing claim, making it an easier target to combat (for instance, if insurance policies were assignable as chattels, rather than choses in action, defenses by the insurance company against the party procuring the insurance, such as fraud, would not be available against the assignee—a clearly undesirable result). On the difference between assignment of chattels and choses in action, see 1 Williston, *Law of Contracts*, § 404.

42. Horwitz, *Transformation of American Law*, 212.

sory notes, which had the advantage of clear intent of the parties to establish their negotiability, gradually emerged in the United States over the course of the nineteenth century, and was only fully established in 1879.[43] Assignability of choses in action rested on the same principles, but was not supported by the same clear commercial interests Horwitz identifies as favoring negotiability of promissory notes, nor by the long tradition of enforcement among merchants. Thus, the formal rule of assignability carried little force as a counterweight to a convincing argument from public policy. The second reason that the courts resorted primarily to public policy justifications for assignability was that widespread assignment of insurance policies was a relatively recent phenomenon, and in the absence of a well-established formal rule, public policy provided an important rhetorical repertoire to explain how the validation of assignments led to just outcomes in the cases.

Before expanding on this point by looking at a few more cases, I will return briefly to *Manhattan Life v. Cohen*, to examine the policy considerations it mentions as controlling the case. The court concentrates in its opinion on the nature of the business relationship between the insured and the assignee that led up to the assignment, diminishing the importance of the consideration paid to the insured, and ignoring the question of whether in addition to the $460 paid directly to the insured, the consideration also included cancellation of an additional debt between them. Since there is no indication that Cohen was nearing insolvency or was in any way coerced into the assignment, and since he had paid premiums on the policy for fourteen years, it is not unreasonable to surmise that an additional debt between Cohen and Hilsman was settled through the assignment. But the court is not interested in settling the case on the basis of the equities between Cohen and Hilsman, since in its view their entire relationship is tainted by gambling. At one point, adopting the estate's proposition of which rule should govern, the court says, "The consideration for the assignment of these policies having been advanced by Hilsman for the express purpose of assisting the insured to participate in a gambling transaction with said Hilsman . . . [,] the consideration was void in law and the attempted assignment of the policies for that reason alone vested no right in Hilsman to either of the policies or the proceeds thereof."[44] While the conflict of laws analysis maintains a balanced judicious tone, when faced with Hilsman's claim in its most direct form, the

43. See id. at 212–26.

44. *Manhattan Life*, 139 S.W. at 58.

court's rhetorical style bursts into a condemnation of the pure immorality of gambling, culminating in a statement of biblical wrath:

> Had [Hilsman] sought to enforce [the policy] through the medium of the courts, he would have been met by the inquiry, "What right have you to the money due on these policies?" His only true answer would have been, "I own them under an assignment from the beneficiary, which the law denounces as illegal and pronounces as void." *Then would the court say unto him, "Depart from me, ye wicked; I know you not."* It would be preposterous to hold that that which is void as against public policy can be validated by a contract which is also void as against public policy.[45]

With or without the unattributed allusion to the gospel, it is clear that the public policy at stake is a moral crusade against the evils of gambling.[46] And in the relationship between Cohen and Hilsman, the court finds two of the dominant modes of commercial behavior often associated with gambling: commodities trading and wagering in lives by assigning insurance policies. The presence of both in one fact situation reinforces the court's crusading energy, allowing it to hold that the use of one mode of gambling to validate another would be "preposterous."[47]

While all courts paid it lip service, those in the majority of jurisdictions seem to have seen the antigambling crusade as a less compelling justification for invalidating the assignments of insurance policies. One concise articulation of the policy justification for allowing the assignment of life insurance policies is the opinion of Justice Holmes in *Grigsby v. Russel.*[48] In that case, the insured, in need of money for a surgical operation, sold the policy to Dr. Grigsby for a hundred dollars. He had up to that time paid two premiums, and was unable to pay the third. Grigsby, who had no insurable interest in the life of the insured, paid the rest of the premiums, and upon the insured's death, claimed the proceeds of the policy. The administrators of the insured's estate also claimed the proceeds of the policy, saying that the assignment was only valid to the extent of the money actually given for the policy and the

45. Id. (emphasis added).

46. "And then will I profess unto them, I never knew you: depart from me, ye that work iniquity." Matthew 7:23.

47. The court's attention to the "gambling" relationship, which takes for granted that commodities futures trading is a form of wagering, allows it to circumvent what might be a deeper problem with assignments, which is the problem of the adequacy of consideration.

48. 222 U.S. 149 (1911).

premiums subsequently paid.[49] The district court ruled for Grigsby, and the circuit court reversed. Holmes, after laying out the facts, summarily presents the legal claim of the estate:

> The ground suggested for denying the validity of an assignment to a person having no interest in the life insured is the public policy that refuses to allow insurance to be taken out by such persons in the first place. A contract of insurance upon a life in which the insured has no interest is a pure wager that gives the insured a sinister counter interest in having the life come to an end.[50]

While Holmes here articulates both the hostility to gambling and the problem of moral hazard as basic policy considerations regarding life insurance, he notes that the gambling aspect is historically more central to insurable interest doctrine. At the same time, he limits its generality, saying that the law does not object to the very idea that a party to a contract would benefit from the other party's death: "The law has no universal cynic fear of the temptation opened by a pecuniary benefit accruing upon a death. It shows no prejudice against remainders after life estates. . . . Indeed, the ground of the objection to life insurance without interest in the earlier English cases was not the temptation to murder, but the fact that such wagers came to be regarded as a mischievous kind of gaming."[51] And yet, while conceding that opposition to gambling was the main impetus for the development of insurable interest doctrine, Holmes does not view it as important, and dismisses the problem almost without real consideration, saying that "when the question rises upon an assignment, it is assumed that the objection to the insurance as a wager is out of the case."[52] On the other hand, Holmes articulates concisely the public policy reason for allowing assignment of policies, almost nonchalantly reminding the reader that "life insurance has become in our days one of the best recognized forms of investment and self-compelled saving. So far as reasonable safety permits, it is desirable to give to life policies the ordinary characteristics of property."[53]

One of the reasons that Holmes could allow himself such telegraphic

---

49. Id. at 154.

50. Id.

51. Id. at 155–56, citing Stat. 14 George III, chap. 48.

52. Id. at 155.

53. Id. at 156.

justification is that the position he espoused had been articulated early on, even when insurance was not a popular means of saving. The position goes back at least as far as the 1855 case of *St. John v. American Mutual Life Insurance Co.*, where the court said that "without the right to assign, insurances on lives lose half their usefulness."[54] A more complete account of the policy argument behind allowing assignments of life policies is given in *Steinback v. Diepenbrock*,[55] where the court notes that sound public policy requires that an insured be permitted to treat the policy as a chose in action, to "go to the best market he can find, either to sell it or borrow money on it," lamenting that an insured without this power would be "limited in his choice of a purchaser to the party having an interest in the continuance of [his] life."[56] In that case, the insured had held the policy for about five years, and its surrender value was only $485. The court explains the insured's predicament:

> He was pressed for money, and finally sold the policy to the defendant . . . for $600, or something like $115 more than he would have received by the surrender of the policy to the company. He had paid a much larger sum in premiums,—something over $2,000,—and there seems to be no good reason why a person owning such a policy, and obliged to sell it, should not be permitted to get back as much as possible of the money that he has paid out for insurance. . . . There is no good reason for saying that an insured person should not have the right, whenever his necessities press him, because of a failing condition of health that assures a speedy death, to realize on his policy, and obtain for it something like a fair price, which may, perhaps, be almost equal to its face value.[57]

Thus, the policy underlying the allowance of assignments is the protection of the insured, by maintaining the liquidity of his or her investment. In the long run, then, allowing assignments rests on the same footing as encouraging insurance as a mode of savings, since people will be encouraged to insure if their investment (in the form of premiums) can be recovered before death.

The question remains, for those courts that take seriously the danger of gambling in lives, of how to protect legitimate insurance without protecting gamblers. The court in *Steinback* takes great pains to establish a means of

---

54. 13 N.Y. 31, 39 (1855).

55. 158 N.Y. 24 (1899).

56. Id. at 31.

57. Id. at 33.

distinguishing between those policies that are legitimate insurances, which should be granted whatever market value the insured can procure, and those policies which are a cover for wager transactions. The means suggested by the court is an examination of the intent of the parties:[58] "The intention of the parties procuring the policy would determine its character, which the courts would unhesitatingly declare in accordance with the facts, reading the policy and the assignment together, as forming part of one transaction."[59] In order to gauge the parties' intentions, "all the facts and circumstances may be proved, and if it then appear that the parties intended by the contract to enable a third and uninterested party to speculate upon the life of another, the court will declare such a contract invalid, not because of the assignment, but in spite of it."[60] And, as far as the *Steinback* court is concerned, the investigation of the intention of the parties should yield an answer to the question of whether the parties acted in good faith: "The materiality of the value of the interest has relation to the question of whether the policy is taken out in good faith, and not as a gambling transaction. If it be taken out in good faith, then a sound public policy would seem to require that the payee should be permitted to treat it as he may any other chose in action."[61]

The *Steinback* court was one of many that announced good faith as the key to the validity of assignment, and the Supreme Court's attitude was typical: "The essential thing is, that the policy shall be obtained in good faith, and not for the purpose of speculating upon the hazard of a life in which the insured has no interest."[62] Other courts expanded, or specified the role of good faith in the context of assignment:

> Another reason sometimes assigned for holding such assignments illegal is that an assignee having no insurable interest is in the position of one who,

58. Recall that this was precisely the maneuver courts employed in dealing with the problem of wagering in commodities. This is still the modern view:

> The standard for determining whether the presumption of validity [of assignment] has been successfully rebutted is the "intentions of the parties" test. Pursuant to this standard, courts examine a number of factors in the quest to determine whether the assignment was a subterfuge for a wagering contract. However, no single factor alone has been identified as controlling on the issue. Each factor must be considered in combination with the underlying facts and circumstances of the case.

Parker, "Lack of Insurable Interest," 87–88.

59. *Steinback*, 158 N.Y. at 31.

60. Id. at 32.

61. Id. at 30–31.

62. *Connecticut Mutual Life*, 94 U.S. at 460.

> in the first instance, takes out a wager policy. But we think not. If an insurable interest exists in the beneficiary at the time the policy is issued, and it is taken out in good faith, the object and purpose of the rule against wager policies would seem to have been sufficiently attained.[63]

Indeed, for those courts interested in allowing the assignment of insurance policies, "good faith" became something of a talisman,[64] with one contemporary writer claiming that good faith, or in his parlance, bona fides, was "the logical test of the propriety, and hence of the validity" of insurance contracts.[65]

However, the widespread use of the term *good faith* does not constitute a guarantee that all courts share an understanding of what "good faith" entails, nor even that the term has any discernible content. A number of examples show the difficulty in establishing a fixed meaning for *good faith* in this context. In *Banker's Reserve Life Co. v. Matthews*, the court adopted the good faith test, saying, "In short, the test is the good faith in taking out the policy for the benefit of one having an insurable interest."[66] The facts of the case, however, suggest a difficulty. The insured procured life insurance (in two policies of five thousand dollars each), assigning seven-tenths of the value to Dr. Matthews and his wife, who was the insured's cousin. In return, Matthews agreed to pay all the premiums on the policies. The policies were taken out with the intention that they be assigned to Matthews, and the court, after an in-depth review of the circumstances surrounding the transactions, validated the assignment.[67] But in many of the cases where

---

63. Chamberlain v. Butler, 86 N.W. 481, 482 (Neb. 1901).

64. For representative rhetoric regarding the adoption of the good faith test, see Finnie v. Walker, 257 F. 698, 700 (2d Cir. 1919) ("A life insurance policy taken out in good faith by the insured, with no idea of assigning it, can afterwards, in good faith, and for a valuable consideration, be sold and assigned to one who has no insurable interest in the life . . ."). For additional cases adopting the good faith test, see, e.g., *Grigsby*, 222 U.S. at 156; Bankers' Reserve Life Co. v. Matthews, 39 F.2d 528, 529 (8th Cir. 1930); Mechanics' National Bank v. Comins, 55 A. 191, 193 (N.H. 1903); Brett v. Warnick, 75 P. 1061, 1064 (Or. 1904).

65. William Reynolds Vance, *Handbook of the Law of Insurance* 103 (1904); see also Patterson, "Insurable Interest in Life," 403–6.

66. 39 F.2d at 529.

67. Similarly, in another case, the Supreme Court of Arkansas validated an assignment, even though the policy was procured with the intention of assigning it to one who had no insurable interest. See Prudential Insurance Co. of America v. Williams, 168 S.W. 1114 (Ark. 1914). In that case, the insured procured the policy with the intention of assigning it to a party who died before the assignment could be executed, and then the insured assigned it to a third party, whose right to the proceeds of the policy was upheld.

assignments are made long after procuring the insurance, the courts raise the hypothetical situation of an assignment agreement made at the time of purchase as the very paradigm of the lack of good faith.[68] In fact, the case most often cited for the invalidation of assignment, *Warnock v. Davis*, had an almost identical fact pattern to the *Matthews* case.[69] On the other hand, in *Finnie v. Walker*, the court voided assignments of a series of policies, some of which were made over a year after the policies had been procured.[70] Thus, the timing of the assignment is not a reliable objective test for "good faith."

Even the cases that invalidate assignments do not offer a conclusive understanding of what "good faith" includes. For instance, in both *Warnock v. Davis* and *McRae v. Warmack*, it was held that the assignment was not of the "fraudulent kind with respect to which the courts regard parties as alike culpable and refuse to interfere with the results of their action. No fraud or deception upon any one was designed by the agreement, nor did its execution involve moral turpitude."[71] Thus, on the one hand, one need not have an evil intent or be guilty of "moral turpitude" to run afoul of the prohibition on assignments that amount to wagers; on the other hand, there is no clear objective test, for example the time of assignment, through which a lack of good faith can be definitively determined. Noting the difficulty in administering the test of "good faith," one contemporary critic lamented that it had become a "touchstone for identifying wagering contracts of insurance":

> Does "good faith" mean that the parties must be free from any consciousness of wrong-doing in procuring the policy? In *Warnock v. Davis, supra*, and

68. See, e.g., *Steinback*, 158 N.Y. at 31: "The insured, instead of taking out a policy payable to a person having no insurable interest in his life, can take it out to himself, and at once assign it to such person. But such an attempt would not prove successful, for a policy issued and assigned, under such circumstances, would be none the less a wagering policy because of the form of it." For additional cases where courts raise the hypothetical case of assignment at the time of procuring the policy, see, e.g., *Grigsby*, 222 U.S. at 156; *Chamberlain*, 86 N.W. at 483; *Rylander*, 53 S.E. at 1037:

> Of course, one cannot do indirectly what the law prohibits him from doing directly, and as it is unlawful for a person to effect insurance upon the life of another in the continuance of whose life he has no interest, an invasion of this rule by the issue of a policy to one who has an insurable interest, and its immediate assignment, pursuant to a preconceived intent, to one without such interest, who undertakes to pay the premiums for his chance of profit upon his investment, is ineffective, and such assignment is void.

69. *Warnock*, 104 U.S. The only real difference was that in Warnock, nine-tenths of the insurance was assigned to a mutual agency of which the insured was a member, rather than, as in Matthews, to his cousin.

70. *Finnie*, 257 F. at 701.

71. *Warnock*, 104 U.S. at 781; McRae v. Warmack, 135 S.W. 807, 811 (Ark. 1911).

> *McRae v. Warmack, supra,* the court distinctly said that the transaction did not involve any "moral turpitude." Does "good faith" mean that the purpose is not to evade the law against wagering? If so, what is the law, and as a corollary, when is it evaded? The "good faith test" answers neither of these questions. Or, to put it another way, is the absence of the intent to make a "wager," "good faith"? Then what is a "wager," and how are the parties to know when they are making one, unless each man is the sole judge of his own "good faith"? It is submitted that the law's standard of harmfulness is objective, not subjective, and that "good faith" is not only futilely ambiguous, but also positively misleading. . . . The phrase "good faith" is valueless as a universal test of insurable interest.[72]

Good faith is introduced in this context as a mechanism to solve the difficulty of distinguishing between wagers and legitimate insurance when the form of the transactions is identical. But the displacement is a failure: determining whether a contract is entered into in good faith turns out to be as difficult, and as dependent on social consequences and cultural values, as the distinction between wagers and insurance was in the first place.

The courts' treatment of commodities and insurance cases reveals the following parallel structure. In both types of cases, the courts take a stand in limiting freedom of contract by distinguishing between an approved and a forbidden contractual form, that is, between legitimate and illegitimate transactions, between permitted contracts and gambling. They discover that analytically the forms are indistinguishable, and in response, they formulate a second set of distinguishing maneuvers, invoking intent and good faith. The problem of fixing a meaning for those terms, however, reenacts the anxieties that generated the initial distinction between the approved and prohibited contracts. Avenues for overcoming those anxieties are the focus of the last chapter in this part of the book.

---

72. Patterson, "Insurable Interest in Life," 404–5.

EIGHT

Acquisitive Individuality Versus Communal Efficiency

Conflicting Policies and the Love-Hate Relationship with Risk

The analytical emptiness of the good faith standard as a tool for distinguishing legitimate from illegitimate contracts exposes a gap in the law. As in the case of the intent of the parties to commodities futures contracts, the gap is filled, not with a technical legal test, but with a conflict among policies. On the one hand, there is the policy of limiting wagers. It bears emphasis that the law is not interested in eradicating wagers, since elements of risk exist in the most legitimate transactions and the law has no way of definitively distinguishing wagers from legitimate contracts. Rather, the policy in its most defensible form is more modest, limiting wagers in such a way that gambling as a vocation does not become attractive. Thus, the limitation of the capacity to wager is positioned within a wider goal of the law and of emerging capitalistic culture generally, which is to foster acquisitive individuality. The chief objection to the wagering contract is that it leads to unearned gain. And, while the law does not attempt to eliminate every unearned gain, it does attempt to limit the harmful social consequences of a mechanism that allows people to get something for nothing. Edwin Patterson, writing in 1918 and defending the limitation of wagers through insurance, explains why the law must combat a vocation of wagering, while wagers that do not amount to a vocation will not have the same harmful consequences:

> Vaguely, a sense of antagonism is aroused in a community of workers against persons who obtain a means of livelihood without participating in the machinery of social or economic production and distribution—in short, against "social slackers." More specifically, unearned gains lead to idleness, and the wagerer becomes a social parasite. Useful business and industry are thereby discouraged. On the moral side, idleness leads to vice; and the impoverishment of the loser entails misery, and, in consequence, crime.[1]

Similarly, modern commentators have noted that gambling, in its various forms and especially when it offered itself as a vocation, stood in defiance of an ethic of industry deemed necessary to support a productive labor force. By holding out the promise of instant wealth, gambling undermined individual motivation to accumulate money gradually through employment.[2]

An ideal of communal efficiency stood on the other side of the gap exposed by the lack of a technical legal mechanism to distinguish gambling from legitimate contract. In the simplest terms, "Life insurance emerged as the most efficient secular risk-bearing institution to handle the economic hazards of death through cooperative self-help."[3] But the principle of efficient risk bearing was hardly limited to life insurance, and the policy of efficient risk management bears further elaboration, especially in its relation to both insurance and speculation in commodities futures. Commentators who tried to legitimize various forms of economic activity that resembled gambling repeatedly resorted to the vocabulary of professionalism and specialization. New York Life's commissioned history, referred to earlier, is a prime example, where the author distinguishes modern life insurance from the older, wagering form, by claiming that insurance "has become an exact science in which predictions can be made with all the certainty of mathematical calculations."[4] Other expressions of the policy were less vulgar and more detailed.

---

1. Edwin W. Patterson, "Insurable Interest in Life," 18 *Colum. L. Rev.* 381, 386 (1918) (footnotes omitted).

2. Viviana A. Rotman Zelizer, *Morals and Markets: The Development of Life Insurance in the United States* 88 (1979). See also, Karen Halttunen, *Confidence Men and Painted Women: A Study of Middle-Class Culture in America, 1830–1870*, p. 17 (1982); Ann Fabian, *Card Sharps, Dream Books, and Bucket Shops: Gambling in 19th Century America* 61 (1990); Vicki Abt et al., *The Business of Risk: Commercial Gambling in America* 208 (1986).

3. Zelizer, *Morals and Markets*, 89.

4. Lawrence F. Abbot, *The Story of NYLIC: A History of the Origin and Development of the New York Life*

Early in the century, economists elaborated the relationship between increasing efficiency and encouraging speculation, laying the basis for the market consciousness that to a great extent still governs modern conceptions of economic activity. In *Risk, Uncertainty, and Profit*, Frank Knight explained that the principles behind insurance practice, namely consolidation and specialization, actually underlay even the basics of production for a market.[5] Knight identified the problem of uncertainty as the central obstacle to rational economic behavior. Uncertainty is reduced by grouping like instances, in other words, consolidation, which can then be subjected to probabilistic calculation. Whereas for the individual, specific instances of uncertainty are unpredictable, when an institution can group instances, it can treat the results as known on the basis of probabilities, and thus plan rationally for the outcomes. Secondly, those institutions that can best group instances are selected to deal with uncertainties. This is known as specialization. Knight went on to explain that while this model of action is the conscious and overt principle in organizing the insurance industry (which groups together the instances of death, uncertain for the individual but highly certain for large groups on the basis of actuarial statistics), the same principle actually explains the relationship of consumers to producers: while individual consumers' wants are unknown in advance even to the consumers themselves, producers are able to plan for the future by producing for an anonymous group, whose wants can be predicted.

> The clue to the apparent paradox is, of course, in the "law of large numbers," the consolidation of risks (or uncertainties). The consumer is, to himself, only one; to the producer he is a mere multitude in which individuality is lost. It turns out that an outsider can foresee the wants of a multitude with more ease and accuracy than an individual can attain with respect to his own.[6]

The two principles of reducing uncertainty to measurable risk are consolidation and specialization, and each is associated with specific economic institutions or practices. The best-known device for dealing with uncertainty through consolidation is insurance, with life insurance being its most

---

Insurance Company from 1845 to 1929, p. 12 (1930).

5. Frank H. Knight, *Risk, Uncertainty, and Profit* 233–63 (1921). See also Henry Crosby Emery, *Speculation on the Stock and Produce Exchanges of the United States* (Faculty of Political Science of Columbia Univ. ed., 1896).

6. Knight, *Risk, Uncertainty, and Profit*, 241.

highly developed form.[7] And significantly, "the most important instrument in modern economic society for the specialization of uncertainty . . . is *Speculation*," the hedging contract being its best illustration in business at large:

> By this simple device the industrial producer is enabled to eliminate the chance of loss or gain due to changes in the value of materials used in his operations during the interval between the time he purchases them as raw materials and the time he disposes of them as finished product, "shifting" this risk to the professional speculator. It is manifest at once that even aside from any superior judgment or foresight or better information possessed by such a professional speculator, he gains an enormous advantage from the sheer magnitude or breadth of the scope of his operations.[8]

Thus, when Justice Holmes calls speculation through the commodities futures markets "the self-adjustment of society to the probable,"[9] or when Professor Patterson devotes an article to legitimating hedging contracts in commodities,[10] they are actually relying on an incipient form of the policy argument fleshed out by economists such as Knight. Speculation, according to this argument, is an important part of the forward motion of a capitalistic market, a sort of engine of the progress of economic rationality. Taken to its extreme, this policy would allow for the development of vocations in risk management, despite the fact that these can be characterized by some as getting something for nothing. But, while it is easy to accept this vision as if it offers a simple and sweeping solution to the tension generated by the law's antipathy to gambling (by seemingly eradicating that antipathy entirely), it is important to note that the tension is not in fact resolved. And the lack of resolution is not dependent merely on an anachronistic attachment to a premodern deterministic or religious worldview. In fact, the policy of limiting gambling advances the goal of constructing acquisitive individuality, nourishing the work ethic which is also presented as a necessary engine of economic progress. In other words, the conflict among policies is not between a premarket or anticapitalist policy and a promarket or capitalist policy; rather, both sides of the policy divide fit squarely into an emerging capitalist society. The policies simply represent conflicting positions within

7. Id. at 245–48.

8. Id. at 255–56.

9. Board of Trade of Chicago v. Christie Grain and Stock Co., 198 U.S. 236, 247 (1905).

10. Edwin W. Patterson, "Hedging and Wagering on Produce Exchanges," 40 *Yale L.J.* 843 (1931).

a market-oriented society regarding the question of which cultural attributes of that society require the law's support or censure.

If analyzed closely, there are many aspects of the judicial rhetoric just canvassed that would yield clues to the shift to a modern market sensibility, and even a theory of the individual that underlies that shift. While it is impossible to undergo a thorough examination of these issues here, a few brief comments may be suggestive. One example is the issue of time. The opinions examined herein have a special concern with time, and its changing meaning and value. "From the time he plants his seed" the farmer has lost control of the value of time, and he is gambling.[11] Theorists examining cultural formations have concentrated on the shifting conceptions of time as a central aspect of the shift to modernity.[12] The Marxist cultural theorist Georg Lukacs lamented that industrial capitalism had alienated individuals through a process of reification, a central aspect of which was the reduction of time into an uncontrollable, external influence on people, who were transformed into cogs in a machine. "The contemplative stance adopted towards a process mechanically conforming to fixed laws and enacted independently of man's consciousness and impervious to human intervention, *i.e.* a perfectly closed system, must likewise transform the basic categories of man's immediate attitude to the world: it reduces space and time to a common denominator and degrades time to the dimension of space."[13] Lukacs's fundamental concern seems to be that time, once an intangible and infinitely meaningful quality, is reduced under conditions of industrial capitalism to yet another one-dimensional and measurable function of money. While they did not use the philosophical articulations available to Lukacs, turn-of-the-century judges shared some of the same perceptions. Insurance

---

11. Albers v. Lamson, 42 N.E.2d 627, 630 (Ill. 1942).

12. See, e.g., Stephen Kern, *The Culture of Time and Space, 1880–1918* (1983); Peter Galison, *Einstein's Clocks, Poicaré's Maps: Empires of Time* (2003).

13. Georg Lukacs, *History and Class Consciousness* 89 (Rodney Livingstone trans., MIT Press 1968) (1923). He continues:

> Thus time sheds its qualitative, variable, flowing nature; it freezes into an exactly delimited, quantifiable continuum filled with quantifiable "things" (the reified, mechanically objectified "performance" of the worker, wholly separated from his total human personality): in short, it becomes space. . . . On the other hand, the mechanical disintegration of the process of production into its components also destroys those bonds that had bound individuals to a community in the days when production was still "organic". In this respect, too, mechanisation makes of them isolated abstract atoms whose work no longer brings them together directly and organically; it becomes mediate to an increasing extent exclusively by the abstract laws of the mechanism which imprisons them.

Id. at 90.

and commodities trading, with their constant reminders of many "futures" on the one hand, and the promise of turning time into money without intervening production on the other, are contexts where the shifting nature of time heightens the uncertainty and even the fear surrounding a transition to modernity.

Cultural critic Walter Benjamin's work is even more pointed in drawing the connections between time, modernity, and gambling. Writing on Baudelaire, Benjamin notes that the image of the gambler became the characteristically modern complement to the archaic image of the fencer, both being heroic figures.[14] He then elaborates suggestively that time itself is different in modernity, a difference understood in part by reference to the gambler. Benjamin's critique of modern subjectivity is more layered and complex than Lukacs's. Rather than relying directly on economic form as a motivation of change, Benjamin analyzes the relationship between cultural forms such as architecture, literature, and technological innovations such as assembly-line work, comparing the repetition involved in such work to the narcotic effect of gambling.[15]

Benjamin's conception of consciousness in modernity links, in a series of complex correspondences, a change in the experience of time with changing cultural conditions, from traffic signals to matches to automated factories, and all of these in turn with the experience of the gambler. The gambler becomes emblematic of modernity. The negotiations of the place of gambling in commodities and insurance contracts, then, take their place as part of a change in the notion of individuality, and a construction of a market consciousness that accompanies a shift to modernity. Benjamin quotes these lines of Baudelaire, which seem to draw out the insecurities that animate much of the conscious and unconscious policy discussion in the cases: "Keep in mind that Time's a rabid gambler / Who wins always without cheating—it's the law!"[16]

The policy divide identified in the case law should be read as a cultural conflict central to the capitalist market economy taking shape in the United

---

14. Walter Benjamin, *Illuminations* 178 (Harry Zohn trans., Schocken Books 1968) (1955).

15. See id. at 174–85; see also Walter Benjamin, "Paris, Capital of the Nineteenth Century," in *Reflections* 146, 159–62 (Edmund Jephcott trans., 1978) ("To the phantasmagorias of space to which the flaneur abandons himself, correspond the phantasmagorias of time indulged in by the gambler. Gambling converts time into a narcotic").

16. Quoted in Benjamin, *Illuminations*, 179.

States around the turn of the century. Both sides in this conflict accepted capitalism as the central mode of economic organization for the country. However, they divided on the question of how to conceptualize risk, and especially on the question of the relationship between uncertainty and the individual. When looked at as a whole, this conflict can be characterized as a love/hate relationship with risk, or an economy of appropriation and distance.[17] The advantage to reading this conflict as such an economy is that it allows us to see expressions of both sides of the policy within the same work; thus, a commitment to an outcome on one side of the policy divide does not cancel the possibility of resorting to rhetoric that favors the other side. It also allows us to read, rather than one case for one judge's view, a discourse and its effects, despite the fact that none of them were willed by any particular actor.

Certain descriptions of the development of contract law early in the century point to the centrality of coming to terms with uncertainty.[18] However, these descriptions elide the cultural aspect of uncertainty, while miscasting the role of uncertainty itself as a phenomenon new to contract law as industrial concentrations grow larger.[19] By assuming an objective uncertainty in economic affairs, these descriptions confuse economics with culture. Economic factors may or may not have become more uncertain, but the crisis of uncertainty was cultural.

The most visible feature in the discursive economy of appropriation and distance is the positioning of risk, chance, or hazard, in relationship to contract. On the one hand, all these types of uncertainty are marginalized as objects of contract. Thus, the rhetoric of contract law is at pains, even in its nonchalant repetitions, to show that commodities futures contracts or insurance contracts are in some way a special, marginal category of contracts.

---

17. By using the term *economy*, I mean to draw attention to a way of looking at rhetorical maneuvers, not merely as independent isolated arguments, but rather as part of a larger rhetorical structure. The rhetorical structure lends arguments intelligibility, but not every piece of rhetoric that seems to favor a given outcome requires that particular outcome.

18. See, e.g., Melvin Aron Eisenberg, "Probability and Chance in Contract Law," 45 *U.C.L.A. L. Rev.* 1005 (1998); Walter F. Pratt, Jr., "American Contract Law at the Turn of the Century," 39 *S.C. L. Rev.* 415 (1988).

19. As Knight shows, the increase of industrial concentration and the rise of larger institutions that can group instances (whether of deaths or of consumer demand) actually decrease the objective manifestations of uncertainty. Legal scholarship often takes at face value the rise in the importance of uncertainty in legal rhetoric, simply assuming that an industrial economy generates more uncertainty than some idealized, simpler economy. From my perspective, it is more interesting to inquire into why uncertainty becomes such an important category for legal thought.

They are even given a special appellation, *aleatory contracts*, implying that all other contracts are free from risk and uncertainty. Thus the common refrain that a transaction, whatever its content, is valid, "provided it not be by way of cover for a wager."[20] This construction masquerades as a simple legal proposition, often presented as a bottom line, and often included in the headnotes of the reports. But we should pause over what it actually entails in the cases. From the sentence itself, we would be tempted to believe that the "wager" is a known quantity, visible to the discerning eye wherever it raises its ugly head. But in fact, in most of these cases, the court spends most of its opinion trying to divine whether the transaction in question is or is not obnoxious to public policy. And recall, this is precisely the question on which the different jurisdictions, and sometimes different courts in the same jurisdiction, simply cannot agree. The courts are engaged in a constructive process of naming certain contracts "wagers," or allowing those contracts to escape that label. But while this process goes on, the refrain allows the courts to repeat the mantra, implying that while there is a question as to the legitimacy of each and every transaction, the "mere wager" itself is always a marginal, exterior category, which has no home within contract.[21]

The language of marginalization is the rhetoric of containment and mastery. On its face, it implies complete control. The very act of incessant, nearly compulsive repetition, found in almost every jurisdiction, implies that the law controls the wager, and thus, even chance itself. Rhetorically, wager is controlled, tamed, expelled from contract discourse. But this almost ritualistic repetition is only a substitute for the control of gambling that the law cannot achieve.[22]

---

20. Hawkes v. Mobley, 163 S.E. 494, 497 (Ga. 1932). For additional cases using substantially the same construction, i.e., calling the transaction valid provided it not be done by way of cover for a wager, see, e.g.: Prudential Insurance Co. of America v. Williams, 168 S.W. 1114, 1115 (Ark. 1914); Page v. Metropolitan Life Insurance Co., 135 S.W. 911, 912 (Ark. 1911); Rylander v. Allen, 53 S.E. 1032, 1036 (Ga. 1906); Guaranty Life Insurance Co. v. Primo, 140 S.E. 780, 781 (Ga. App. 1927); Volunteer St. Life Insurance Co. v. Buchannan, 73 S.E. 602, 604 (Ga. App. 1912); Elkhart Mutual Aid Benevolent Relief Ass'n v. Houghton, 2 N.E. 763, 767 (Ind. 1885); Reilly v. Penn Mutual Life Insurance Co., 207 N.W. 583, 585 (Iowa 1926); Chamberlain v. Butler, 86 N.W. 481, 483 (Neb. 1901); Mechanics' National Bank v. Comins, 55 A. 191, 195 (N.H. 1903); Empire Development Co. v. Title Guarantee and Trust Co., 121 N.E. 468, 469 (N.Y. 1918); In re Phillips' Estate, 86 A. 289, 290 (Pa. 1913); Cronin v. Vermont Life Insurance Co., 40 A. 497, 497 (R.I. 1898); Roberts v. National Benefit Life Insurance Co., 148 S.E. 179, 180 (S.C. 1929); Rogers v. Atlantic Life Insurance Co., 133 S.E. 215, 217 (S.C. 1926); Crosswell v. Connecticut Indem. Ass'n, 28 S.E. 200, 201 (S.C. 1897); Shoemaker v. Harrington, 30 S.W.2d 539, 543 (Tex. Civ. App. 1930); Manhattan Life Insurance Co. v. Cohen, 139 S.W. 51, 54 (Tex. Civ. App. 1911).

21. Courts also favor this construction ("mere wager") when attacking wagering, in the abstract.

22. In this, the courts reenact the child's game of disappearance and return, *fort-da*, described by Freud

On the other hand, an opposed rhetoric is also at work, dispersing or disseminating the wager rather than marginalizing it. Instead of claiming that the uncertainty inherent in gambling is somehow exterior to contract, this rhetoric claims it is the essence of contract, and even that contract can be defined as the assumption of risk. This view is at least as old as Holmes's *The Common Law*,[23] and is popular today in the contract opinions of Chief Judge Richard Posner.[24] Indeed, it has become a commonplace of legal opinions to speculate on the ubiquity of something akin to gambling in contract specifically, and in economic life generally. A rich example, complete with literary allusion, comes from a case regarding a joint venture in stock investment:

> Except for those endowed with the blessings of prescience or omnipotence, the agreements of all men as to the future depend on some degree upon chance and unknown and fortuitous events.
>
> The best laid schemes o' mice and men / Gang aft a-gley;
> An lea'e us nought but grief and pain, / For promis'd joy.
>
> One of our most substantial and respected businesses, insurance, is premised upon the most unknowable and unpredictable contingency of all—death. The stock market, as a barometer of business success, international and domestic outlook, sales, taxes, profits, competition, and a hundred variables, not the least of which is the irrationality of mass psychology, is a notoriously volatile indicator whose fluctuations, largely beyond individual control, bestow fortunes on some men while leaving others shattered and

---

in *Beyond the Pleasure Principle*. There, the child enacts the controlled disappearance and return of his toys in order to compensate himself for his mother's disappearance, which is beyond his control. See Sigmund Freud, *Beyond the Pleasure Principle* 12–17 (James Strachey ed. and trans., W. W. Norton 1961) (1920).

23. See Oliver Wendell Holmes, Jr., *The Common Law* 299–301 (1881) ("In the case of a binding promise that it shall rain to-morrow, the immediate legal effect of what the promisor does is, that he takes the risk of the event, within certain defined limits, as between himself and the promisee. He does no more when he promises to deliver a bale of cotton") Id. at 300.

24. See, e.g., Nicolet Instrument Corp. v. Lindquist and Vennum, 34 F.3d 453, 456 (7th Cir. 1994) ("It is not a novel idea that an essential function of contracts is to allocate particular risks to the parties best able to bear them"); Market Street Assocs. v. Frey, 941 F.2d 588, 595 (7th Cir. 1991) (contrasting contractual functions of allocation of risk on the one hand and the setting in motion of a cooperative enterprise on the other); Spartech Corp. v. Opper, 890 F.2d 949, 955 (7th Cir. 1989) ("A principle purpose of contracts . . . is to allocate the risk of the unexpected . . . not to place it always on the promisee"); Northern Ind. Pub. Serv. Co. v. Carbon County Coal Co., 799 F.2d 265, 275–78 (7th Cir. 1986) (asking how the parties would have assigned the risk that the performance of the contract might become impossible); Fidelity and Deposit Co. v. City of Sheboygan Falls, 713 F.2d 1261, 1269 (7th Cir. 1983) ("An important function of contracts is to allocate risk; and the performing party to a contract usually guarantees performance against at least some contingencies that are beyond his control").

> penniless. Chancy, yes. A gamble in the legal sense rather than the vernacular, no. "Business may involve speculation but unless the latter is illegal it does not get down to what in modern times is the lower classification known as gambling." Risk, then, is not the element which makes the transaction a gamble.[25]

Contract law, then, has learned to live with risk. It has set itself up as a higher order, to be contrasted with that "lower classification," gambling. Contract discourse has taken the teeth out of gambling, devolving "chance and fortuitous events" in the first sentence quoted above into a mere colloquialism, "chancy," later in the passage. Chance intrudes everywhere in life, but only in a moderate, controlled fashion, at least as far as the "legal sense rather than the vernacular" is concerned.

This quotation is only a hint of the fact that insecurity over the status of speculative transactions arises in almost the same form today, regarding two distinct contexts closely analogous to the turn-of-the-century cases discussed here. The first context is activity in the market for complex derivatives; the second is the new industry of viatical settlement. A brief word regarding these two issues should suffice to show that while attitudes toward gambling have changed over the last hundred years, the basic problematic of distinguishing legitimate risk allocation from illegitimate speculation is still alive and unsettled, and perhaps unsettling.

The market for financial instruments known as derivatives has grown to staggering proportions since the early 1980s.[26] For the most part, this growth is perceived as part of an extension of the rationalization of pricing risk. However, periodically, scandals involving huge losses plague the industry and generate a different kind of discourse.[27] Popular discourse surrounding the derivatives markets, particularly following scandals, is full of references to betting and gambling, and to the fact that investment and gambling are difficult to distinguish, "since all financial products straddle that very fine

---

25. Liss v. Manuel, 296 N.Y.S.2d 627, 630–31 (Civ. Ct. 1968) (citation omitted).

26. The derivatives market was estimated to have a notional value of $70 trillion in 1998, 100 trillion in 2000, and 340 trillion in 2005. See *Bank for International Settlements Quarterly Review*, Sept. 2005, available at *www.bis.org/publ/quarterly.htm.*

27. Among the more publicized scandals in derivatives trading are the collapse of Barings Bank in 1995; the bankruptcy of Orange County, California, in 1994; the losses incurred by Procter and Gamble and Gibson Greetings, Inc., in derivatives trades with Bankers Trust in 1994; and the collapse of the Long Term Capital "hedge fund" in 1998. For an account of the tendency of derivatives markets to resemble gambling, see Timothy L. O'Brien, *Bad Bet: The Inside Story of the Glamour, Glitz, and Danger of America's Gambling Industry* (1998).

line separating temperate, calculated gambles from irrational, impassioned betting."[28] Each new scandal brings with it a call for tighter regulation, with its familiar dynamic of paternalism pitted against those who claim that flexible self-regulation will always be more efficient.[29] Finally, defenders of the derivatives markets today make a claim for specialization and expertise, reminiscent of Justice Holmes's crocodile tears over the fact that "the success of the strong induces imitation by the weak, and that incompetent persons bring themselves to ruin by undertaking to speculate in their turn."[30] The moral aversion to gambling has dissipated, but the theoretical difficulty of determining the proper way to regulate the market in risk lives on.[31]

The difficulty in regulating the assignment of life insurance replays itself even more starkly. Since 1990, a "new" industry of viatical settlement has sprung up. Viatical settlements are agreements to buy insurance policies from terminally ill policy holders, usually people suffering from AIDS, for a percentage of the value of the policy, typically between 55 and 70 percent of the face value of the policy.[32] In essence, viatical settlements are identical to the assignments of life policies discussed above, except that the AIDS epidemic has created a population base in dire need of cash, primarily for medical expenses, before the policies mature (at death). Seeing the

---

28. Id. at 274. For journalistic accounts of investment in derivatives characterized as betting, see, e.g., Michael Lewis, "How the Eggheads Cracked," *N.Y. Times Mag.*, Jan. 24, 1999, at 24; Steven Lipin et al., "Fancy Footwork: Bankers Trust Thrives Pitching Derivatives, but Climate Is Shifting," *Wall St. J.*, Apr. 22, 1994, at A1; Steven Lipin et al., "Portfolio Poker: Just What Firms Do with Derivatives Is Suddenly a Hot Issue," *Wall St. J.*, Apr. 14, 1994, at A1; Robert Trigaux, "Firms' Stretch for Profits Could Backfire," *St. Petersburg Times*, Apr. 14, 1994, at 1E.

29. See, e.g., Jaye Scholl, "The Big Fizzle: Beware of Leveraged Rocket Scientists with an Attitude," *Barron's*, Sept. 28, 1998, at 23; Randall Smith and Steven Lipin, "Beleaguered Giant: As Derivatives Losses Rise, Industry Fights to Avert Regulation," *Wall St. J.* Aug. 25, 1994, at A1; Steven Lipin and Anita Raghavan, "GAO to Join Hot Debate on Derivatives, " *Wall St. J.*, May 19, 1994, at C1.

30. *Board of Trade of Chicago*, 198 U.S. at 248.

31. One recent article on the issue claims, using economic analysis, that pre-1930s antipathy toward gambling may have had its basis in efficiency, and that the current support for lax regulation of speculative transactions in derivatives may be economically unsound. See Lynn Stout, "Why the Law Hates Speculators: Regulation and Private Ordering in the Market for OTC Derivatives," 48 *Duke L.J.* 701 (1999). Legal scholarship surrounding derivatives sometimes touches on the gambling issue, but it is more often focused on the question of whether derivatives can be regulated by federal authorities as securities. See Procter and Gamble Co. v. Bankers Trust Co., 925 F. Supp. 1270 (S.D. Ohio 1996); see also William K. Maready, Jr., "Comment, Regulating for Disaster: Federal Attempts to Control the Derivatives Market," 31 *Wake Forest L. Rev.* 885 (1996).

32. See Timothy P. Davis, "Should Viatical Settlements Be Considered 'Securities' Under the 1933 Securities Act?" 6 *Kans. J.L. and Pub. Pol'y*, 75 (1997). See also Dave Luxenberg, "Comment, Why Viatical Settlements Constitute Investment Contracts Within the Meaning of the 1933 and 1934 Securities Acts," 34 *Willamette L. Rev.* 357 (1998).

potential for profits, the industry has grown at a very rapid pace,[33] and is expanding its client base from AIDS patients to numerous terminally and chronically ill patients.[34] While most of the legal discourse, again, revolves around the question of how to regulate the viatical industry,[35] one commentator opened her discussion with the claim, "Viatical companies gamble on people's lives,"[36] and another notes, "Critics claim that it is 'ghoulish' to allow companies to financially succeed by gambling on the life expectancies of others."[37] The focus of the discussion has shifted—gambling has been displaced as the center of regulatory discourse—but the core conflict over what kinds of speculation will be deemed legitimate retains its resonance.

I have focused on a transformative moment in the development of contract law, where the question of gambling was eventually swallowed and internalized as if the problem were solved. What has come to light, instead, is that the conflict over what was gambling and what was allocation of risk was handled, and settled, not according to an analytical formula that successfully distinguished between them, but rather through a more complex and less decisive cultural negotiation and displacement of the question. The close reading of judicial rhetoric I have engaged in serves to show that legal discourse is a productive endeavor. More than straightforward prohibitions on certain types of conduct, judicial grappling with risk and uncertainty offers its audiences an image with which to identify; rhetoric does not stop at telling us what to do, it tells us what to be.

Today, the gambling label is less of a stigma, not only for dubious financial transactions, but even for plain, straightforward gambling, which has

---

33. Viatical settlements were estimated at $5 million in 1989, $500 million in 1996, and were projected to grow to $4 billion by the year 2000. Miriam R. Albert, "Selling Death Short: The Regulatory and Policy Implications of Viatical Settlements (Symposium on Health Care Policy: What Lessons Have We Learned from the AIDS Pandemic?)," 61 *Alb. L. Rev.* 1013, 1018 (1998); Joy D. Kosiewicz, "Comment, Death for Sale: A Call to Regulate the Viatical Settlement Industry," 48 *Case W. Res. L. Rev.* 701 (1998).

34. Kosiewicz, "Death for Sale," 725.

35. 35. See SEC v. Life Partners, Inc., 87 F.3d 536 (D.C. Cir. 1996); Davis, "Should Viatical Settlements Be Considered Securities"; Luxenberg, "Why Viatical Settlements Constitute Investment Contracts"; Michael R. Davis, "Note, Unregulated Investment in Certain Death: *SEC v. Life Partners, Inc.*," 42 *Vill. L. Rev.* 925 (1997); Katherine DePeri, "Recent Decisions: Brokered Viatical Settlement Contracts Are Not Securities," 70 *Temp. L. Rev.* 857 (1997); Elizabeth L. Deeley, "Note, Viatical Settlements Are Not Securities: Is It Law or Sympathy?" 66 *Geo. Wash. L. Rev.* 382 (1998); Shanah D. Glick, "Comment, Are Viatical Settlements Securities Within the Regulatory Control of the Securities Act of 1933?" 60 *U. Chi. L. Rev.* 957 (1993).

36. Kosiewicz, "Death for Sale," 701.

37. Denise M. Schultz, "Comment, Angels of Mercy or Greedy Capitalists? Buying Life Insurance Policies from the Terminally Ill," 24 *Pepp. L. Rev.* 99, 103 (1996).

been legalized in almost all the states in some form, from numbers (the state lotteries) to poker (casino gambling). All of these legalized forms are seen as productive economic endeavors, at least as much as any of the rest of the entertainment industry. In the modern setting, then, the normative question of the legitimacy of specific types of transactions is not played out by arguing over whether they are gambling (everyone is willing to admit they are), but rather, is displaced onto the question of how they should be regulated, and particularly, whether they should be regulated by the ultimate father figure—the federal government in the shape of the Securities and Exchange Commission or the Commodities Futures Trading Commission. This displacement represents a shift of the same normative debate, over how and how heavily transactions of this sort should be regulated and (the other side of the coin) enforced.

Commenting on the workings of legal discourse as an ideological function, Robert Gordon has argued that lawyers' main importance derives from their contribution to the forms and categories of public discourse.[38] Judicial discourse surrounding the problem of gambling in contract law around the turn of the century was involved in such an ideological function. By spinning out an economy of appropriation and distance with regard to risk, chance, and hazard in the economic processes of contracting, contract discourse helped its audiences come to terms with the deep fears and uncertainties that accompanied the transition into modernity. By retaining its condemnatory critique of gambling, or "banishing its gambling doubles," it played the protector of souls.[39] And by recognizing that efficient economies required speculative activity, and that an element, albeit a controlled element, of gambling existed in all economic activity, contract discourse made way for the emergence of an individual who could claim mastery even while acknowledging uncertainty. Throwing itself between the devil and the deep sea, contract helped Americans stop worrying and learn to love risk.

---

38. Robert W. Gordon, "Legal Thought and Legal Practice in the Age of American Enterprise, 1870–1920," in *Professions and Professional Ideologies in America* 81–82 (Gerald L. Geison ed., 1983).

39. Fabian, *Card Sharps*, 5.

PART THREE

The Narratives of Incomplete Contracts

NINE

Framing Incomplete Contracts

There is a long-running debate in legal scholarship and judicial opinion over incomplete contracts and the implication of terms in contract disputes. Like many fundamental issues in legal theory, the debate is apparently not susceptible to final settlement; it is inconclusive. The chapters in this part of the book do not endeavor to advance an argument *within* the debate. Instead, this part is an attempt to understand the productive power of the framework of the debate itself, by raising questions such as the following: What is the common ground of the positions in the debate? How does the frame of the debate shape our wider understanding of contract, or of private law more generally? And most importantly, how does a historical narrative shape our conception of contract and our disputations over contract doctrine?

The debate over the incompleteness and implication plays an oblique role in a cultural conflict over the individual subject. While arguments within the debate do not flow as logical necessities from positions in the conflict over the nature of the individual, they are granted intelligibility by their association with such positions. Viewed as a whole, the debate may mean less to deciding disputes and influencing contracting behavior than to the extension of legal discourse into this cultural conflict. One reason for this is that the debate on a general level is unwinnable. Thus, it is the common formation of relevant questions that has real effects, rather than any debatable answer to those questions. This view allows us to query the kinds of interests served by the creation of a particular language regarding implication. But such speculations gain persuasive power only by means of extensive analysis of the debate.

For that reason, the chapters of this part proceed somewhat differently than the previous parts. Rather than beginning directly with an analysis of historical material, this chapter opens by examining the current debate over contractual incompleteness, with an eye toward the uses of history in that debate. The middle chapter of this part is concerned with exposing a recurrent flaw that reappears on both sides of the debate. The burden of the final chapter is to show that this flaw has significant effects on current contract thinking. In brief, the argument is as follows: The debate over incompleteness is premised on an historical narrative that claims that contract law moved, over the course of the twentieth century, from rigid, formalist, noninterventionism, toward flexible interventionism. The current debate revolves around the attempt to define the ideal level of interventionism, and thus relies on the assumption that nonintervention is not only possible, but an option exercised in recent history. Put bluntly, that historical narrative is wrong. Even at the height of the classical period—the period that is considered the model of rigid formalist adjudication—judges actively completed parties' incomplete contracts. They did so by applying standard common law modes of interpretation, and also, significantly, by employing the very paradigm of flexible intervention, the implied obligation of good faith and fair dealing. By analyzing a host of cases from around the turn of the century, Chapter 10 exposes the flaw in the underlying historical narrative on which the incompleteness debates are premised. This allows us to see the framework of debate for what it is—a series of repetitive rhetorical maneuvers that make the private ordering paradigm a taken-for-granted backdrop to the discussion of contract. By positing a golden age of contracting, in which a preexisting individual could expect that his contracts would be *enforced* but not *rewritten,* both sides of the debate over incompleteness encourage a limited view of contract law: a view that makes private ordering the legitimate core, and societal involvement a potential threat.

GRAPPLING WITH INCOMPLETE CONTRACTS: THEORY

It has become commonplace that almost all contracts are incomplete.[1] Increasingly over the past decade, scholars of contract have focused their energies intensely on questions of how courts should supply missing terms, and what those missing terms should be. In a moment of exaggeration, one commentator suggested that this was the only debate in contemporary contracts scholarship.[2] Countless contracts disputes are implicated in the struggle over how courts should determine the operative effect of the parties' language or silence, or the background rules that govern their relationship: all of these issues are aspects of the problem of incompleteness. Rather than embarking on another contribution to the literature on the problems of incompleteness, I intend to comment on the significance and effects of the debate itself. To that end, I begin by mapping the major attempts to deal with the problem in the scholarly literature. After the overview of the literature, the next part of the chapter goes on to explain the relationship of the various scholarly discussions of incompleteness to a particular instance of the problem, the implied covenant of good faith.

The intensity of the debate and the wide range of applications have resulted in a multiplicity of methods and terminologies for dealing with incompleteness. Traditionally, the issue was discussed under the headings of interpretation and construction, with much of the specific discussion classed under the topic of constructive conditions. As the century progressed, the term "gap-filling" was popularized, and there were important discussions of supplying omitted terms in contracts. I will discuss these traditional (and ongoing) contributions together.[3] Since the 1980s, a growing literature on

---

1. For the argument that virtually all contracts are incomplete, see Eyal Zamir, "The Inverted Hierarchy of Contract Interpretation," 97 *Colum. L. Rev.* 1710 (1997); Randy E. Barnett, "The Sound of Silence: Default Rules and Contractual Consent," 78 *Va. L. Rev.* 821 (1992); David Charny, "Hypothetical Bargains: The Normative Structure of Contract Interpretation," 89 *Mich. L. Rev.* 1815 (1991); Victor P. Goldberg, "Discretion in Long-Term Open Quantity Contracts: Reining in Good Faith," 35 *U.C. Davis L. Rev.* 319 (2002); Gillian K. Hadfield, "Problematic Relations: Franchising and the Law of Incomplete Contracts," 42 *Stan. L. Rev.* 927 (1990).

2. See Lawrence A. Cunningham, "Hermeneutics and Contract Default Rules: An Essay on Lieber and Corbin," 16 *Cardozo L. Rev.* 2225, 2225, n. 1 (1995).

3. The mainstream discussions of incompleteness do not have a commonly accepted theoretical label. If pressed to attach such a label, I would follow Ian Macneil in calling the theoretical underpinnings of this work "liberal pragmatism." See Ian R. Macneil, "Relational Contract Theory: Challenges and Queries," 94 *Nw. U. L. Rev.* 877, 882–83, esp. n. 28 (2000).

hypothetical bargains has made inroads to becoming the dominant terminology in discussing the problems traditionally addressed under interpretation and construction. Finally, over the past two decades, filling the gaps in incomplete contracts has increasingly been termed a problem of choosing default rules. While there are significant differences among these three discourses, as well as much overlap, a review of the literature is useful for understanding the scope of the current chapter.

Interpretation, Construction, Gap-Filling, Supplying Terms, Implied Terms

A naive conception of contract might hold that all contractual relations are a function of the parties' intentions, and those intentions only. While courts often give lip service to the idea that they will not make contracts for the parties, legal scholarship long ago abandoned the idea that contracts can never be enforced beyond the intentions of the parties.[4] The opening salvo in the critique of the naive conception emphasizes that unintended legal relations exist regardless of the conscious expectation of the parties, and thus that courts must inquire into those legal relations, as well as those actually intended by the parties.[5]

The basic insight that contractual relations include intended and unintended relations concentrates within it two themes: the first is a division of functions between interpretation on the one hand, and the determination of legal relations, or construction, on the other; the second is the scope of the factors that will impact on construction. Interpretation comprises an inquiry into actual intentions of the parties and an inquiry into the meaning of the words to a reasonable and disinterested third party, but only rarely are these two inquiries consciously distinguished by courts.[6] Whether objective or subjective, interpretation proper is confined to determining the meaning

4. "It is common form among judges to deny that they ever read into a contract or other document anything other than what, in their view, the parties actually intended; and occasionally they have even gone so far as to say that the implication must be collected from the words of the document itself. These statements cannot be taken seriously." Glanville Williams, "Language and the Law—IV," 61 *L.Q. Rev.* 384, 402–3 (1945). For admissions that intention alone cannot control by theorists who might prefer that it could, see Barnett, "The Sound of Silence," 822–23, 898–902; Charles Fried, *Contract as Promise* 60–61, 69, 73 (1981).

5. Arthur L. Corbin, "Conditions in the Law of Contract," 28 *Yale L.J.* 739, 740 (1919). The following paragraphs track Corbin's analysis of the distinction between intended and unintended legal relations and the implications of that distinction for legal doctrines of contract interpretation and construction.

6. Id. at 740–41. The implicated distinction between objective and subjective interpretation is of only

of the words used by the parties in reaching and framing an agreement. But interpretation is a limited endeavor when trying to determine the legal effects of the contract. Instead, the crucial work of the court is to determine the jural relations of the parties, a determination that depends not on the meaning of the words the parties used, but rather on "general rules of law even though they were unknown by the parties, to rules of fairness and morality, to the prevailing *mores* of the time and place."[7]

Beyond the acknowledgment that interpretation and construction often merge, the analysis underscores two issues: the first is the function of construction generally, which is to determine the overall legal effect of the contract.[8] The second issue is the source for that determination, and here the traditional view gives a confident but controversial answer. The source of obligations must be found not in the parties' intentions or in their agreement, but in "general rules of law," "rules of fairness and morality," and "the prevailing *mores*," all with an eye toward fulfilling the requirements of "the welfare of society."[9] The identification of the source of obligations is in part a function of the scope of the factors that affect construction: whereas some would have interpretation and construction concentrate solely on the allocation of duties at the time of formation of the contract, the traditional analysis embraces the view that facts occurring after acceptance may be crucial when a court determines the legal effects of the contract.

By claiming that the courts inevitably do their most important contracts work in construction, the distinction between interpretation and construction undermines the popular fiction that the terms of the contract are always and only products of the parties' intentions. The distinction, while still occasionally mentioned, has faded from judicial and scholarly usage.[10] The

---

marginal significance for this section of the chapter. For a detailed analysis, see generally Larry A. DiMatteo, *Contract Theory: The Evolution of Contractual Intent* (1998).

7. Corbin, "Conditions in the Law of Contract," 741.

8. For a more detailed statement of the merger between interpretation and construction, see 3 Arthur L. Corbin, *Corbin on Contracts: A Comprehensive Treatise on the Working Rules of Contract Law* 280 (1960): "As is stated at other points in this treatise, it is very often unnecessary for the court to distinguish between contract and quasi contract, between promise implied in fact and promise 'implied by law,' between interpretation and construction, in order to make a just decision. This is true, however, only when 'justice' requires the result reached in either case." For an overt judicial acknowledgment of such merging, see Martin v. Campanero, 156 F.2d 127, 130, n. 5 (2d Cir. 1946).

9. Corbin, "Conditions in the Law of Contract," 741.

10. See Cunningham, "Hermeneutics and Default Rules"; but see Charny, "Hypothetical Bargains," 1816. See also Williams v. Metzler, 132 F.3d 937, 946–48 (3d Cir. 1997).

functions of construction, even though sometimes distinguished from interpretation, are often discussed in the same breath, most importantly under the heading "gap-filling," which was favored by the realists and has become a standard term in discussing the Uniform Commercial Code, and supplementation or supplying terms.[11] Discussion of construction is described in the Restatement (Second) of Contracts under the heading of supplying omitted terms.[12]

Parallel to the discussion of construction or supplying terms, there is also a discussion of implied terms. The language of implied terms is predominantly a feature of English law, though there are many American applications and some American scholarly discussion.[13] While still the active nomenclature in English decisions and texts,[14] the attempt to distinguish true implication from imposition through rules of law is more than a half-century old.[15] By now, the acknowledgment that implied terms are often unrelated to the intentions of the parties is common in English treatments of the issue.[16]

---

11. For an example of how the terms *gap-filling* and *supplying* are used almost interchangeably and in close connection with interpretation, see Richard E. Speidel, "Restatement Second: Omitted Terms and Contract Method," 67 *Cornell L. Rev.* 785, 790–92, 803–5 (1982).

12. *Restatement (Second) of Contracts* § 204 reads: "When the parties to a bargain sufficiently defined to be a contract have not agreed with respect to a term which is essential to a determination of their rights and duties, a term which is reasonable in the circumstances is supplied by the court." A comment to the section attempts to clarify the distinction between interpreting and supplying terms. See *Restatement (Second) of Contracts* § 204 cmt. c (1981). For a discussion of this section, see generally Speidel, "Omitted Terms"; see also E. Allan Farnsworth, "Disputes over Omission in Contracts," 68 *Colum. L. Rev.* 860 (1968).

13. Applications are all over the case law, and in the UCC, where some of the most important "gap-fillers" are the provisions on "implied warranties." See *UCC* §§ 2-314 (implied warranty of merchantability); 2-315 (implied warranty of fitness for particular purpose). For an academic usage, see Charles J. Goetz and Robert E. Scott, "The Limits of Expanded Choice: An Analysis of the Interactions Between Express and Implied Contract Terms," 73 *Cal. L. Rev.* 261 (1985).

14. *Chitty on Contracts* §§ 13-001–13-010 at 619–26 (A. G. Guest ed., 27th ed. 1994).

15. In his series of articles on *Language and the Law*, Glanville Williams candidly explained that under the guise of implication, courts often imported terms into a contract regardless of whether the parties had considered them, or whether they were logically implied by the agreed upon terms. Such terms, Williams thought, "might better be called 'constructive' than 'implied,'" because they "are in fact merely rules of law that apply in the absence of an expression of contrary intent." Williams, "Language and the Law," 403–4. Like Corbin's exploitation of the distinction between construction and interpretation, Williams's critique was based on the idea that the terminology of implication served to obscure the judicial function of applying rules of law to determine the effects of contracts on the parties, even though the parties had never expressed any opinion regarding those rules. For an analogous critique of the language of implied terms on this side of the Atlantic, see Farnsworth, "Disputes over Omissions," 862 ("It would be a significant contribution to clarity of thought in this important area of contract law if courts would abandon the façade of the implied term and expose the process of inference that lies behind it"; id. at 879); see also 3 Corbin, *Corbin on Contracts*, 300.

16. See *Chitty on Contracts*, § 13-003, 619. See also Hanoch Sheinman, "Contractual Liability and Vol-

Stated at this level of generality, there is a staggering range of issues that could be viewed as problems of construction. Contracting parties often fail to foresee contingencies that arise during performance, and perhaps just as often avoid express negotiation (much less agreement) on issues that are foreseeable. Parties rarely elaborate on their obligations in the eventuality of breach, and while they sometimes agree to a particular mechanism of modification or adjustment of the relationship based on foreseeable contingencies, they rarely provide for the eventuality that performance in fact will deviate from those mechanisms. Mistake, frustration of purpose, impossibility, warranties, remedies, and a host of other contractual issues could conceivably be presented as subheadings of the problem of construction.[17] "Gap-filling," and "supplying an omitted essential term," carry connotations of completing an obvious lack, a term that is clearly needed, like the price in a contract with an open price term.[18] But more detailed discussions acknowledge that the issue extends into almost every area of contract law.[19]

For many theorists, the problem with construction or supplying omitted terms as a framework for solving problems of incompleteness is that they do not offer sufficient guidance, either for decision making or for predictions about decision making. When faced with a problem of construction in general, traditional proponents counsel reliance on fairness and justice.[20]

---

untary Undertakings," 20 *Oxford J. Legal Stud.* 205, 207–8 (2000) ("Contractual liability is liability for obligations the content of which is [to a large extent] superimposed, rather than voluntarily shaped. . . . The doctrine of implied terms points in the direction of a more realistic picture, in which much of the content of a contract may owe little to any agreement"). For an analogous argument regarding implying terms in the context of the requirements of good faith, which will be considered extensively below, see J. F. O'Connor, *Good Faith in English Law* 19 (1990).

17. One reason most of these issues are not considered problems of construction is that they have developed a specialized set of considerations or rationales, thus separating them from those issues of construction for which general grounds of fairness and justice are still thought to be the primary form of guidance in decision making. The commentary to the Restatement clarifies:

> This Section states a principle governing the legal effect of a binding agreement. The supplying of an omitted term is not technically interpretation, but the two are closely related; courts often speak of an "implied" term. In many common situations the principle has been elaborated in more detailed rules, applicable unless otherwise agreed. See the rules on the effect of failure of performance stated in §§ 231–49 and the rules on impossibility and frustration stated in Chapter 11, and compare §§ 158 and 272, regarding the supplying of terms in cases of mistake and impracticability or frustration.

Restatement (Second) of Contracts § 204 cmt. a (1981).

18. See *Restatement (Second) of Contracts* § 204 cmt. d (1981).

19. An instructive discussion is Zamir, "Inverted Hierarchy," which in the framework of incompleteness treats problems ranging from interpretation of contract language to waiver, to limitation of damages, to choice of remedies, to misrepresentation and undue influence and beyond.

20. See 8 Catherine M. A. McCauliff, *Corbin on Contracts* 127–28 (Joseph M. Perillo ed., rev. ed. 1999);

Modern theorists working within the mainstream framework have tried to supply additional guidance, usually relying on the concept of reasonability generally, or sometimes more specifically on reasonable expectations.[21] In some cases, scholars have tried to glean insight about supplying terms from particular commercial contexts,[22] or from detailed theoretical extrapolations regarding what the relevant aspects of context might be.[23]

Hypothetical Bargains and Default Rules Analysis

Many scholars have found the idea of filling contractual gaps by supplying terms that judges find just or fair normatively deficient and intellectually unsatisfying. One response to the problem has been hypothetical bargain theory. At its most capacious, hypothetical bargain theory sets out to achieve two goals: to establish a method for choosing particular gap-filling terms, and to offer a justification for both the method and the choices. The

---

Farnsworth, "Disputes over Omission in Contracts," 878–79. In addition to fairness, theorists who take construction seriously often single out specialized contracts for more specific guidance. Thus, they deal separately with, for instance, constructive conditions in the sale of land, the sale of goods, service contracts, charter parties, leases, and so on. See, e.g., 8 McCauliff, *Corbin on Contracts*, chaps. 33–35. See also Todd D. Rakoff, "The Implied Terms of Contracts: Of 'Default Rules' and 'Situation Sense,'" in *Good Faith and Fault in Contract Law* 191 (Jack Beatson and Daniel Friedmann eds., 1995).

21. See, e.g., Speidel, "Omitted Terms," 801–5; W. David Slawson, *Binding Promises* 44–73 (1996); W. David Slawson, "The New Meaning of Contract: The Transformation of Contracts Law by Standard Forms," 46 *U. Pitt. L. Rev.* 21 (1984); Michael I. Meyerson, "The Reunification of Contract Law: The Objective Theory of Consumer Form Contracts," 47 *U. Miami L. Rev.* 1263 (1993). For a critique of the use of reasonable expectations as a test for default rules, see Richard Craswell, "The Relational Move: Some Questions from Law and Economics," 3 *S. Cal. Interdisc. L.J.* 91, 111 (1993).

22. See, e.g., Robert A. Hillman, "Court Adjustment of Long-Term Contracts: An Analysis Under Modern Contract Law," 1987 *Duke L.J.* 1; Richard E. Speidel, "Court-Imposed Price Adjustments Under Long-Term Supply Contracts," 76 *Nw. U.L. Rev.* 369 (1981); John P. Dawson, "Judicial Revision of Frustrated Contracts: The United States," 64 *B.U. L. Rev.* 1 (1984); Ian R. Macneil, "Contracts: Adjustments of Long-Term Economic Relations Under Classical, Neoclassical, and Relational Contract Law," 72 *Nw. U. L. Rev.* 854 (1978); John E. Murray, Jr., "The Chaos of the 'Battle of the Forms': Solutions," 39 *Vand. L. Rev.* 1307 (1986); David V. Snyder, "The Law of Contract and the Concept of Change: Public and Private Attempts to Regulate Modification, Waiver and Estoppel," 1999 *Wis. L. Rev.* 607.

23. The most sustained effort to detail the relevant aspects of context is Ian Macneil's, suggesting up to ten behavioral patterns and norms to be considered, including role integrity; reciprocity; implementation of planning; effectuation of consent; flexibility; solidarity; creation and restraint of power; and harmonization with the social matrix. See Macneil, "Relational Contract Theory," 879–80; Ian R. Macneil, "The Many Futures of Contracts," 47 *S. Cal. L. Rev.* 691 (1974); Ian R. Macneil, *The New Social Contract* (1980); Ian R. Macneil, "Values in Contract: Internal and External," 78 *Nw. U. L. Rev.* 340 (1983). See also Robert W. Gordon, "Macaulay, Macneil, and the Discovery of Solidarity and Power in Contract Law," 1985 *Wis. L. Rev.* 565; Peter Linzer, "Uncontracts: Context, Contorts, and the Relational Approach," 1988 *Ann. Surv. Am. L.* 139.

methodology may be articulated at various levels of detail and sophistication, but the core idea is encapsulated in a simple formulation: "To interpret contracts, lawyers ask: what would the parties have agreed to had they explicitly adverted to the issue?"[24]

Thus, when faced with language whose application to a particular dispute is ambiguous, or with the more common problem of the parties' silence regarding a particular contingency, a court following the hypothetical bargain method should not impose its own vision of fairness under the circumstances, but rather should supply terms "to which the parties would have agreed ex ante. . . . If the contract is a scheme of rational cooperation for mutual advantage, then it should be completed by imagining the terms of a hypothetical rational agreement between them."[25]

Hypothetical bargain methodology has achieved wide popularity, even though it is less prevalent among contracts theorists than among scholars in other fields, ranging from corporate law, to bankruptcy, to trusts, criminal procedure, and family law.[26] The apparent advantage of the method is that it purports to give judges guidance in supplying terms, and in so doing, it aspires to limit the discretion of judges who would otherwise be forced to rely on ad hoc determinations of the requirements of justice. The first assumption of hypothetical bargain theory, then, is that parties would not

24. Charny, "Hypothetical Bargains," 1815–16. He continues: "That is, the interpreter constructs a 'hypothetical bargain': he determines how the parties would have bargained to treat the situation that has arisen had it been directly presented to them at the time they were forming the contract."

25. Jules L. Coleman, *Risks and Wrongs* 165 (1992). Coleman continues by explaining that gaps are a result of transaction costs, and then makes a succinct statement of the paradigm: "When transaction costs make an explicit agreement too costly ex ante, the court should apply a default or gap-filling rule that 'mimics' the outcome of a hypothetical contract between them. The hypothetical contract is the one the parties would have made had the transaction costs not made their doing so irrational."

26. The Restatement, here seen as a representative of mainstream contract scholarship, explicitly rejects the hypothetical bargain model: "Where there is in fact no agreement, the court should supply a term which comports with community standards of fairness and policy rather than analyze a hypothetical model of the bargaining process." *Restatement (Second) of Contracts* § 204 cmt. d (1981). For an analysis of the differences between using hypothetical bargain theory in contract and in other fields, see Ian Ayres, "Empire or Residue: Competing Visions of the Contractual Canon," 26 *Fla. St. U. L. Rev.* 897, 899–900 (1999). For use of the model in various fields, see, e.g., Frank H. Easterbrook and Daniel R. Fischel, *The Economic Structure of Corporate Law* 22, 34 (1991); Thomas A. Smith, "The Efficient Norm for Corporate Law: A Neotraditional Interpretation of Fiduciary Duty," 98 *Mich. L. Rev.* 214 (1999); Eric Talley, "Turning Servile Opportunities to Gold: A Strategic Analysis of the Corporate Opportunities Doctrine," 108 *Yale L.J.* 277 (1998); Milton C. Regan, Jr., "Spousal Privilege and the Meanings of Marriage," 81 *Va. L. Rev.* 2045 (1995); Elizabeth S. Scott and Robert E. Scott, "Marriage as Relational Contract," 84 *Va. L. Rev.* 1225 (1998); John H. Langbein, "The Contractarian Basis of the Law of Trusts," 105 *Yale L.J.* 625 (1995); Alan Schwartz, "A Contract Theory Approach to Business Bankruptcy," 107 *Yale L.J.* 1807 (1998).

bargain to accept judicial determination of fair or just solutions to problems that are not explicitly addressed in the contract language. In other words, they would not bargain in advance to accept the solution proposed by mainstream contract theory (construction or supplying terms). And the theoretical bite comes from focusing not on the totality of circumstances up to the time of the dispute, but rather on the preferences of the parties at the time of contract formation. For some scholars, the focus on the time of formation is an avenue to finding justificatory force for what otherwise would be considered the imposition of terms without the parties' consent.[27] At the same time, hypothetical bargain theory has come under sustained criticism regarding its methodology and justification.[28]

Much of the recent contracts scholarship on the problems of contractual incompleteness has been carried out under the heading of default rules analysis.[29] Default rules analysis begins from the same premises as gap-filling or construction. Contracting parties cannot foresee all possible contingencies, and rationally ignore certain contingencies because it would be costly to provide for them. Therefore, almost all contracts will be incomplete, and "it falls to public institutions—courts and legislatures—to create background, or 'default,' rules to govern private relationships when such unaddressed contingencies arise and private ordering, thus, has failed."[30]

Based on this articulation, it appears that the analysis of default rules is nearly identical to the analysis of gap-filling, supplying terms, or construc-

---

27. Disregarding for the moment some important refinements, this is the position adopted by a number of scholars who have focused on the justification for supplied terms based on some form of hypothetical bargains. See, e.g., Barnett, "Sound of Silence"; Randy E. Barnett, "Rational Bargaining Theory and Contract: Default Rules, Hypothetical Consent, the Duty to Disclose, and Fraud," 15 *Harv. J.L. and Pub. Pol'y* 783, 784–94 (1992); Coleman, *Risks and Wrongs*, 164–82.

28. See, e.g., Steven J. Burton, "Default Principles, Legitimacy, and the Authority of a Contract," 3 *S. Cal. Interdisc. L.J.* 115 (1993); Charny, "Hypothetical Bargains"; Juliet P. Kostritsky, "'Why Infer'? What the New Institutional Economics Has to Say About Law-Supplied Default Rules," 73 *Tul. L. Rev.* 497 (1998).

29. See, e.g., "Symposium, Default Rules, and Contractual Consent," 3 *S. Cal. Interdisc. L.J.* 1 (1993); Ian Ayres and Robert Gertner, "Majoritarian vs. Minoritarian Defaults," 51 *Stan. L. Rev.* 1591 (1999); Morten Hviid, "Default Rules and Equilibrium Selection of Contract Terms," 16 *Int'l Rev. L. and Econ.* 233 (1996); Alan Schwartz, "Relational Contracts in the Courts: An Analysis of Incomplete Agreements and Judicial Strategies," 21 *J. Legal Stud.* 271 (1992); Clayton P. Gillette, "Commercial Relationships and the Selection of Default Rules for Remote Risks," 19 *J. Legal Stud.* 535 (1990); Jason Scott Johnston, "Strategic Bargaining and the Economic Theory of Contract Default Rules," 100 *Yale L.J.* 615 (1990); Ian Ayres and Robert Gertner, "Filling Gaps in Incomplete Contracts: An Economic Theory of Default Rules," 99 *Yale L.J.* 87 (1989); Barnett, "Sound of Silence"; Kostritsky, "Why Infer?"

30. Russell Korobkin, "The Status Quo Bias and Contract Default Rules," 83 *Cornell L. Rev.* 609, 609–10 (1998).

tion generally. There are, however, a number of apparent distinctions. First of all, the founding documents of default rules analysis take pains to distinguish immutable or mandatory rules from default rules, that is, those rules that the parties can contract around by setting express terms that govern a particular contingency.[31] Thus, default rules are not necessarily binding on the parties, but they are binding if the parties have not replaced them with express terms.[32] While the same could be said for most court-supplied contract terms, the discussion of default rules serves to place renewed emphasis on the distinction between mandatory and mutable rules. Secondly, the debate has been dominated by a law and economics perspective. The two issues are related: the renewed emphasis on the distinction between mandatory and mutable terms has led some theorists to conclude that contract default rules are particularly apt for efficiency analysis, and in some cases, that efficiency is the only important concern to be addressed.[33]

---

31. See, e.g., Ayres and Gertner, "Economic Theory of Default Rules," 87:

> The legal rules of contracts and corporations can be divided into two distinct classes. The larger class consists of "default" rules that parties can contract around by prior agreement, while the smaller, but important, class consists of "immutable" rules that parties cannot change by contractual agreement. Default rules fill the gaps in incomplete contracts; they govern unless the parties contract around them. Immutable rules cannot be contracted around; they govern even if the parties attempt to contract around them.

See also Alan Schwartz, "The Default Rule Paradigm and the Limits of Contract Law," 3 *S. Cal. Interdisc. L.J.* 389, 389–92 (1993).

32. "What makes the default rule approach to gap-filling distinctive in both word processing and contract law is that default rules are binding in the absence of manifested assent to the contrary—which means that a manifested assent to the contrary will displace the default rule." Barnett, "Sound of Silence," 825.

33. The typical view suggests that where the parties can vary the terms, law-supplied rules that are inefficient will be futile. See *Foundations of Contract Law* 28–29 (Richard Craswell and Alan Schwartz eds., 1994). A number of methodological innovations have been introduced in the default rule literature. The most basic insight of economic analysis regarding default rules is based on transaction costs. In the absence of transaction costs and with perfect information, parties would contract efficiently. By allocating risk to the superior risk bearer or superior risk avoider, they would increase the gains from trade, in other words the gains from the transaction that they could then divide among themselves. Assuming that transaction costs were the main reason for contractual incompleteness, early efforts in economic analysis concluded that default rules that mimic efficient transactions, that is, those rules that mimic what most parties would have wanted, or their hypothetical bargain, would generate efficiency. The efficiency of such "majoritarian" defaults arises in two ways: first, such defaults reduce the number of inefficient contract terms, because if the parties fail to reach an efficient term on their own and remain silent regarding a particular contingency (because of transaction costs), the law will supply the efficient term; second, such terms minimize the transaction costs themselves, because they offer parties "off the rack" provisions that are efficient, so the parties need not incur the cost of drafting them. For explanations of these initial claims, see, e.g., Korobkin, "Status Quo Bias," 613–15; Ayres and Gertner, "Economic Theory of Default Rules," 92–93. For an early articulation of the model, see Richard A. Posner and Andrew M. Rosenfield, "Impossibility and Related Doctrines in Contract Law: An Economic

Summary

Current contracts scholarship has a number of different terminologies or discourses to deal with the problems raised by incomplete contracts. There is significant overlap among discussions of supplying terms, hypothetical bargains, and default rules. However, while none of these discourses presents a unified picture within itself, there are at least two sets of distinctions. The first distinction is one of method: scholars working in the supplying-terms discourse are, as a general matter, willing to consider events up to and including the time of the dispute when deciding how to resolve a matter of incompleteness; hypothetical bargain theorists and most default rules analysts are committed to determining the proper default rule on the basis of the situation between the parties ex ante, in other words, limiting themselves to the situation at the time of formation of the contract.[34] But there are also more subtle differences of method, related to the basic distinction between mutable and immutable rules. For default rules analysts, this distinction animates the entire project, because it is the mutability of the rules that allows the efficiency analysis to proceed.[35] Hypothetical bargain theory and the discourse of supplying terms both have a more nuanced vision of the distinction, noting that the problems of incompleteness often

---

Analysis," 6 *J. Legal Stud.* 83 (1977). Recent economic analyses have proposed additional refinements, and highlighted additional reasons why parties might not reach efficient solutions on their own, and the difficulties of formulating default rules that necessarily generate efficient results. See, e.g., Ian Ayres and Robert Gertner, "Strategic Contractual Inefficiency and the Optimal Choice of Legal Rules," 101 *Yale L.J.* 729 (1991); Barry E. Adler, "The Questionable Ascent of *Hadley v. Baxendale*," 51 *Stan. L. Rev.* 1547 (1999); Ayres and Gertner, "Majoritarian vs. Minoritarian Defaults"; Schwartz, "Default Rule Paradigm." Noneconomists have also made several significant contributions to the default rules literature, often in dialogue with economists. See, e.g., Burton, "Default Principles"; Coleman, *Risk and Wrongs*; Barnett, "Sound of Silence."

34. One speculation on the reasons for such differences in orientation runs thus: Scholars interested in supplying terms share a common law adjudication focus. When presented with a dispute arising from an incomplete contract, they are drawn to evaluating the reasons for resolving the concrete dispute in a particular way, and thus are drawn to the context from which the dispute arises. Default rules analysts, on the other hand, and especially the economists among them, are interested primarily in the incentive effects of rules. The focus is actually on the legislative effects of the rules, even if they are laid down in the context of an adjudicated dispute.

35. This is a necessary corollary to the oft-stated idea that the contracting parties know their interests best: if some centralized figure could know in advance without consulting the parties what transactions were efficient, it would be possible to organize the economy without need for private ordering. The efficiency of private ordering rests on the assumption that there can be no such centralized knowledge (or at least that attaining such knowledge is deeply problematic), and therefore the parties' choices are the basis for the efficiency of transactions. See Michael J. Trebilcock, *The Limits of Freedom of Contract* 7–8 (1993).

hinge on the interplay of compulsory and suppletive terms, and as such, it is often difficult and possibly unnecessary to decide whether a term is mutable or immutable.[36]

The second set of distinctions lies in the realm of justification. For scholars working in the tradition of supplying terms, the issue of justification for court-supplied terms is almost a nonissue. Based on the work of the legal realists, mainstream contracts scholarship has come to see the completion of the incomplete contract in dispute as an inevitability: courts have, throughout the modern period, completed contracts by implication or by supplying terms, and to do so without a view to justice and fairness would be absurd. Whether influenced by a Mansfieldian or Llewellynesque sense that contract adjudication should mirror commercial practice, or by a realist-inspired view of contract as public law, these scholars come close to taking for granted the necessity of completing incomplete contracts when such disputes reach adjudication. The fact that contracts are routinely completed by courts, on this view, has implications for understanding contract and "private" law, but judicial discretion of this sort does not entail problems of legitimacy. In part, such a view rests on a forthright admission that once a dispute reaches adjudication, supplying a term or refusing to supply one rests on the same footing in terms of justification. At the stage of adjudication, there is no option not to decide. Default rules analysis and hypothetical bargain theory, on the other hand, have both been engaged in periodic assessments and reassessments of the legitimacy of their framework for dealing with incompleteness. Grounding principles for some theorists have ranged from consent, to game-theoretic accounts of rationality, and to a Rawlsian account of fairness and coordination, but the overwhelmingly most popular justificatory principle is efficiency, with the refinements of what constitutes efficiency growing more delicate over time.

---

36. For instance, corporate law hypothetical bargain discussions often focus on the content of fiduciary duties. Rarely is it denied that fiduciary duties are compulsory, and yet parties can tailor their relationships such that the content of these duties shifts significantly. On the blurred distinction between compulsory and mutable terms, see Zamir, "Inverted Hierarchy," 1735–48. A contribution in what seems to be a similar direction from within the economic analysis of default rules is Korobkin, "Status Quo Bias." In contract discourse, a similar dynamic plays itself out regarding the duty of good faith, which is often considered nondisclaimable, and yet which allows for almost unlimited tailoring of obligations and discretions.

OF INCOMPLETE CONTRACTS AND THE DUTY OF GOOD FAITH IN CONTRACT PERFORMANCE: APPLIED THEORY

Most observers readily admit that the duty of good faith is one of the central mechanisms in American contract law for coming to terms with incomplete contracts. At the same time, the doctrine has an ambiguous status in the various discourses whose central aim is dealing with incompleteness. At least two factors combine to generate this ambiguity. First of all, there is a lack of clarity over whether good faith is a compulsory or suppletive (or default) term. Second, there is disagreement, or possibly confusion, over the role of good faith vis-à-vis contractual freedom. I take these up in turn.

The central documents that are considered authoritative statements of American contract law treat good faith as an immutable term, announcing that every contract *imposes* an obligation of good faith in its performance or enforcement.[37] But the picture is more complicated. While the obligation of good faith may not be disclaimed, the parties may tailor their agreement to such an extent that they will agree in advance on what will be considered good faith and what will not, or at least on what the standards for deciding will be.[38] The rule seems immutable externally (contracting parties cannot expunge the obligation of good faith entirely), but mutable internally (they can decide what it will include, and probably limit its content with respect to a particular contingency to the vanishing point).[39] One commentator summed up the ambiguity: "The precise interaction of the duty of good faith with express contract language thus remains an important jurisprudential mystery."[40] Of course, this type of mystery does not pose the same kind of problem for every theorist. Some default rules analysts appear to consider the label of immutability enough to preclude analysis of the obligation; on the other hand, scholars working on supplying terms have made good faith into a major focus for dealing with problems of incompleteness. This ambiguity is perhaps enough to suggest that a clear distinction between mutable

---

37. *Restatement (Second) of Contracts* § 205 (1981); *UCC* § 1-203 (1990).

38. *UCC* § 1-102(3) (1990).

39. "It is possible to so draw a contract as to leave decisions absolutely to the uncontrolled discretion of one of the parties and in such a case the issue of good faith is irrelevant." MacDougald Construction Co. v. State Highway Department, 188 S.E.2d 405, 407 (Ga. App. 1972).

40. Michael P. Van Alstine, "Of Textualism, Party Autonomy, and Good Faith," 40 *Wm. and Mary L. Rev.* 1223, 1227 (1999).

and immutable terms does not accurately reflect the workings of particular rules or provisions.

Closely related to the question of whether good faith is compulsory or suppletive is the wider question of the relationship of the duty of good faith to the idea of contractual freedom. There is often a tendency to conflate the requirements of good faith in contract performance with straightforwardly paternalistic terms, especially unconscionability. This conflation is in part the result of the multiple uses of the term *good faith*, making a clarification worthwhile. *Good faith* is a notoriously slippery term. As the reporter of the Restatement noted, "the phrase 'good faith' is used in a variety of contexts, and its meaning varies somewhat with the context."[41] Considering the intensity of academic debate over the subject, the comment's admission that meaning "varies somewhat" is an understatement.[42] Rather than offering another definition, then, I concentrate here on clarifying the function of good faith in the performance context.

The conceptual distinction at stake in understanding the function of good faith is the difference between policing the market and policing the performance or behavior of the parties in carrying out their contract. There are occasional conceptualizations of good faith that link it to policing the market generally. Such conceptualizations perceive that arrangements reached by individual parties may be so unfair that they are unworthy of enforcement. The reason usually given for the existence of such contracts, or more specifically, for the presence of such terms within contracts that are otherwise unobjectionable, is an imbalance in the parties' bargaining position at the outset of the relationship.[43] At least in the context of American contracts discourse, however, the problems of policing the market are more accurately assessed under the rubric of unconscionability.[44]

---

41. *Restatement (Second) of Contracts* § 205 cmt. a (1981).

42. Regarding the proliferation of meanings of good faith, Professor Farnsworth has commented, "Indeed, it can almost be said that there are as many definitions of good faith as there are purported experts in the field." E. Allan Farnsworth, "The Concept of Good Faith in American Law," in 10 *Saggi, conferenze e seminari* 1, 3 (Centro di studi e ricerche di diritto comparato e straniero ed., 1993); and elsewhere: "The Americans have, or so it might seem, too many meanings of good faith." "Good Faith in Contract Performance," in *Good Faith and Fault*, 153, 161.

43. For example, this is the model of good faith that animates the European Community's Council Directive on Unfair Terms in Consumer Contracts (Council Directive 93/13/EEC), Art. 3(1): "A contractual term which has not been individually negotiated shall be regarded as unfair if, contrary to the requirement of good faith, it causes a significant imbalance in the parties' rights and obligations arising under the contract, to the detriment of the consumer."

44. See *UCC* § 2-302(1). See also James J. White and Robert S. Summers, *Uniform Commercial Code*

To use good faith to police the performance of the contract, on the other hand, is to perceive good faith as an instrument for implementing the parties' agreement, rather than to overturn some aspect of it. According to this conception of good faith, the doctrine is "a compact reference to an implied undertaking not to take opportunistic advantage in a way that could not have been contemplated at the time of drafting, and which therefore was not resolved explicitly by the parties."[45] In other words, good faith is a doctrinal mechanism with which judges can complete incomplete contracts. Good faith, on this reading, is an interpretive doctrine used to determine the content of the parties' obligations according to the agreement, especially in situations where the explicit terms of the contract have provided one party with discretion in performance.[46] When the terms of the contract are indefinite,[47] when performance requires cooperation,[48] when one party has the power to accept or reject the performance on the basis of its satisfaction, or in similar situations where the explicit terms of the contract do not clearly determine what is required of the parties, good faith is one part of a judicial arsenal that supplies standards of performance. Other parts of that arsenal include the rules of interpretation of the contract language itself, statutory provisions or case law on construction or gap-filling, or default terms, the course of dealing and course of performance, custom, and usage.[49] Frequently, rather than use the appellation good faith, judges speak of implying terms.[50] But the combined effect of the various parts of the

---

133–35 (4th ed. 1995); Todd D. Rakoff, "Contracts of Adhesion: An Essay in Reconstruction," 96 *Harv. L. Rev.* 1173 (1983). For an argument that policing the market, and in particular the relative power of market agents, is an active consideration beyond the doctrine of unconscionability, see Daniel D. Barnhizer, "Inequality of Bargaining Power," 76 *U. Colo. L. Rev.* 139 (2005).

45. Kham and Nate's Shoes No. 2, Inc., v. First Bank of Whiting, 908 F.2d 1351, 1357 (7th Cir. 1990).

46. For the distinction between good faith and unconscionability, see Steven J. Burton and Eric G. Andersen, *Contractual Good Faith* 50–51 (1995). On the misuse of contractual discretion, see Steven J. Burton, "Breach of Contract and the Common Law Duty to Perform in Good Faith," 94 *Harv. L. Rev.* 369 (1980).

47. E.g., contracts with open price or quantity terms; see *UCC* § 2-311(1) (1990).

48. E.g., contracts where brokers are responsible for procuring clients, where the ultimate seller has to go through with the sale in order to entitle the broker to a commission; see Republic Group, Inc., v. Won-Door Corp., 883 P.2d 285 (Utah App. 1994); Cantrell-Waind and Associates, Inc., v. Guillaume Motorsports, Inc., 968 S.W.2d 72 (Ark. App. 1998); Cauff, Lippman, and Co. v. Apogee Finance Group, Inc., 807 F. Supp. 1007 (S.D.N.Y. 1992).

49. See Robert S. Summers, "'Good Faith' in General Contract Law and the Sales Provisions of the Uniform Commercial Code," 54 *Va. L. Rev.* 195, 233 (1968).

50. See E. Allen Farnsworth, "Good Faith Performance and Commercial Reasonableness Under the Uniform Commercial Code," 30 *U. Chi. L. Rev.* 666, 672 (1963).

arsenal is to evaluate the parties' behavior according to standards of fairness, efficiency, reasonableness, and decency, and to fill in gaps in the agreement according to those norms.

When good faith is discussed in the context of policing the market, the primary concern is prevention of the abuse of the power to dictate contract terms. Therefore, the standard looks to the formation of the contract, and to whether the circumstances surrounding it warrant enforcing the agreement. Technically, these uses of a standard of good faith are closely linked to the doctrines of fraud, duress, undue influence, and unconscionability. Policing performance, on the other hand, looks to good faith as a substantive standard, a measure of content, and a way to monitor behavior in performance; thus, it refers predominantly to a tool of construction or gap-filling through which courts enforce a particular version of the bargain reached by the parties. That particular version is one that allows the inclusion of norms of reasonability and the avoidance of arbitrariness or caprice, but it does not generally set out to reallocate the market power of the parties. Rather, it is an attempt to uphold the court's understanding of how reasonable parties would behave under the circumstances, preventing opportunistic advantage taking or sharp practice during the performance of the contract.[51] Stating the distinction in this way serves two functions. First, it clarifies the differences among various uses of the terminology of good faith, which are too often confused.[52] Second, it groups uses of the term under two relatively

51. The distinction between policing the market and policing behavior could be stated at various levels of generality. One possible distinction would be between standards of validity and standards of substantive content of obligations. Another, much discussed opposition centers on the question of whether "honesty" is a sufficient standard. But upon closer examination, honesty is usually only appropriate to contexts of formation, and inappropriate as a standard of behavior, where it is difficult to imagine what honesty might mean as a standard of performance. Consider the following typical scenarios where good faith claims have been entertained: (a) an employer terminates a relationship with an at-will employee in order to avoid paying commissions; (b) a supplier who has discretion to accept or reject the clients solicited by its distributor rejects a major client, and then makes the sale directly to avoid paying the distributor its fees; (c) a borrower agrees to return a loan upon the sale of a piece of property, but then does nothing to sell the property. In all these situations, honesty simply is not a category that is helpful in determining whether the obligations of the contract have been fulfilled. Good faith beyond honesty offers courts a loosely related set of norms by which to evaluate contractual performance, most importantly reasonableness, but also fairness, fidelity to the purpose of the contract or the spirit of the deal, lack of caprice or arbitrariness, sometimes even cooperation. Scholarship on good faith has been nearly uniform in criticizing honesty as a standard of performance. See Farnsworth, "Good Faith Performance," 672. See also Summers, "'Good Faith' in General Contract Law," 206; Burton, "Breach of Contract."

52. The argument has been forwarded that such a confusion was responsible for the UCC's adoption of "honesty in fact" as the general definition of good faith for the Code. See Farnsworth, "Good Faith Performance," 673.

stable categories, each of which represents a different set of concerns. Distinguishing those concerns should clarify to some extent the connection between the doctrines that lawmakers resort to and the goals they are trying to achieve.

THE POLARIZED DEBATE OVER GOOD FAITH

The debates over good faith as a mechanism for completion of incomplete contracts are polarized. At times, the polarization comes through in overtly ideological terms; at other times, it remains couched in technical or doctrinal discussions that mediate ideological polarization. Interestingly, the schism over incompleteness is not the exclusive province of legal scholarship: increasingly over recent decades, there is a developing polarization in adjudication as well.

Recent writing on the obligation of good faith in contracts evinces a tendency toward polarization. At one pole of the spectrum, we find the argument that contract law threatens to be overrun by "vague community standards" that bring contract to the point of "implied fiduciary liability."[53] This view asserts that good faith jurisprudence is emblematic of a trend in contract law of expanding duties beyond written agreements; that the rise of relational duties of good faith in contract is not an isolated doctrinal development, but rather represents a position on a "road from individualism to sharing";[54] and finally, that the trend undermines the meaning of contract and the function of law more generally. The opposite view is a mirror image of the first, arguing that the obligation of good faith has been constricted to the point where it hardly serves as a significant source of obligation, exhibiting a retrenchment from an earlier trend toward expanding the obligations flowing from good faith.[55] This view sees the retrenchment as entailing "profoundly conservative political dimensions."[56]

The endpoints of the polarized spectrum may overstate or oversimplify the ideological stakes of the debate over the implications of the doctrine

---

53. Douglas K. Newell, "Will Kindness Kill Contract?" 24 *Hofstra L. Rev.* 455, 455–56 (1995).

54. Id. at 456.

55. Ralph James Mooney, "The New Conceptualism in Contract Law," 74 *Or. L. Rev.* 1131, 1133 (1995); Emily M. S. Houh, "The Doctrine of Good Faith in Contract Law: A (Nearly) Empty Vessel?" 2005 *Utah L. Rev.* 1.

56. Mooney, "New Conceptualism," 1135, 1186–87.

of good faith in contract, but they are not alone in legal academia in attributing direct ideological significance to shifts in the usage of good faith. Charles Fried, for example, sets out to refute an entire genealogy of critique of promise-based contract law that relies on altruism as a competing morality for contractual relations. According to Fried, the proposed connection between the concept of good faith and altruism is "subversive of individualism" in denying individualism a "contractual refuge."[57] Fried attempts to answer this line of critique by developing a conception of good faith that requires "not loyalty to some undefined relationship but only loyalty to the promise itself—the faithful carrying out of the mutual promises that the parties, having come to understand their *separate* purposes, chose to exchange."[58] Critique of Fried's position on good faith has often been formulated in overtly ideological terms.[59]

More widespread than the directly ideological polarization over gap-filling through good faith discussed above is the doctrinal polarization of the debate. Most academic discussions of good faith steer clear of direct treatment of the ideological implications of its use. This does not prevent polarization, however, over the direct normative questions of how good faith should be employed in filling gaps. At opposing ends of the spectrum are positions that mirror the views on incompleteness more generally. At one end of the spectrum, then, is the position that good faith is a mechanism for dealing with incompleteness on the basis of an encompassing view of the parties' relationship and community standards of fairness and reasonableness. The position includes two controversial elements: first, that gap-filling through good faith should take into account all the circumstances leading up to the dispute, including circumstances occurring after formation of the contract that the parties did not foresee, or for some other reason chose to leave indefinitely determined at the time of formation; second, that the standard for filling the gap should be based on ideas of justice, reasonableness, and fairness, rather than on a search for the putative intentions of the parties.

57. See Fried, *Contract as Promise*, 76–77.

58. Id. at 88. The relationship between this concept of loyalty to the promise and the other aspects of gap-filling remain unclear. On the one hand, Fried acknowledges that gap-filling requires resort to nonpromissory principles such as sharing and altruism (even to the extent that contractual partners have some obligation to share unexpected benefits and losses of the relationship); on the other hand, he seems to assume that the function of gap-filling, which is not necessarily tied to the promise principle, is somehow qualitatively different from the use of good faith, which is. See id. at 69–73, 85–91.

59. See Macneil, "Values in Contract," 390–97; Anthony T. Kronman, "A New Champion for the Will Theory," 91 *Yale L.J.* 404 (1981).

The other end of the spectrum is occupied by scholars concerned primarily with ensuring that good faith does not undermine the allocation of risks undertaken by the parties through the express terms of their contract, where the contract is understood as the agreement as it stood at the time of formation. This concern takes several forms. For some scholars, it leads to a focus on making sure that good faith does not undermine the explicit terms of the agreement; for others, it leads to the more extreme conclusion that good faith should be purged from most contexts of gap-filling. Illustrations from the ends of the spectrum and various positions in between abound.[60]

Proponents of a context-dependent reading of good faith assert the propriety and necessity of looking beyond the written or express terms of an agreement in order to gauge the parties' obligations. Thus, whether writing on general matters of contract interpretation or gap-filling, or analyzing a variety of specific transactional contexts, scholars with varying theoretical predilections have argued that the application of good faith should be based on a wide-ranging inquiry as to the relationship of the parties, including circumstances and changes occurring after formation of the contract. The substantive standards by which to apply good faith, according to the contextualist pole, range from general conceptions of fairness, reasonable expectations, or contractual morality,[61] to incorporation of "relational norms,"[62] to some form of efficiency criterion.[63] Other scholars, meanwhile, have argued

60. One of the transactional contexts that has generated intense debate over good faith is what has become known as lender liability. In response to widespread litigation of good faith claims of debtors against lenders, there has been an outpouring of academic literature on the topic, including calls for the abolishment of the doctrine of good faith. For a representative sample of the lender-liability good faith debate, see, e.g., Dennis M. Patterson, *Good Faith and Lender Liability* (1990); Mark Snyderman, "Comment, What's So Good About Good Faith? The Good Faith Performance Obligation in Commercial Lending," 55 *U. Chi. L. Rev.* 1335 (1988); Loeb Granoff, "Emerging Theories of Lender Liability: Flawed Applications of Old Concepts," in *Lender Liability: Definitions, Theories, Applications* 119 (Dennis M. Patterson ed., 1990); Robert D. Wilson and William H. Lawrence, "Good Faith in Calling Demand Notes and in Refusing to Extend Additional Financing," 63 *Ind. L.J.* 825 (1987); Janine S. Hiller, "Good Faith Lending," 26 *Am. Bus. L.J.* 783 (1989); A. Brooke Overby, "Bondage, Domination, and the Art of the Deal: An Assessment of Judicial Strategies in Lender Liability Good Faith Litigation," 61 *Fordham L. Rev.* 963 (1993); Barbara A. Fure, "Contracts as Literature: A Hermeneutic Approach to the Implied Duty of Good Faith and Fair Dealing in Commercial Loan Agreements," 31 *Duq. L. Rev.* 729 (1993); Dennis M. Patterson, "A Fable from the Seventh Circuit: Frank Easterbrook on Good Faith," 76 *Iowa L. Rev.* 503 (1991); Glenn D. West and Michael P. Haggerty, "The 'Demandable' Note and the Obligation of Good Faith," 21 *U.C.C. L.J.* 99 (1988).

61. See Robert S. Summers, "The General Duty of Good Faith: Its Recognition and Conceptualization," 67 *Cornell L. Rev.* 810, 826 (1982).

62. See, e.g., Hadfield, "Problematic Relations," 984–86; Linzer, "Uncontracts," 68–89.

63. See Mark P. Gergen, "The Uses of Open Terms in Contract," 92 *Colum. L. Rev.* 997, 1064–81 (1992);

for the importance of limiting good faith to effectuating the intentions or expectations of the parties at the time of formation. Thus, scholars writing with an economic perspective have advanced such a position by claiming that a broader contextual analysis, while also generating uncertainty, would have the especially destructive effect of undermining presumptively efficient risk-allocations undertaken by the parties at the time of formation.[64] Non-economists in this camp have justified a focus on formation by asserting that overriding the parties' expressions of intent at formation by imposing a court's view of fairness would be an impingement on party autonomy.[65]

Polarization on questions of good faith is not the sole province of legal academia. Courts are also deeply divided on questions of whether and how to apply a standard of good faith to contract disputes. Many courts have at least paid lip service to the proposition that every contract contains an "implied covenant of good faith,"[66] or more simply imposes a duty of good faith and fair dealing in performance and enforcement of the contract.[67] But the application of the duty of good faith has varied widely among jurisdictions and transactional contexts. Thus, many courts have ruled that the implied covenant of good faith applies to most contracts, but does not apply in certain critical contexts, particularly employment and lender-borrower contracts.[68] Other courts have flipped the presumption, saying that while good faith might apply in certain specialized contexts that entail special relationships of trust, there is no general obligation of good faith.[69] Perhaps the clearest rhetorical evidence of polarization is the contrast between "matter of fact" approaches to good faith and approaches that view good faith as a deep threat to established tenets of contract law. For example, one of the most widely cited cases on the obligation of good faith portrayed good faith

---

Charles J. Goetz and Robert E. Scott, "Principles of Relational Contracts," 67 *Va. L. Rev.* 1089 (1981); Charles J. Goetz and Robert E. Scott, "The Mitigation Principle: Toward a General Theory of Contractual Obligation," 69 *Va. L. Rev.* 967 (1983); Hadfield, "Problematic Relations"; Gillian K. Hadfield, "Judicial Competence and the Interpretation of Incomplete Contracts," 23 *J. Legal Stud.* 159 (1994).

64. See Gillette, "Commercial Relationships." For a variation on this theme, see Goldberg, "Reining in Good Faith"; Alan Schwartz and Robert E. Scott, "Contract Theory and the Limits of Contract Law," 113 *Yale L.J.* 541 (2003).

65. See Fried, *Contract as Promise*, 72–73, 86–88.

66. See Burton, "Breach of Contract," 369, 404.

67. See *Restatement (Second) of Contracts* § 205 (1981).

68. See, e.g., Kastner v. Blue Cross and Blue Shield of Kansas, Inc., 894 P.2d 909, 919 (Kans. App. 1995); see also Westwood-Booth v. Davy-Loewy, Ltd., 1999 WL 219897 (E.D. Pa. April 13, 1999).

69. See, e.g., Guzman v. El Paso Natural Gas Co., 756 F. Supp. 994 (W.D. Tex. 1990).

as "simply a rechristening of fundamental principles of contract law."[70] On the other hand, one state supreme court called the implied covenant of good faith a novel theory contrary to the adversary system, and sounded a general alarm: "The novel concept [of the implied covenant of good faith] advocated by the courts below would abolish our system of government according to settled rules of law and let each case be decided upon what might seem 'fair and in good faith' by each fact finder. This we are unwilling to do."[71]

At nearly every turn, a student of the subject would be struck how wide the spectrum of judicial positions on particular issues of good-faith performance actually is. Even among courts that nominally accept the application of a duty of good faith, there is wide variation. For any given area where good faith has become an important issue in litigation, there are cases supporting an expansive interpretation of good faith alongside cases that deny the application of good faith to the problem altogether, alongside a third position, nominally accepting a role for good faith but in fact narrowly constricting the effects of the doctrine.

In the employment context, for instance, many courts have found the duty of good faith applicable to wrongful dismissal claims, and plaintiffs have been successful in pursuing claims against employers who dismissed them in bad faith.[72] On the other hand, other courts have ruled that the duty of good faith does not apply to employment contracts, either because at-will employment is not contractual and therefore there is no obligation to which the duty may be applied,[73] or because even though contractual, the relationship is not amenable to a duty of good faith.[74]

---

70. Tymshare Inc. v. Covell, 727 F.2d 1145, 1152 (D.C. Cir. 1984) (Scalia, J.). See also Market Street Associates Ltd. v. Frey, 941 F.2d 588, 595 (7th Cir. 1991) (Posner, J.) ("The contractual duty of good faith is thus not some newfangled bit of welfare-state paternalism . . . and we are therefore not surprised to find the essentials of the modern doctrine well established in nineteenth-century cases") (citations omitted).

71. English v. Fischer, 660 S.W.2d 521, 522 (Tex. 1983). For critiques of this position, see the concurring opinion by Spears, J., id., at 524–25, and especially the dissent of Kilgarlin, J., id. at 525–528.

72. See, e.g., Koepping v. Tri-County Met. Trans. Dist. of Or., 119 F.3d (10th Cir. 1997); Atwood v. Western Construction, Inc., 923 P.2d 479 (Idaho App. 1996); Maddaloni v. Western Mass. Bus Lines, Inc., 422 N.E.2d 1379 (Mass. App. 1981); Magnan v. Anaconda Industries, Inc., 429 A.2d 492 (Conn. Super. 1980); K-Mart Corp. v. Ponsock, 732 P.2d 1364 (Nev. 1987); Fortune v. National Cash Register Co., 364 N.E.2d 1251 (Mass. 1977); Monge v. Beebe Rubber Co., 316 A.2d 549 (N.H. 1974); Foley v. Interactive Data Corp., 765 P.2d 373 (Cal. 1988). See also 2 E. Allen Farnsworth, *Farnsworth on Contracts* §§ 7.17–7.17a, at 359–71 (2d ed. 1998).

73. See Dodgens v. Kent Manufacturing Co., 955 F. Supp. 560 (D.S.C. 1997).

74. See, e.g., McIlravy v. Kerr McGee Corp., 119 F.3d 876 (10th Cir. 1997); Nunez v. A-T Financial Information, Inc., 957 F. Supp. 438 (S.D.N.Y. 1997); *Kastner v. Blue Cross and Blue Shield of Kansas*; Murphy v. American Home Products Corp., 58 N.Y.2d 293 (1983); *Guzman v. El Paso Natural Gas*; Lawhorn

The most important development in the judicial treatment of good faith is more subtle than a statement that good faith does not apply to the dispute. Instead, a more delicate undermining of good faith may be seen in cases where courts declare that the doctrine applies, but their mode of application has the result of minimizing or eliminating any practical effect of the duty. One way of doing this is by declaring that while there is a duty of good faith in all contracts, good faith will not trump explicit terms, and then reading an express term that grants discretion as an absolute grant of unfettered discretion.[75] Courts dealing with assignment clauses in leases (and often in combined dealership-lease agreements) often run up against the problem of a clause requiring that assignment gain the consent of the lessor. Granting consent to an assignment is a typical case of a discretionary power, and the prevention of an arbitrary or unreasonable refusal to allow assignment seems like a perfect situation in which to use the duty of good faith.[76] However, many courts faced with such situations have ruled good faith has little to contribute to the analysis.[77]

---

and Associates, Inc. v. Patriot General Insurance Co., 917 F. Supp. 539 (E.D. Tenn. 1996). For surveys of the conflicting decisions on good faith in the employment context, see Monique C. Lillard, "Fifty Jurisdictions in Search of a Standard: The Covenant of Good Faith and Fair Dealing in the Employment Context," 57 *Mo. L. Rev.* 1233 (1992). See also Burton and Andersen, *Contractual Good Faith*, 91–95.

75. See, e.g., United Airlines, Inc. v. Good Taste, Inc., 982 P.2d 1259, 1263 (Alaska 1999); Metro Communications Co. v. Ameritech Mobile Communications, Inc., 984 F.3d 739 (6th Cir. 1993); Acetylene Gas Co. v. Oliver, 939 S.W.2d 404 (Mo. App. 1996); Flight Concepts LP v. Boeing Co., 38 F.3d 1152 (10th Cir. 1994); Goodyear Tire and Rubber Co. v. Whiteman Tire, Inc., 935 P.2d 628 (Wash. App. 1997). See also Van Alstine, "Of Textualism," 1260–65.

76. See, e.g., Elliot v. Staron, 735 A.2d 902 (Conn. Sup. Ct. 1997) aff'd, 736 A.2d 196 (Conn. App. Ct. 1999); Kendall v. Ernest Pestana, Inc., 709 P.2d 837 (Cal. 1985); see also *Restatement (Second) Property* § 15.2(2) (landlord's consent to alienation cannot be withheld unreasonably, unless the lease includes an absolute right to withhold consent). For a critique of this position, see Alex M. Johnson, Jr., "Correctly Interpreting Long-Term Leases Pursuant to Modern Contract Law: Toward a Theory of Relational Leases," 74 *Va. L. Rev.* 751 (1988). The use of good faith to limit discretion is the theme of Burton and Andersen's analysis. See Burton and Andersen, *Contractual Good Faith.*

77. For example, in Johnson v. Yousoofian, 930 P.2d 921 (Wash. App. 1996), plaintiffs ran a deli on defendant's property, and made an agreement to sell. The lease had a provision by which assignment could only be made with the consent of the lessor, and the lessor withheld consent in order to pressure plaintiffs to give in regarding a separate dispute they had over costs for remodeling on the property. Plaintiffs were victorious in the dispute over remodeling, but the delay resulted in their selling the deli on less favorable terms. Rejecting their claim that the defendant had abused his discretion in withholding consent to the assignment, the court held that good faith only applied to specific contract obligations, and that the lease did not impose an obligation to consent. Thus, the court agreed, ostensibly, that the obligation of good faith applies to every contract; but by a sleight of hand, it made the obligation completely meaningless. See also James v. Whirlpool Corp., 806 F. Supp. 835 (E.D. Mo. 1992); Pacific First Bank v. New Morgan Park Corp., 876 P.2d 761 (Or. 1994); Delta Air Lines, Inc., v. Norris, 949 S.W.2d 422 (Tex. App. 1997); *Goodyear Tire and Rubber Co. v. Whiteman Tire;* Stern v. Great Western

One recent decision in this vein merits examination here because of the process by which the court reached its conclusions. In *Taylor Equipment, Inc., v. John Deere Co.*, a jury awarded damages to a dealer upon finding that the manufacturer had violated the duty of good faith by arbitrarily withholding consent to assign the dealership.[78] The trial court had excluded evidence of the dealer's prior breach of the contract, and of the prospective buyer's subsequent financial difficulties, which tended to show that the manufacturer's withholding of consent was based on reasonable business judgment. On appeal, the eighth circuit court held that the evidentiary rulings would have been enough to warrant reversal of the judgment, but it went on to analyze the holding on good faith, concluding that only a limited duty of honesty would apply, and more generally that good faith would not limit or temper an express term granting discretion to the manufacturer. As pointed out by the dissent, the analysis overstates the court's position, and is colored throughout by the fact that the court believes that on the facts, the manufacturer acted completely reasonably. In fact, in response to the dealer's earlier breach, the manufacturer had not simply terminated the agreement as it was entitled to do, but offered to allow the dealer to sell to an approved buyer. On the court's view of the facts, the party who had behaved decently was being charged with a breach of good faith, and this led to a backlash and significant narrowing of the duty. In this and other cases, courts are faced with something of a challenge when they find a claim of breach of good faith to be unworthy. The difficult road is to explain why they see the facts the way they do (always a tricky business for courts); sometimes, perhaps unfortunately, the easier way seems to be to tailor the legal duty narrowly so as to limit its application.

Lender liability is another transactional context that has become rife with good faith litigation. Some jurisdictions have elected to bypass the problem so far as possible, by holding that the duty of good faith simply does not apply to lender-borrower relationships.[79] But elsewhere, borrowers have used claims based on good faith with some success. Much of the discussion

---

Bank, 959 F. Supp. 478 (N.D. Ill. 1997); *Westwood-Booth v. Davy-Loewy*; Pasha Auto Warehousing, Inc., v. Philadelphia Regional Port Authority, 1998 WL 633692 (E.D. Pa. Aug. 17, 1998); Alan's of Atlanta, Inc., v. Minolta Corp., 903 F.2d 1414 (11th Cir. 1990).

78. 98 F.3d 1028 (8th Cir. 1996).

79. See *Westwood-Booth v. Davy-Loewy*; Temp-Way Corp. v. Continental Bank, 139 B.R. 299 (E.D. Pa. 1992); Chrysler Credit Corp. v. B.J.M., Jr., Inc., 834 F. Supp. 813 (E.D. Pa. 1993). "So far as possible" because some lender-borrower cases are governed by the UCC, which mandates a good faith standard.

has centered around the celebrated case of *K.M.C. Co., Inc., v. Irving Trust Co.*,[80] where the sixth circuit court held that the duty of good faith required that the lender give reasonable notice before refusing to advance credit under an existing credit line, so as to allow the borrower a reasonable opportunity to seek alternative financing.[81] But cases with the opposite holding, often explicitly rejecting the reasoning in *K.M.C. v. Irving Trust*, have been numerous.[82] Given the fact that good faith is primarily a doctrine policing behavior within the contract, and not a doctrine that upsets market ordering, perhaps the most intriguing element of the lender liability cases is the extent to which good faith strikes courts as dangerous.[83]

The intensity of the debate over good faith may be read as a symptom that the stakes in the debate extend beyond the technicalities of contract interpretation. In the following chapter, I concentrate on the historical backdrop to the debate, in an attempt to show how the doctrinal history of good faith opens up an understanding of those stakes.

---

80. 757 F.2d 752 (6th Cir. 1985).

81. See also Reid v. Key Bank of S. Me., Inc., 821 F.2d 9 (1st Cir. 1987); In re Martin Specialty Vehicles, Inc., 87 B.R. 752 (D. Mass. 1988).

82. See, e.g., Needham v. The Provident Bank, 675 N.E.2d 514 (Ohio App. 1996); *Kham and Nate's Shoes No. 2, Inc., v. First Bank of Whiting*; Bennco Liquidating Co. v. Ameritrust Co. Natl. Assn., 621 N.E.2d 760 (Ohio App. 1993); Solar Motors, Inc., v. First National Bank of Chadron, 537 N.W.2d 527, (Neb. App. 1995); Flagship National Bank v. Gray Distribution Systems, Inc., 485 So.2d 1336 (Fla. App. 1986); Spencer Companies, Inc., v. Chase Manhattan Bank, N.A., 81 B.R. 194 (D. Mass. 1987); Government Street Lumber Co., Inc., v. AmSouth Bank, N.A., 553 So.2d 68 (Ala. 1989); National Westminster Bank, U.S.A. v. Ross, 130 B.R. 656 (S.D.N.Y. 1991); Centerre Bank of Kansas City v. Distributors, Inc., 705 S.W.2d 42 (Mo. Ct. App. 1985).

83. An example from a recent case shows that this sense of danger is visible even in decisions that ultimately recognize the possibility of relief on the basis of good faith. In Travel Services Network, Inc., v. Presidential Financial Corp. of Mass., 959 F. Supp. 135 (D. Conn. 1997), plaintiffs acquired and operated travel agencies, and contracted with defendant for a line of credit to acquire another agency. When defendants reneged on verbal assurances that they would not cut off credit, and eventually denied funding altogether, the deal fell through and plaintiffs claimed damages on the basis of a breach of good faith. The court denied defendants summary judgment, saying that false assurances, if proved, would be a violation of good faith. At the same time, the court went out of its way to analyze the holding in *K.M.C. v. Irving Trust* and to rule, first, that the case was distinguishable on its facts, and second, that Massachusetts courts would read the ruling narrowly if they were to adopt it at all. For additional cases limiting the effects of the doctrine of good faith even while nominally accepting its application to the case, see United States National Bank v. Boge, 814 P.2d 1082 (Or. 1991); Tolbert v. First National Bank, 823 P.2d 965 (Or. 1991); *Pacific First Bank v. New Morgan Park Corp.*; Uptown Heights Associates v. Seafirst Corp., 891 P.2d 639 (Or. 1995). See also James A. Webster, "Comment, A Pound of Flesh: The Oregon Supreme Court Virtually Eliminates the Duty to Perform and Enforce Contracts in Good Faith," 75 *Or. L. Rev.* 493, 525–55 (1996).

TEN

The Use and Abuse of Historical Narrative

Debates over Incomplete Contracts

THE COMMON HISTORICAL NARRATIVE

Given the polarization in the debates over incompleteness, it may be somewhat surprising that both poles in the debates rely on a common historical narrative as part of the justification for their positions. In fact, however, each side takes a common descriptive narrative and uses it to generate opposing normative conclusions. In a nutshell, the common description goes as follows: Up until the Great Depression, American contract law was highly formal and individualistic, characterized by a wide latitude of freedom of contract and extreme contracting power. Since then, we have seen a progressive socialization of contract law, characterized by wide-scale intervention into contract relations, both by legislative initiative and through the judiciary.[1] This concerted intervention, the story goes, has aimed at neutralizing

---

1. As an influential source put it: "The most striking feature of nineteenth century contract theory is the narrow scope of social duty which it implicitly assumed. In our own century we have witnessed what it does not seem too fanciful to describe as a socialization of our theory of contract." Friedrich Kessler and Grant Gilmore, *Contracts: Cases and Materials* 1118 (2d ed. 1970).

the excessive bargaining power of large concentrations of wealth, and its effects can be seen primarily in consumer protection and the empowering of organized labor.

It bears emphasis that this description is not primarily associated with legal historians. Significantly, however, this description forms one of the underlying messages typically presented to first-year law students in a basic course on contracts.[2] In addition, there is a widespread reliance on this general narrative by contract scholars writing, in one way or another, about incompleteness of contracts. For example, in a recent book, David Slawson argues that twentieth-century reforms have combined to increase consumers' bargaining power vis-à-vis producers and insurers.[3] He opens his account with a historical description:

> The courts of England and the United States had completed the law of what we now call "classical contract" by the beginning of the twentieth century. Contract law remained in its classical state until late in the twentieth century, when the courts of the United States began the reforms that are the subject of this book.
>
> Classical contract had three distinguishing characteristics: nearly unlimited freedom of contract, nearly unlimited contracting power, and a clear separation from tort. . . . These characteristics enabled people to make the contracts they chose, practically without limitation as to kind or extent.[4]

The passage encapsulates two propositions often taken for granted as historical background in discussions of contractual incompleteness: the first is that the beginning of the twentieth century was a period of classical contract,[5] where contract law accorded with the theoretical accounts of contract of classical scholars; the second is that classical law did not provide for judicial gap-filling along the lines of modern contract law, but rather accorded explicit agreement of the parties complete deference. Another recent

---

2. See, e.g., Friedrich Kessler, Grant Gilmore, and Anthony T. Kronman, *Contracts: Cases and Materials* 1–17 (3d ed. 1986); Charles L. Knapp, Nathan M. Crystal, and Harry G. Prince, *Problems in Contract Law: Cases and Materials* 595 (4th ed. 1999).

3. See generally W. David Slawson, *Binding Promises* (1996). Slawson identifies the reforms as "reasonable expectations," "relational torts," "bad faith breach," and "remedies reform." All of these are in some measure answers to the problems of incompleteness or default rules.

4. Id. at 3. This theme is expanded throughout the book. For instance: "Courts have created duties for parties to certain relationships since time immemorial, but they did not generally create them for contractual relationships until about 1960." Id. at 74.

5. "Freedom of contract reached its zenith in the United States in the so-called Lochner era, when courts constitutionalized it. The era lasted from about 1890 to 1920." Id. at 13.

account claims that the most important feature of twentieth-century contract law has been the judicial reformation of contract through the implication of terms, alongside statutory intervention to ensure fairness.[6]

The historical description comports with a popular conception that twentieth-century developments in contract law have witnessed a decline in the importance of assent. In other words, it relies on a conception of contract history that posits that up until well into the century, explicit consent was the lynchpin of contractual obligation, and that contracts were enforced only on the basis of explicitly specified intent at the time of contract formation.[7] The reliance on this historical narrative is varied, and often implicit. For many theorists, it is an almost unstated basis for the discussion of incompleteness, and it is often mentioned in passing, nearly taken for granted.[8] The historical description is sometimes proposed in general terms (i.e., contract law used to be formalist), and sometimes in more specific terms (i.e., contract interpretation used to rely on strict application of the plain-meaning rule and the parol-evidence rule).

Significantly, the historical description mentioned here is not limited to theorists who try to portray the shift in contract law as progressive. Even scholars whose account is ostensibly ahistorical, notably economic analysts of the law, rely at times on the same narrative.[9] Recent discussions of commercial law particularly, at varying levels of explicitness, have relied on ver-

---

6. Larry A. DiMatteo, "Equity's Modification of Contract: An Analysis of the Twentieth Century's Equitable Reformation of Contract Law," 33 *New Eng. L. Rev.* 267 (1999).

7. For a brief account of classical law along these lines, see K. M. Sharma, "From 'Sanctity' to 'Fairness': An Uneasy Transition in the Law of Contracts?" 18 *N.Y.L. Sch. J. Int'l and Comp. L.* 95, 106–10 (1999).

8. See, e.g., Randy E. Barnett, "The Sound of Silence: Default Rules and Contractual Consent," 78 *Va. L. Rev.* 821, 822 (1992).

9. For an explicit use of the historical narrative, see Charles J. Goetz and Robert E. Scott, "The Limits of Expanded Choice: An Analysis of the Interactions Between Express and Implied Contract Terms," 73 *Calif. L. Rev.* 261, 273 (1985):

> Until recently, the state had a relatively restrained role in developing contractual formulations. The traditional common law interpretive approach . . . focused intensively on the written agreement. . . . The common law rules thus strained mightily to avoid confronting many of the sources of formulation error just described, relying on the maxim "the courts do not make a contract for the parties." . . . Pressure mounted steadily to imply informal understandings and usages into contracts. The dam, which had begun to leak earlier in the twentieth century, finally burst with the adoption of the Uniform Commercial Code, the triumph of a dramatically changed, activist approach that has come to permeate other aspects of contract law as well.

Id. at 273–74. See also Eric A. Posner, "The Decline of Formality in Contract Law," in *The Fall and Rise of Freedom of Contract* 61 (F. H. Buckley ed., 1999); Victor P. Goldberg, "Discretion in Long-Term Open Quantity Contracts: Reining in Good Faith," 35 *U.C. Davis L. Rev.* 319 (2002).

sions of the same narrative. The key feature in these discussions is the claim that commercial law had a formalist basis until the adoption of the Uniform Commercial Code, which is seen as a radical departure from prior commercial law.[10] Similarly, there is a widespread consensus that the obligation of good faith in the performance of contracts is a relatively recent addition to contract doctrine.

The shared historical description of the state of contract law is the foundation upon which contract scholars have conducted a long-running argument over the desirability of what has traditionally been considered state intervention into contractual relations.[11] In its simplest terms, the argument is about

---

10. David Charny opened his comment on the new formalism with a concise description of the shared background assumptions:

> Over the past century, contract and commercial law have been prime sites for the debate about formalism in law. Two stages are familiar. In the formalist moment of classical legal thought, lawyers aspired to deduce the vast edifice of contractual rules from an essentialist understanding of the nature of promise and consent. Even details of performance and remedy, such as the perfect tender rule or the preference for expectation damages, were thought to be derivable from the essential nature of promissory obligation.
>
> Equally familiar, the modernist or progressive phase of twentieth century American legal thought—epitomized by figures like Holmes, Corbin, and Llewellyn—rejected the classical aspiration to formality and dismantled ruthlessly the deductive system that the classicists had constructed. The critique drew its impetus from two complementary postulates. First, "abstract rules do not decide concrete cases." The claim to deduce outcomes from an austere set of formal rules, grounded in an essentialist conception of promissory consent, was a fake. Second, contract and commercial law should instead seek guidance from the concrete, everyday perceptions and understandings of the transactors, "men of affairs" whose innate or inarticulate understanding of commercial needs guided practice and should provide the basis for the rules coercively imposed by the law. At the limit, the law would simply adopt or embody what these men of the world understood, instinctively, to be their transactional obligations. Most notably incorporated into the Uniform Commercial Code, this view also provided a foundation for the "relational" approach to contract.

David Charny, "The New Formalism in Contract," 66 *U. Chi. L. Rev.* 842, 842 (1999) (footnote omitted). For additional recent work on commercial law relying on the same narrative, see, e.g., Robert E. Scott, "The Case for Formalism in Relational Contract," 94 *Nw. U. L. Rev.* 847 (2000); Lisa Bernstein, "The Questionable Empirical Basis of Article 2's Incorporation Strategy: A Preliminary Study," 66 *U. Chi. L. Rev.* 710 (1999); Omri Ben-Shahar, "The Tentative Case Against Flexibility in Commercial Law," 66 *U. Chi. L. Rev.* 781 (1999); Dennis M. Patterson, *Good Faith and Lender Liability* 11–45 (1990). For an early version of the argument that the code was a radical departure from classical or formalist positions on interpretation and gap-filling, see Eugene F. Mooney, "Old Kontract Principles and Karl's New Kode: An Essay on the Jurisprudence of Our New Commercial Law," 11 *Vill. L. Rev.* 213 (1966).

11. The traditional view has been that contract law is facilitative insofar as it respects the right of the parties to make law between themselves. On this view, the state intervenes only at the margins of contract, to ensure that only contracts that actually represent the parties' consent are enforced, for instance by prohibiting fraud and duress. Early in the twentieth century there was an effort by some scholars to undermine this characterization, and to point out instead that all contract enforcement, whether its sources were regulatory-statutory or traditional common law doctrines, was equally interventionist, and thus that contract law was actually a branch of public law. See, e.g., Morris R. Cohen, "The Basis of Contract," 41 *Harv. L. Rev.* 553 (1933); Robert L. Hale, "Coercion and Distribution in a Supposedly

how to interpret the socialization of contract law. On one side of the argument is the position, for convenience characterized here as the "right" pole, that claims that such socialization is misguided and that current contract doctrine should revert to a model that more closely approximates classical law. On the other side, the "left" argues that the socialization of contract was and remains a necessary result of changed economic conditions.

The argument merits fleshing out in several particulars. The right pole in the argument comprises an uneasy coalition of autonomy theorists on the one hand, and devotees of the economic analysis of the law on the other. While their methods and ultimate goals diverge, autonomy and efficiency theorists often converge in their conclusions regarding the proper judicial handling of contractual incompleteness. The most detailed elaboration of autonomy theory on incompleteness is Randy Barnett's theory of default rules.[12] Barnett argues that courts should enforce "conventionalist" default rules, consent to which could be traced to the moment of formation of the contract. When default rules conform as closely as possible to the subjective agreement of the parties, when they are sufficiently knowable in advance, and when there is a reasonable opportunity to opt out of a particular default rule, the basis for using conventional defaults is the same as the basis for contractual enforcement generally: consent. Barnett expends a great deal of theoretical energy distinguishing among the various things that contractual parties could conceivably consent to at the time of formation. The focus on formation allows him to limit the creation of obligation to a given point at which parties agreed to relinquish entitlements they held prior to entering the contract.[13] Taken at face

---

Non-coercive State," 38 *Pol. Sci. Q.* 470 (1923). While this countervision of the role of contract in private law remains important, its proponents did not succeed in supplanting the dominant idea that intervention into contract was a marginal activity.

12. See Barnett, "Sound of Silence"; Randy E. Barnett, "Rational Bargaining Theory and Contract: Default Rules, Hypothetical Consent, the Duty to Disclose, and Fraud," 15 *Harv. J.L. and Pub. Pol'y* 783, 784–94 (1992); Randy E. Barnett, "Conflicting Visions: A Critique of Ian Macneil's Relational Theory of Contract," 78 *Va. L. Rev.* 1175 (1992).

13. To be fair to Barnett, his theory is very flexible. Thus, if the conventional understanding of defaults includes the idea that gaps will be filled by a court according to what it finds to be reasonable and fair when considering all the circumstances up to the time of the dispute (as the Restatement suggests), then such a default rule would still accord with consent theory, and would take into account events after the time of formation. To return to a critical view, however, such a situation would obviate the role of consent in just the way the legal realist view of gap-filling suggested, which is the problem Barnett set out to combat. For a more rigid version of claim arising from a focus on entitlement theory, see Peter Benson, "The Unity of Contract Law," in *The Theory of Contract Law: New Essays* 118 (Peter

value, Barnett's theory highlights the role of consent at formation in order to elevate the role of consent as the marker of party autonomy.[14] In turn, the focus on formation (whether phrased in terms of consent or promise) is meant to be an antidote to the realist or contextual view that courts (must) impose duties that the parties never had in mind. In this, Fried and Barnett and, more recently, Peter Benson set out to save a view of contract associated with classical contract law that privileges the parties' lawmaking power and minimizes the extent to which contract (necessarily) involves state imposition of obligations.

Commercial law scholars on what I have termed the right have been even clearer about their reliance on the historical narrative of the socialization of contract law. Recent influential work by Lisa Bernstein and by Robert Scott has developed a common theme, and expanded on it with empirical research. The common theme is that UCC-inspired contextualism, or incorporation of relational norms, is inappropriate for adjudication of disputes arising from incompleteness. Scott sums up the theme in a recent article by claiming that in a complex economy, it is difficult for courts to supply efficient default terms. He thus recommends a "rigorous application of the common-law plain meaning and parol evidence rules," and concludes that "a formalist approach to interpretation would advance the standardization norm by expanding the established menu of legally blessed standard-form terms and clauses."[15]

Claims like Bernstein's and Scott's show that even the most sophisticated current contract theory makes use of the narrative of the socialization of contract in its justifications. Reduced to its simplest form, the claim is that up until the adoption of the Uniform Commercial Code, commercial law adjudication was formalistic and closely tracked the parties' express agree-

---

Benson ed., 2001); Peter Benson, "The Idea of a Public Basis of Justification for Contract," 33 *Osgoode Hall L.J.* 273 (1995).

14. Charles Fried's theory of gap-filling offers a similar perspective, though he is willing to supplement the promise principle, which represents autonomy, with other principles including reliance and sharing, in situations where true gaps in the agreement signal that the agreement has run out. See Charles Fried, *Contract as Promise* 71–73 (1981). For critiques of autonomy theories as they apply to default rules, see David Charny, "Hypothetical Bargains: The Normative Structure of Contract Interpretation," 89 *Mich. L. Rev.* 1815, 1825–35 (1991); Richard Craswell, "Contract Law, Default Rules, and the Philosophy of Promising," 88 *Mich. L. Rev.* 489 (1989).

15. Scott, "Case for Formalism," 866; Robert E. Scott, "The Uniformity Norm in Commercial Law: A Comparative Analysis of Common Law and Code Methodologies," in *The Jurisprudential Foundations of Corporate and Commercial Law* 149 (Jody S. Kraus and Steven D. Walt eds., 2000).

ment. The code instituted contextual interpretation and construction in search of the parties' agreement in fact, including the relational norms built up during performance. But the code's contextualism has failed, and the proper task for the courts is to *return* to formalistic adjudication.

Commercial law neoformalism, or anti-antiformalism, is only the latest version of the critique of contextual gap-filling.[16] But the novelty of recent anti-antiformalism lies in the empirical basis and the nuance of its claims. The main thrust of the claims, however, has been familiar for some time. And scholars on the right have supported limitation of the role of courts in gap-filling in similar terms over many contexts. These scholars justify the limitation of courts' roles by saying that an extensive judicial role in this capacity: (a) diminishes the law's traditional respect for individual autonomy; (b) increases transactions costs and thus reduces the overall gains from trade; and (c) creates regressive distributional effects.[17] Thus, on the right, the arguments against contextual construction of contract parties' duties stem from a normative evaluation of the historical narrative that paints the developments either as a decline from some more noble standard, or as a well-meaning but failed attempt to achieve goals that could not be addressed in contract law.

Scholars on the left, in contrast, tend to portray the same historical description as a progressive story. Classical contract, on this view, may have been appropriate for an individualistic economy in the nineteenth century, but the large-scale concentration of wealth and power in the twentieth century make it inappropriate for current economic conditions, under which a classical law of contract would perpetuate inequality. An early and influential articulation of the position was Friedrich Kessler's essay "Contracts of Adhesion." Kessler argued that the development of large-scale enterprise with mass production and distribution made standardized contracts inevitable, and that under a regime of standardization, "the individuality of the parties which so frequently gave color to the old type contract has disappeared."[18]

---

16. See Charny, "New Formalism," 842.

17. For a paradigmatic example of such an argument that brings up each of these elements in turn, complete with a resort to a backward-looking respect for a traditional rule in the face of attempts to incorporate relational norms, see Richard A. Epstein, "In Defense of the Contract at Will," 51 *U. Chi. L. Rev.* 947 (1984). For additional work making use of some or all of the elements, see Alan Schwartz, "Relational Contracts in the Courts: An Analysis of Incomplete Agreements and Judicial Strategies," 21 *J. Legal Stud.* 271 (1992).

18. Friedrich Kessler, "Contracts of Adhesion: Some Thoughts About Freedom of Contract," 43 *Colum. L. Rev.* 629, 631 (1943).

The vision of the consent of the parties creating law in a decentralized process animated classical theories of contract, but the vision was undermined by concentrated power, especially the power to dictate standardized terms. Kessler critiques the "individualism of our rules of contract law" by claiming that they are based on a vision of an economy of small enterprise, a vision that does little to describe American reality at mid-century. Noting that contemporary capitalism has an innate trend toward monopoly, Kessler warns that the existence of freedom of contract does nothing to ensure that all members of society will enjoy that freedom: "On the contrary, the law, by protecting the unequal distribution of property, does nothing to prevent freedom of contract from becoming a one-sided privilege. Society, by proclaiming freedom of contract, guarantees that it will not interfere with the exercise of power by contract."[19]

A similar justification for contextual interpretation or construction undergirds much of mainstream contract theory. The same historical narrative is often used both in justifying mandatory protections, such as unconscionability, and in justifying contextualist modes of dealing with incompleteness.[20]

Significantly, while there are points of divergence, there are also points of overlap regarding the values that the left and the right attempt to justify in their differing normative assessments of the common historical description. Thus, on the one hand, scholars associated with the left sometimes claim that contextualist approaches to gap-filling rest primarily on the value of fairness or sharing.[21] On the other hand, some scholars on the left

---

19. Id. at 640. At first glance, it may appear that Kessler's discussion is geared generally toward questions of policing the market, and not toward contractual incompleteness. In fact, however, his concrete examples, taken from insurance cases, are as much about implication, constructive conditions, and the interpretation of silence, as about any overarching legislative market intervention. See id. at 637–38. Kessler's essay has the virtue and the defect of not distinguishing sharply between policing the market and policing party behavior within the bargain. The defect is that the lack of distinction leaves crucial questions of institutional role unaddressed. The more important virtue, however, is that the combined treatment exposes the ideological connection (which Kessler refers to as emotional) between the two issues. One key passage reads: "Technical doctrines of the law of contracts cannot possibly provide the courts with the right answers. . . . All the technical doctrines resorted to by the courts in the insurance cases denying liability are in the last analysis but rationalizations of the court's emotional desire to preserve freedom of contract." Id. at 639.

20. For an extended example of overt reliance on this narrative to justify contract supplementation according to reasonable expectations as well as legislative action, see Slawson, *Binding Promises.*

21. See, e.g., Walter F. Pratt, Jr., "American Contract Law at the Turn of the Century," 39 *S.C. L. Rev.* 415, 461–62 (1988):

> The courts had come to realize that the essence of the new contractual practices was sharing. . . . The

have argued that contextual gap-filling is a better way to serve the values of autonomy or efficiency. One context for this argument is standardized agreements, where consent to the terms of the agreement is largely fictive, and reliance on the parties' reasonable expectations from the agreement seems the better vehicle toward realizing autonomy.[22] In addition, scholars have sometimes claimed that realizing autonomy may be a justification for an expanded conceptualization of good faith.[23] And several scholars have argued that contextual gap-filling in relational settings would be a way to achieve efficient outcomes.[24] The distinctive feature in these analyses, whatever values they emphasize, is the familiar argument: classical contract law is inappropriate to modern economic conditions because it cannot adequately come to terms with the two most important characteristics of the market: large-scale inequalities and the complexity of relationships. The palliative prescribed for these faults is contextual treatment of incompleteness.[25]

> typical relationship between the contracting parties was no longer a discrete transaction based on a particular performance, promised for an assured future. Instead, the parties left open a term in the agreement, binding themselves to move together into the uncertain future. . . .
>
> The close ties between the parties prompted the realization that the relationship between them was akin to one of sharing. Thereafter, courts were able to view parties to the new contracts as being more like partners or co-adventurers than like atomistic elements of a larger economy.

See also Peter Linzer, "Uncontracts: Context, Contorts and the Relational Approach," 1988 *Ann. Surv. Am. L.* 139; K. M. Sharma, "From 'Sanctity' to 'Fairness': An Uneasy Transition in the Law of Contracts?" 18 *N.Y.L. Sch. J. Int'l and Comp. L.* 95, 106–10 (1999).

22. See, e.g., Kessler, "Contracts of Adhesion"; Slawson, *Binding Promises.* This theme is also recurrent in the work of Richard Speidel, both in the context of standardized agreements and regarding relational exchanges, where the parties' actual expectation includes adjustments over the course of long-term contractual performance. See, e.g., Richard E. Speidel, "Afterword: The Shifting Domain of Contract," 90 *Nw. L. Rev.* 254, 260–61 (1995); Richard E. Speidel, "Contract Theory and Securities Arbitration: Whither Consent?" 62 *Brook. L. Rev.* 1335 (1996).

23. See Richard E. Speidel, "The Characteristics and Challenges of Relational Contracts," 94 *Nw. L. Rev.* 823, 846 (2000); Michael P. Van Alstine, "Of Textualism, Party Autonomy, and Good Faith," 40 *Wm. and Mary L. Rev.* 1223, 1227 (1999).

24. See Mark P. Gergen, "In Defense of Judicial Reconstruction of Contracts," 71 *Ind. L.J.* 45 (1995).

25. Not everyone on the left makes use of the common narrative. There are at least two crucial exceptions. Critical legal scholars, especially Duncan Kennedy, have argued for contextualist interventionist contract adjudication without relying on the common narrative. See, e.g., Duncan Kennedy, "Form and Substance in Private Law Adjudication," 89 *Harv. L. Rev.* 1685 (1976); Duncan Kennedy, "Distributive and Paternalist Motives in Contract and Tort Law, with Special Reference to Compulsory Terms and Unequal Bargaining Power," 41 *Md. L. Rev.* 563 (1982); Roberto Unger, *The Critical Legal Studies Movement* (1986). The second exception is Ian Macneil. Macneil's relational theory rejects the classical vision of contract, not because of changing historical conditions, but because classical theory was never a plausible account of contracting in fact. See, e.g., Ian R. Macneil, *The New Social Contract* (1980); Ian R. Macneil, "The Many Futures of Contracts," 47 *S. Cal. L. Rev.* 691 (1974).

RETHINKING THE HISTORICAL BACKGROUND

The common historical narrative is based on three interrelated ideas on varying levels. The most general (but least seriously propounded) idea is that prior to its twentieth-century socialization, contract law was characterized by unlimited freedom of contract that fit into a system of laissez-faire. The second idea is that the reigning conception of contract was one of private lawmaking. Contract as private lawmaking entails that the parties are sole authors of their own obligations, which are created out of whole cloth at the moment of the formation of contract. The third idea, seemingly flowing from the second, is that courts engaged in narrow or formalistic interpretation and construction, refusing to import relational norms like reasonableness or good faith to fill gaps in incomplete contracts. All three of these ideas are flawed, and I treat them in turn.

Unlimited Freedom of Contract

Simply put, late nineteenth-century law was not characterized by unlimited freedom of contract or by laissez-faire. I do not expect this to be a controversial claim, and accordingly I will give it short shrift here. The idea that it was characterized by unlimited freedom of contract seems to be part of a hard-dying heuristic, even though few people who have devoted much attention to the nineteenth century actually believe it anymore.[26] To the extent that the image of the late nineteenth century as a period of unlimited freedom of contract holds sway, it is the product of an overemphasis on labor contracts and the constitutionalization of freedom of contract in that context. However, as Charles McCurdy has shown, legislatures promulgated much interventionist regulation around the turn of the century, and courts typically rejected challenges to regulation, even when its effects were redistributive. The exception to courts' deference to regulative action was the labor contract, where many legislative attempts (and the attempts were numerous) to offset labor's weak bargaining position were overturned as unconstitutional.[27] The focus on cases like *Lochner v. New York* and *Coppage v. Kansas* often obscures the fact that regulation of many basic contract issues

---

26. For a detailed exposition, see generally William J. Novak, *The People's Welfare: Law and Regulation in Nineteenth-Century America* (1996).

27. See Charles W. McCurdy, "The 'Liberty of Contract' Regime," in *The State and Freedom of Contract* 161, 165–67 (Harry N. Scheiber ed., 1998).

was widespread, and whole industries were heavily regulated before the end of the nineteenth century.[28]

Legislative intrusion into contractual relations was extensive, especially in regulating businesses whose contracts had "community-wide" effects, such as "contracts between utility company and customer, insurer and insured and railroad and farmer. By the 1880s there was a real gulf between the accepted abstraction of laissez-faire theory and actual state regulation of public utilities, labor relations, insurance, banking, health and social welfare."[29] In fact, widespread regulation was a fundamental part of the American economy throughout the nineteenth century, though it probably intensified after 1870. As William Novak points out, "In theory, the nineteenth century market was 'free.' In practice, it was 'well-ordered' and 'well-regulated.' The legal and local regulation of economic life in early America was pervasive."[30]

It is possible that laissez-faire is compatible with a wide range of different rules within contract doctrine, but the characterization of the late nineteenth century as a time of laissez-faire or of extreme freedom of contract is strained, at best. It is easy to compose a short list of obvious infringements on freedom of contract. Legislatively or administratively prescribed prices for gas and electricity services, grain elevators, and railroads, legislatively imposed contracts in insurance and banking, and legislative and judicial limitations if not prohibitions on the types of "speculation" central to the economy can hardly be reconciled with extreme freedom of contract. Com-

---

28. Lochner v. New York, 198 U.S. 45 (1905); Coppage v. Kansas, 236 U.S. 1 (1915).

29. Kevin M. Teeven, *A History of the Anglo-American Common Law of Contract* 296 (1990).

30. Novak, *The People's Welfare*, 112. Novak is not alone in noting the range of regulation—the ubiquity of regulation in nineteenth-century America has been a theme for legal historians:

> We ought not overlook the considerable vigor and strong continuity of the regulatory tradition. Constitutional decisions upholding regulatory powers of the state, such as Munn v. Illinois in 1877, did not manifest a startling doctrinal break with the past, as has often been contended. Rather, they had deep roots in the prior history of jurisprudence in water rights, eminent domain, and police power in the state courts—in what I have argued was a coherent body of law expressing the principle of public purpose and public rights. This regulatory tradition . . . forms one of the iron chains that links modern administrative law to historic mooring. It is a line of substantial, often dramatic continuity that extends into the contemporary legal culture of the regulatory state.

Harry N. Scheiber, "Doctrinal Legacies and Institutional Innovations: Law and the Economy in American History," in *American Law and the Constitutional Order: Historical Perspectives* 451, 462 (Lawrence M. Friedman and Harry N. Scheiber eds., enlarged ed. 1988). See generally James Willard Hurst, *Law and the Conditions of Freedom* (1956). Regarding the widely discussed interventionism of rate regulation, see Stephen A. Siegel, "Understanding the Lochner Era: Lessons from the Controversy over Railroad and Utility Rate Regulation," 70 *Va. L. Rev.* 187 (1984). For a similar assessment of the situation in England, see Anthony Ogus, *Regulation: Legal Form and Economic Theory* 7 (1994).

mon carriers could not choose their trading partners, could not decide on the prices they charged, and could not "contract out" of liability for negligence.[31] Even in the labor context, where some famous decisions raised freedom of contract to its greatest gains and constitutional status, free contract was intensely contested, with legislatures often passing maximum-hours statutes, child labor protections, and "antitruck" laws mandating payment in cash rather than company scrip.[32]

Whether the actual state of affairs late in the nineteenth century is important to the current dispute over incompleteness is unclear. At the same time, while few people might be willing to defend the image of the turn of the century as a period of laissez-faire, the image still forms an assumed part of the background for the discussion. Like the other elements of the narrative, it posits an imaginary starting point from which to trace and evaluate developments, and a point of comparison when abstracted individuals were free to relinquish entitlements and undertake obligations without the interference of societal strictures, whether in the shape of legislative protections or judicial adjustment of their contracts.[33]

Contract as Private Lawmaking: Consent as Sole Source of Obligation

On the level of sophisticated contract theory, the role of consent in contractual obligation is hotly contested.[34] At another level however, that of

---

31. In fact, even carriers who were not common carriers could not, according to most authorities, contract to exempt themselves from liability for negligence; see 2 Samuel Williston, *The Law of Contracts* § 1073 (1st ed. 1920). The most cited case on contracting out of liability for negligence is New York Cent. Railroad Co. v. Lockwood, 84 U.S. 357 (1873). See discussion in McCurdy, "The Liberty of Contract Regime," 174–76.

32. On the contested meanings and applications of free contracting in the labor context, including evidence that many trades exhibited custom determined duties and wages that were not subject to contract, see William E. Forbath, "The Ambiguities of Free Labor: Labor and the Law in the Guilded Age," 1985 *Wis. L. Rev.* 767.

33. An exception to the lack of support for characterizing the late nineteenth century as an era of laissez-faire is Richard A. Epstein, "Contracts Small and Contract Large: Contract Law Through the Lens of Laissez-Faire," in *Fall and Rise of Freedom of Contract*, 25. Epstein distinguishes between the narrow rules of contract doctrine, which he says are for the most part unimportant in establishing or critiquing laissez-faire, and wider issues of freedom of contract. One of the problems with the essay, however, is that it seems to classify the system according to some of its popular rhetoric, rather than according to the standard that Epstein himself proposes, which is an evaluation of the way systems "respond to grand social problems—the trusts and the utilities." Id. at 61.

34. For parameters of the debate, compare Randy E. Barnett, "A Consent Theory of Contract," 86 *Colum. L. Rev.* 269 (1986), with Linzer, "Uncontracts," 142.

common assumptions about contract, consent is king. It is on this foundation that the common historical narrative proceeds, likening "classical contract" to a regime of pure consent that existed before society began to impose obligations on contractors regardless of their intentions. Like the claim about unlimited freedom of contract, nobody is willing to defend this claim in detail. However, on the level of the basic understanding of what contract law is about, almost everybody makes use of the idea.

It seems important to unpack at least two different levels of this argument. First, there is a relatively technical level, dealing with specific rules of contract. On this level, almost all students of the issue freely admit that the leaders of the classical movement in contract, led by Williston, were committed to the objective theory of contract, and were thus willing to sacrifice subjective intention in some instances, in return for achieving deeper security of exchange. Williston went to the extreme of saying that contractual liability could arise when neither party intended it.[35] However, the impact of accepting objective interpretation of contracts for one's view of the source of contractual obligation remains contested.[36] For the most part, objective in-

---

35. Williston was fond of quoting Learned Hand's pronouncement, "A contract has, strictly speaking, nothing to do with the personal, or individual, intent of the parties. A contract is an obligation attached by the mere force of law to certain acts of the parties, usually words, which ordinarily accompany and represent known intent." Hotchkiss v. National City Bank, 200 F. 287, 293 (S.D.N.Y. 1911) aff'd, 231 U.S. 50 (1913). The passage is quoted twice in the first volume of the first edition of Williston's treatise, once in the text and once in a note, and in a note in a law review article Williston published the year before the treatise came out. See 1 Williston, *Law of Contracts*, § 21, n. 13; § 94; Samuel Williston, "Mutual Assent in the Formation of Contracts," 14 *Ill. L. Rev.* 85, 87, n. 8 (1919). See also 1 Williston, *Law of Contracts*, § 95 ("It is even conceivable that a contract shall be formed which is in accordance with the intention of neither party").

36. For instance, Morton Horwitz has shown how legal realists argued that the rise of an objective theory of contract erased any basis for a clear distinction between contract and tort. See Morton J. Horwitz, *The Transformation of American Law, 1870–1960*, pp. 46–51 (1992). James Gordley has expanded the discussion to include continental theorists:

> Towards the end of the [nineteenth] century, the will theorists were challenged by the proponents of an "objective" theory of contract. The objectivists claimed that the parties did not will the legal consequences of their transaction, or at least that the law did not arrive at these consequences because the parties had willed them. One step in their argument was to claim that the parties could not have willed all the legal consequences of their transaction. . . .
>
> For the objectivists, to show that some consequences of the parties' transaction were not willed was one step towards their ultimate conclusion that the will of the parties was not, in principle, the source of their obligations.

James Gordley, *The Philosophical Origins of Modern Contract Doctrine* 209–10 (1991). On the other hand, Randy Barnett's consent theory incorporates objective interpretation while clinging to the centrality of individual consent as the key to creation of legal obligation. See Barnett, "Consent Theory." If the realist critique was as effective as Horwitz claims, the roots of a reconstruction of contract around the concept of consent are visible in Lon Fuller, "Consideration and Form," 41 *Colum. L. Rev.* 799, 808 (1941). For earlier, continental theories attempting to reconcile objectivism and will theory, see Gordley, *Philosophi-*

terpretation is seen as a concession to security and certainty, something of a practical necessity to ease evidentiary problems. And many would admit that at the margins, an objective law of contract overrides intent. However, this is typically seen as a minor adjustment to make contract law practical, without changing the basic idea of contract as the obligation that flows from agreement. Thus, at the level of technical rules, nobody feels required to deny the fact that classical law was not actually committed to pure consent.

The second level of this argument is the more general and interesting. Here, I refer to the broad idea that the law of contract is the law of obligations created exclusively by the parties, as distinguished from those obligations that are imposed by law. Everyone seems willing to admit that there are exceptions to the general idea, but most people are committed to a conception of contract that holds the exceptions are minor and anomalous. Moreover, to the extent that the exceptions are important, they are seen as modern innovations, outgrowths of a twentieth-century trend that blurs the distinction between public and private law.[37] Almost everyone proceeds on

---

cal Origins, 211–12. Williston himself was ambiguous, if not contradictory, on these questions. On the one hand, when distinguishing between quasi contract and contract proper, he seems to rely on the intention of the parties. See 1 Williston, *Law of Contracts*, § 3. On the other hand, Williston was adamant in rejecting the will theory as wholly inapplicable to the common law of contracts, and with it, he rejected the idea that parties to a contract were required to have an intent to form a legal relation. Thus, possibly contrary to popular belief, Williston did not believe in a modified will theory or in promise as the basis of contract. In explaining that the history of the common law supports his position that an expression of assent rather than genuine consent is required to form a contract, he writes:

> The original basis of the action of assumpsit was consideration, and the essential feature of consideration was the justifiable reliance upon words or acts. The acceptor's justifiable reliance on the offeror's proposal is historically, and it is believed on proper analysis still law to-day, the basis of contract. The view here criticised was developed as part of the system of philosophy, law and economics, which, during the first half of the nineteenth century laid emphasis on the will. This philosophy has had great influence on the law of the continent of Europe and . . . has served to obscure the true foundation of the English law of contracts. . . .
>
> [T]he assertion is ventured that the common law does not require any positive intention to create a legal obligation as an element of contract. The views of parties to an agreement as to what are the requirements of a contract, as to what mutual assent means, or consideration, or what contracts are enforceable without a writing, and what are not, are wholly immaterial. They are as immaterial as the views of an individual as to what constitutes a tort. In regard to both torts and contracts, the law, not the parties, fixes the requirements of a legal obligation.

1 Williston, *Law of Contracts*, §§ 20–21 (footnotes omitted).

37. This is the half of Grant Gilmore's thesis that everyone takes issue with. Gilmore's thesis had two parts: the contemporary, attempted prophetic part said that contract was being swallowed up by tort into a cohesive law of obligations, in part through the mechanism of promissory estoppel. See generally Grant Gilmore, *The Death of Contract* (2d. ed. 1995) (1974). The past twenty-five years have seen an outpouring of writing suggesting that Gilmore's obituary for contract as independent was premature. For a recent and mostly charitable assessment, see "Symposium: Reconsidering Grant Gilmore's *The Death*

the assumption that classical contract and everything that preceded it took that distinction more seriously, and that up until the twentieth century, contract was always conceived of as purely private lawmaking. This claim seems to hold heightened relevance for the debate over incompleteness, since only if contract is conceived of as consent-based and private does legal (judicial, societal) intervention to remedy incompleteness become problematic.

I would like to posit here that the view of contract as historically purely private and consent-based is flawed, and that the reason the view is unproblematically espoused is that we underestimate the impact of the classical revolution on contract thinking. Now, it is a truism (one that happens to be true) that judicial and scholarly rhetoric have treated contract as a party-generated obligation for at least three hundred years. My goal is not to erase those dominant statements of the nature of contract. However, until the classical scholars began to dominate the field, contract was at the same time considered the law of relations: the law of vendor and purchaser; of factors or of brokers; bailor and bailee; master and servant; principal and agent; landlord and tenant; lessor and lessee; shipper and carrier; and on and on. And the content of the duties or obligations in each of these relations was supplied by law, in accordance with recognized contract types.[38] True, individuals entering the relations could sometimes vary the obligations by "special" contract. But for many relations, this only happened at the margins, and was not considered very important. Thus, even the contracts treatise that is the bridge to the classics spends most of its energies in delineating the obligations within the relations.[39]

---

of Contract," 90 *Nw. U. L. Rev.* 1 (1995). But the historical half of the thesis was that the disaggregation of the law of obligations was only as old as the classical period (1870 onward). This part of his thesis has attracted less attention. A major exception is James Gordley, "The Death of Contract," 89 *Harv. L. Rev.* 452 (1975) (book review).

38. James Gordley has discussed the relationship between contract types and the shift to a general theory that ignores contract types, or relations:

> Unlike the natural lawyers, nineteenth-century treatise writers did not discuss the reasons there were different types of contracts, each with different terms. The treatises written in the earlier part of the century often solemnly define contract in terms of mutual assent and then leap without explanation into the welter of rules applicable to various types of contracts. The question why the parties are bound to these rules to which they never expressly consented is hardly considered. Towards the end of the century, particularly in the works of Langdell and Holmes in the United States and Anson and Pollock in England, the discussion of the particular rules of various types of contracts all but disappears. These authors describe general contract law without trying to relate it to the law of sales, the law of leases, and so forth.

Gordley, *Philosophical Origins*, 158. See also id. at 208.

39. Parsons's discussions of duties within, for instance, the various sorts of bailments or the relations of

Beyond the elaborate attention bestowed on detailing the content of law-supplied obligations, we can glean some indication of the role of law vis-à-vis private agreement from the following passages from Parsons:

> The law, as we have already had occasion to say in reference to various topics, frequently supplies by its implications the want of express agreements between the parties. . . . If the parties expressly provided not any thing different, but the very same thing which the law would have implied, now this provision may be regarded as made twice; by the parties and by the law. And as one of these is surplusage, that made by the parties is deemed to be so; and hence is derived another rule of construction, to wit, that the expression of those things which the law implies works nothing.[40]

Note that according to Parsons, when the parties and the law provide the same term, the term implied by law is the one considered binding. In other words, the term implied by law has priority over the provision by the parties, despite the fact that the parties may choose to vary the terms. Now, one might say that this only shows that there were a great many default rules and that the parties could use the ready-made rules when they chose. But it seems that more is at stake, at least conceptually. The common view is that contract had always been about abstract parties combining in transactions of their own making. The view that emerges from Parsons's discussion of implication, on the other hand, suggests that webs of patterned relationships preexist the parties, who can then choose to enter them. And the fact that the former view is such a taken-for-granted part of our current vision of contract is not evidence about the history of contract, but rather a testament to the success of the classical revolution in contract theory.[41]

---

agent and principal, or duties of factors and of brokers are granted more than three times the space of his discussions of general contract questions such as assent or consideration. See Theophilus Parsons, *The Law of Contracts* (1st ed. 1853). Parsons was Dane Professor of Law at Harvard, the same chair eventually held by Williston, who, before writing his own treatise, edited the eighth edition of Parsons's treatise, which appeared in 1893.

40. 2 Parsons, *Law of Contracts*, 27. Note that the examples of the principle are not given in abstractions of *A* and *B*, but rather as concrete relations, including lessor and lessee, mortgagor and mortgagee, charter party shipper, and so on. See id. at 27–28.

41. The question arises as to how the view of contract as a relation with societally defined duties into which the parties may enter can coexist with a view of contract as obligation created by the intent of the parties. At least two issues, one substantive and one of legal reasoning, come up in an attempted explanation. On the substantive level, one would have to question even the short-lived dominance of the will theory. Thus, while it is clear that the will theory became popular among contract treatise writers around the end of the eighteenth century (see, e.g., the first English-language treatise devoted to contract, John Joseph Powell, *Essay upon the Law of Contracts and Agreements* [1st ed. 1790]), contract

Completing Incomplete Contracts

The common narrative critiqued here holds that completion of incomplete contracts by the courts is a relatively recent phenomenon, that courts used to interpret and construe contracts formalistically and narrowly. Sometimes, this view manifests itself in statements that assume that interpretive tools like custom and usage, or gap-fillers like reasonable time for performance, are recent developments.[42] To the extent that statements like this are taken at face value to mean that custom and usage or the supply of a reasonable time term are modern (say, UCC-era) innovations, they are easily refuted.[43] The more serious claim is that courts did not intervene to complete incomplete contracts, and especially that they did not do so by imposing a duty of good faith in the performance of contracts. Thus, contracts scholars who have dealt intensively with good faith commonly hold that the obligation to perform a contract in good faith was relatively undeveloped until the middle of the twentieth century, and that the main impetus to its elevated status was the work of Karl Llewellyn in drafting the UCC.[44] This claim seems at first glance to be borne

---

doctrine continued to be influenced as much by a tradition of commercial law, which was not a product of will theory, as by the treatises. In other words, the recognized contract types of commercial relationships and customs formed the backbone of the mechanics of contract doctrine, while the treatise writers were proceeding with the task of generalizing and rationalizing. On the level of legal reasoning, the issue is how much force first principles were to have over concrete rules, and what kinds of mediating devices were available to deal with contradictions. In simplest terms, up until the classical period, students of contract were concerned with showing how the various principles of contract and the rules of contract cohered. They were not, however, in the business of deriving particular rules (or critiquing the existing rules) by deduction from the principles. This was the methodological revolution instituted by classical theorists. On the relationship between contract types and general contract theory, see Gordley, *Philosophical Origins* 158–60. On the way preclassical treatise writers like Parsons used principles, see Duncan Kennedy, "The Rise and Fall of Classical Legal Thought" chap. 4 (unpublished manuscript, 1975). For an indication that the priority of legally implied terms was still an issue for classical contract theory, see 2 Williston, *Law of Contracts*, § 615.

42. See, e.g., Douglas K. Newell, "Will Kindness Kill Contract?" 24 *Hofstra L. Rev.* 455–56 (1995) (implying that resort to "usage" arises with the UCC) and 472 (contrasting resort to usage with "the classical theory of Williston"); Scott, "Case for Formalism"; Scott, "Uniformity Norm."

43. If we take Parsons as a representative of preclassical law, and Williston as representative of the classics, their clear incorporation of these interpretive tools is enough to refute the strong version of the claim. See 2 Parsons, *Law of Contracts*, 47–59; 2 Williston, *Law of Contracts*, §§ 648, 652.

44. See E. Allen Farnsworth, "Good Faith Performance and Commercial Reasonableness Under the Uniform Commercial Code," 30 *U. Chi. L. Rev.* 671 (1963). Elsewhere, Farnsworth articulates the position thus:

> Credit for the contemporary recognition of the doctrine of good faith instead goes to Professor Karl Llewellyn, Chief Reporter for the Uniform Commercial Code. Llewellyn, who had taught at Leipzig, was inspired not by Mansfield, but by the Treu und Glauben provision of the German Civil Code. Although the common law doctrine of a few states—notably, New York and California—mentioned

out by those cases in which courts declared that where there was an express contract regarding a particular subject matter, the courts would not imply terms or a contract regarding the same subject matter.[45] On the other hand, it was far more common for courts to say that "what the law will imply in an express contract is as much part and parcel of it, and as much to be dwelt on in construing it, as if stated in such contract in direct terms."[46]

---

good faith before the adoption of the UCC, it was not until good faith was included in the Code that the doctrine reached national prominence.

E. Allen Farnsworth, "Duties of Good Faith and Fair Dealing Under the UNIDROIT Principles, Relevant International Conventions, and National Laws," 3 *Tul. J. Int'l and Comp. L.* 47, 51–52 (1995). See also E. Allan Farnsworth, "The Concept of Good Faith in American Law," in 10 *Saggi, conferenze e seminari* 12 (Centro di studi e ricerche di diritto comparato e straniero ed., 1993); Steven J. Burton and Eric G. Andersen, *Contractual Good Faith* 21 (1995); Van Alstine, "Of Textualism," 1241–42.

45. See, e.g., In re Brose's Estate, 26 A. 766 (Pa. 1893); Ramming v. Caldwell, 43 Ill. App. 175 (1891); Wait's Appeal, 9 A. 943 (Pa. 1887); Brown v. Fales, 29 N.E. 211 (Mass. 1885); Keystone Lumber and Salt Manufacturing Co. v. Dole, 5 N.W. 412 (Mich. 1880); McPherson v. Harris, 59 Ala. 620 (1879).

46. Chouteau v. Missouri Pac. Railway Co., 22 S.W. 458, 460 (Mo. 1893). See also, e.g., Manistee Iron Works Co. v. Shores Lumber Co., 65 N.W. 863, 865 (Wis. 1896) (contract must be construed as if those terms the law will imply were expressly introduced into it); Southern Railway Co. v. Franklin and Pennsylvania Railroad Co., 32 S.E. 485 (Va. 1899) (courts are careful in inferring covenants, but what is necessarily implied is as much a part of the instrument as if plainly expressed); Morrow v. Board of Education of Chamberlain, 64 N.W. 1126 (S.D. 1895) (incidental stipulations necessary to carry a contract into effect, or make it reasonable, or conformable to usage, are implied therefrom); Morier v. Moran, 58 Ill. App. 235 (1895) (what is implied in contract is as much part of contract as what is expressed); Hart v. Otis, 41 Ill. App. 431 (1891) (same); City of St. Louis v. Laclede Gaslight Co., 14 S.W. 974 (Mo. 1890) (same); Hearne v. Marine Insurance Co., 87 U.S. 488 (1874) (in a written contract, what is implied is as effectual as what is expressed). An unsystematic survey of approximately five hundred contracts cases dating from 1850 to 1900 shows that the restrictive statement on implication was relatively rare. This is not to say that courts agreed to imply terms in all cases that they did not resort to a restrictive statement of the rule on implication. The analysis that follows assumes that the general statements of the rules of implication are not enough to understand the actual judicial practice of implication. Many of the cases where courts declared a restrictive rule on implication were situations where plaintiffs claimed recovery "off the contract," in other words, in quasi contract. Such cases are technically beyond the scope of this chapter, but it is worth noting that some courts were willing to grant recovery, in the teeth of claims that an express contract covered the entire obligation of the defendant. See, e.g., Goddard v. Foster, 84 U.S. 123 (1872) (express contract of a factor came to an end, but business begun included another ship's voyage, regarding which the Court held that the factor could recover the reasonable value of his services, with the Court saying that "where the case shows that it is the duty of the defendant to pay, the law imputes to him a promise to fulfil that obligation"; id. at 141); Snowden v. Clemons, 38 P. 475 (Colo. App. 1894) (recovery on promise or express contract denied, but awarded on claim for services actually rendered); Vickery v. Ritchie, 88 N.E. 835 (Mass. 1909) (contract for services rendered void by mutual mistake, but recovery awarded on quantum meruit); Donovan v. Halsey Fire Engine Co., 24 N.W. 819 (Mich. 1885) (plaintiff may recover for services in implied assumpsit despite lacking written contract, which defendant claimed was necessary for company to incur liability); Butterfield v. Byron, 27 N.E. 667 (Mass. 1891) (contract could not be performed because hotel to be built burned down, but builder could recover for value services performed); Casey and Hurley v. MacFarlane Bros. Manufacturing Co., 76 A. 515 (Conn. 1910) (builder recovered for value of extra work and materials despite contract language stating that extra work required architect's order).

Overall, however, general statements regarding the rules of implication tell us less than a closer look at the courts' actual practice of completing incomplete contracts late in the nineteenth century and into the beginning of the twentieth. Modern scholars have underestimated the completion of incomplete contracts by reference to good faith or related concepts like reasonableness, justice, and fairness. The fertile soil for the growth of the doctrine at this time was an increase in litigation over contracts with terms indefinitely expressed. The growth of national commodities exchanges, of the railroads, the expanded scale of construction that accompanied widespread urbanization, the expansion of the insurance industry, and the growth of national advertising all contributed to the growth of complex contracting practices, where the obligations of the parties were open to interpretation.[47] The increase in contracts with open terms highlighted the necessity for court completion of contracts, and good faith and related norms like reasonability were the primary tools of supplementation.

Possibly the paradigmatic open-term contract in the late nineteenth century was one for constructing a railroad, with the vast uncertainty regarding the actual efforts to be required. At the time of contracting, little beyond the endpoints of the railway was a matter of certainty; in other words, the precise trajectory of the railway might not be known yet. Contracts of this sort required the parties to set up mechanisms to deal with eventualities that would arise during performance, and had to rely on a large measure of cooperation in order to see the work to its conclusion. An instructive illustration is *Williams v. Chicago, Santa Fe and California Railway Co.*, decided by the Supreme Court of Missouri in 1899.[48] The defendant began planning for the building of a railroad from Kansas City to Chicago in 1886. When meeting with bidders for the work of construction, the general manager and chief engineer of the defendant told potential contractors that the locations were not yet finally settled but were subject to changes; that crossings on other railroads could be changed to overhead or under crossings; and that difficult ground conditions might be encountered.

The parties agreed that the work would be executed under direction and supervision of the chief engineer of the railway, who would be responsible for determining all measurements and calculations of the amounts and

47. See Harold C. Havighurst, "The Restatement of the Law of Contracts," 27 *Ill. L. Rev.* 910, 916 (1933); see also Pratt, "American Contract Law at the Turn of the Century," 417–19, 433.

48. 54 S.W. 689 (Mo. 1899).

kinds of work to be performed. In other words, the parties delegated to the chief engineer responsibility for determining what performance would consist of and, based on bids and estimates, the value of the work done, including extra work not contemplated at the time of the agreement. Eventually, and maybe predictably, plaintiffs charged that the work requirements and changes imposed were excessive, and that the valuation was too scant. What is noteworthy about the long opinion, however, is the implication of the requirement of good faith regarding the engineer's determinations, and especially the relatively detailed content of the requirement. Over the course of the opinion, the court includes not merely an absence of fraud (though there is that as well, repeatedly), but also the obligation to avoid "gross mistake";[49] to act without caprice and without a motivation of causing the other party loss;[50] to act in a manner that is just and reasonable, and conversely to act in a manner that is neither unreasonable nor arbitrary;[51] and to avoid action motivated by the purpose of lessening the other party's profits in performance.[52]

In the course of the opinion, the court deals with eighteen specific claims, but without examining the treatment of each, it is worthwhile to note the language it adopts when dealing with a claim that a change in the line of the railway warranted additional compensation:

> I find no evidence that this change of line was made by the engineers or other officers or agents of the railway company either capriciously, fraudulently, or for the purpose of causing the plaintiffs to lose money and profits in the performance of their contract. On the contrary, I find that the change was made in good faith and for a lawful and fair purpose. I am of the opinion, and so find, that the change was not an unreasonable one, and that it was one which might fairly be said to be within the contemplation of the parties in framing the above-quoted provisions of the contract.[53]

The passage links many of the main themes of modern good faith scholarship. It links good faith with both fairness and reasonableness, and it explains the kinds of behavior it is trying to exclude, particularly caprice and the

49. Id. at 692, 695, 708.

50. Id. at 693, 695.

51. Id. at 694, 695.

52. Id.

53. Id. at 693.

motivation of causing losses to a contractual partner. In addition, it ties these goals to the parties' expectations in framing the contract the way they did.[54]

---

54. A look at the details of a few additional cases from the period offers the flavor of how courts completed contracts through the mechanism of good faith. In Bradford v. Whitcomb, 32 S.W. 571 (Tex. Civ. App. 1895), plaintiff was a builder hired to make certain renovations in defendant's building, all of which he completed, except for cutting an opening for a cellar door. Plaintiff could easily have cut the opening, which was not a significant addition to the work, but refrained from doing so because a tenant of the building claimed that it would ruin the rooms he occupied. The builder, having otherwise completed the renovations, waited to receive payment and instructions from the defendant, who was out of state. In the meantime, the building was entirely destroyed by fire. Plaintiff claimed payment due on the contract, and defendant claimed that without full compliance, there should be no recovery. The court of civil appeals accepted defendant's claim, but on rehearing, reversed itself, relying this time on a doctrine of good faith substantial performance. Justifying its reversal, the court said, "in this class of contracts, 'embracing many particulars which it is difficult, if not impracticable, to comply with with entire exactness' . . . it is now the rule that, where a builder has in good faith intended to comply with the contract, and has substantially complied with it, although there may be slight defects, caused by inadvertence or unintentional omissions, he may recover the contract price, less the damage on account of such defects." Id. at 224. Good faith here is the measure of performance, and the measure of the excuse, and it is worth noting how reasonableness overtakes intention: the court states the rule as one allowing recovery where there had been an intention to comply, or if defects were caused by unintentional omissions. But in the case at hand, plaintiff made a clear conscious decision not to cut the door. In fact, the intention was to prevent damage to the building, and possibly to the defendant's interests. The court glides over this point, but in actuality the ruling is based on the fact that plaintiff's decision not to cut the door was reasonable and appropriate under the circumstances, and not on the defect being unintentional or inadvertent.

The relationship of estimates to actual deliveries was also a point around which the doctrine of good faith developed. Not all cases of this sort were either output or requirements contracts. In Day v. Cross, 59 Tex. 595 (1883), the parties contracted for the delivery of ten thousand head of specific marks and brands of cattle, "more or less." Payment was to be on the basis of a price per head. The agreement provided for a fixed date of delivery, after which any cattle that had not been delivered and accepted remained property of the sellers. Sellers delivered just over five thousand head, and the buyer's heirs refused to pay, claiming that delivery amounting to only half the estimated number of cattle was a breach of the contract. The court held that the case turned on the construction of the contract, asking whether it raised an absolute obligation to deliver the quantity stated, or whether that number was an estimate, and the number to be delivered "depended upon what [the sellers] could, with the proper use of skill, care and diligence, collect and turn over to [the buyer]." Opting for the latter, the court found that the contract relied on an estimate. From this conclusion, it proceeded to the combined issues of good faith and diligence required of the seller, examining the reason for the difference between estimate and delivery, and concluding that the sellers had acted in good faith, and had, as they had been obliged, used "that care, skill and energy which a good business man engaged in the stock business would use to collect said stock of cattle and deliver them at the place . . . and at the time mentioned in the contract." The motivation of the court is easy to understand. Evidence showed that the total number of the specific marks and brands of cattle involved was close to what was tendered. The sellers were not opportunistically holding back cattle in order to sell them at a higher price to another bidder. The estimate of how many cattle were available was mistaken, but since payment was per head, and since the sellers had used good faith and diligence in making the estimate and the delivery, there was no reason to penalize them for the discrepancy. Thus, the buyer would get what he paid for, and his damage would only be the disappointed expectancy of receiving more. The jury included a partial reward for that damage as well, which, like the rest of the jury verdict, was upheld. For a more extreme example of the same situation, with the court relying again on good faith to determine the nature of the estimate and its relationship to actual performance, see Brawley v. United States, 96 U.S. 168 (1877).

With this detailed illustration in mind, we can turn to the work of trying to establish some order in the case law on good faith. The turn-of-the-century cases that turn on good faith as a substantive standard of contract performance can be classed loosely in four groups. In the first group are cases where, generally stated, one party claims that its obligations under the contract are limited to a narrow or literal reading of the contract language. In these cases, courts regularly imply standards of reasonability and good faith in order to prevent a party from escaping its duties under a broader reading of the contract that the court believes should be controlling. The second group includes cases structurally similar to the first, but instead of claiming a limitation of obligation, one party claims that the contract was indefinite or lacked mutuality, and thus was void, such that no obligation arose. The third group comprises instances where one party raises obstacles to the other party's performance, and courts protect the party attempting to perform. Finally, the fourth group includes cases in which the courts prevent one party from exploiting a technical flaw in the other party's performance to avoid carrying out an obligation. These cases form the root of the doctrine of substantial performance, and good faith becomes a condition for employment of the doctrine.[55]

Attempts to Limit the Obligations Under the Contract

The first group of cases, where one party claims that its obligations are limited to a narrow reading of the contract, includes two subgroups of cases. In the first, one party claims that a satisfaction clause in the contract gives it unfettered discretion to accept or reject performance by the other party. An example of such a case is *City of Chicago v. Sexton*, where plaintiff was a builder responsible for the iron work in the erection of a city hall.[56] The contract held that payment would be made when the work was completed to the satisfaction of the mayor, which the city sought to withhold. The court held that the power of the mayor could not be exercised capriciously or arbitrarily, but could only be exercised in good faith and for reasonable cause.[57] Cases imposing standards of good faith or reasonability in the application of satisfaction clauses are numerous.[58]

---

55. See Robert S. Summers, "'Good Faith' in General Contract Law and the Sales Provisions of the Uniform Commercial Code," 54 *Va. L. Rev.* 237 (1968).

56. 2 N.E. 263 (Ill. 1885).

57. Id. at 264.

58. See, e.g., Fechteler v. Whittemore, 91 N.E. 155 (Mass. 1910) (satisfaction clause on contract for

The second subgroup comprises cases where one party claims that its obligations should be read narrowly, typically excluding an obligation that the other party deems necessary to achieve the contract's purpose. For example, in *Humphreys v. Central Kentucky Natural Gas Co.*, plaintiff was a florist and a gas customer of defendant company that had received the franchise to supply gas for heating to the residents of the city.[59] The plaintiff claimed that a failure through negligence to provide him with adequate gas pressure resulted in the death of the plants and flowers stored at his place of business. The company defended by saying that neither the franchise contract with the city nor the contract with plaintiff specified any quantity of gas to be supplied, so that no express condition or provision of the contract could be relied upon to base a cause of action. The court held that the company was required to carry out the obligations undertaken in good faith, and that in the absence of specified "duties and obligations intended to be assumed by one of the parties, the law will imply a contract on his part to do and perform those things that according to reason and justice he should do to carry out the purpose for which the contract was made."[60] Fleshing out the content of the undertaking by defendant, the court said that "it engaged and undertook to continue the service in such a manner as would reasonably and naturally fulfill the expectations in the minds of the contracting parties when the franchise was granted and accepted, and perform this service in such a manner as was reasonably intended by it and [the] city when the contract was entered into."[61] The court repeatedly states that the implied conditions would be those that "reason and justice" require, and that the undertaking necessarily implied an obligation to "ex-

transfer signs, to be measured by standard of reasonable men acting in good faith); Hunt Co. v. Boston Elevated Railway Co., 85 N.E. 446 (Mass. 1908) (satisfaction clause in contract for construction of hoisting towers and equipment to be used under standard of reasonable man); Doll v. Noble, 116 N.Y. 230 (1889) (satisfaction clause regarding woodwork on a building held to require that satisfaction not be withheld unreasonably or in bad faith); Thomas v. Fleury, 26 N.Y. 26 (1862) (architect's certificate of satisfaction could not be withheld unreasonably or capriciously); Hawkins v. Graham, 21 N.E. 312 (Mass. 1889) (satisfaction clause in contract for heating apparatus judged by standard of reasonable man); Duplex Safety Boiler Co. v. Garden, 101 N.Y. 387 (1886) (satisfaction clause in contract for boiler alteration held to standard of reasonability, with the court saying, "that which the law will say a contracting party ought in reason to be satisfied with, that the law will say he is satisfied with"; id. at 390); Meisell v. Globe Mutual Life Insurance Co., 76 N.Y. 115 (1879) (satisfaction clause regarding certificate of health held to require that satisfaction not be withheld capriciously or without reasonable grounds).

59. 229 S.W. 117 (Ky. App. 1920).

60. Id. at 119.

61. Id. at 120.

ercise reasonable and practicable care and diligence" in carrying it out.[62] Cases of this sort are legion.[63]

---

62. Id.

63. See, e.g., Meyer v. Swift, 11 S.W. 378 (Tex. 1889) (good faith performance of contract to furnish room and board included obligation to furnish reasonable board and lodging for elderly party to contract); O'Hara v. City of Scranton, 54 A. 713 (Pa. 1903) (implied covenant of good faith on part of the city to make assessments necessary to pay for services); Lawler v. Murphy, 20 A. 457 (Conn. 1889) (implied covenant of good faith requires affirmative duty of making assessment to pay claim, with the court saying: "We conclude then that, in connection with the express promises contained in the contract in this case, there is an implied promise to make an assessment to pay the death claim agreed to be paid,—an implied promise which the law, 'in order to promote good faith, and make the parties act up to the spirit as well as to the letter of their engagements, will create and supply as a necessary result and consequence of their contract'"; id. at 459 (internal quotation unattributed); Sanford v. Wheelan, 7 P. 324 (Or. 1885) ("good faith and fair dealing" required paying off encumbrances on land before trying to finalize the sale); Cowling v. Greenleaf, 6 P. 907 (Kans. 1885) (termination of agreement dependent on good faith of party terminating); Walker v. Whipple, 25 N.W. 472 (Mich. 1885) (dissenting opinion holds that termination of agreement while parties were in the midst of business contemplated by contract was a breach of good faith and of the contract); Wigan v. Bachmann-Bechtel Brewing Co., 222 N.Y. 272 (1918) (voluntary discontinuance of the business, even though continuance was not an express term of the contract, held to be inequitable and unjust, violating requirements of good faith and fair dealing); Cullinan v. Standard Light and Power Co., 65 S.W. 689 (Tex. Civ. App. 1901) (exaggerated demand in requirements contract held to be sharp practice); Industrial and General Trust, Ltd., v. Tod, 180 N.Y. 215 (1905) (reorganization agreement had no express term requiring reorganizers to present bondholder with a plan; court uses good faith and the doctrine of implied terms to hold that presentation of such a plan was required); *Mainstee Iron Works Co. v. Shores Lumber Co.* (contract for building an engine on a barge, court held that "where a contract is so framed that it binds the party contracting to do the act, it will imply a correlative obligation on the party to do what is necessary on his part to enable the party so contracting to fulfill his part of the contract," and that "the implication is equally clear that it was the duty of the defendant to deliver or place [the barge at plaintiff's yard] in a reasonably suitable situation or condition to enable the plaintiff to perform its contract"; id. at 865); Patterson v. Guardian Trust Co. of New York, 129 N.Y.S. 807, 811 (App. Div. 1911) (trust company's duty to apply proceeds of sale of bonds to prior indebtedness, where the court said, "It would seem too clear for argument that the plainest principles of justice require the implication of a covenant imposing upon the defendant the obligation to exercise ordinary vigilance and intelligence in protecting the proceeds of the bonds, and to see that they are applied to the payment of the prior mortgages"); Mull v. Touchberry, 100 S.E. 152, 153 (S.C. 1919) (in discussing implied warranties on the sale of a used car, the court said, "From an expressed undertaking, the law will also imply whatever the parties may be reasonably supposed to have meant, and what is essential to render the transaction fair and honest" [citation omitted]); Dunlap Lumber Co. v. Nashville, Chattanooga and St. Louis Railway Co., 165 S.W. 224 (Tenn. 1914) (reasonableness and commercial custom required railway company to continue deliveries to a mill on the mill's track); *Morrow v. Board of Education of Chamberlain* (good faith and reasonability required teacher to continue teaching under changed course assignments); Beatty v. Coble, 41 N.E. 590 (Ind. 1895) (physician's agreement to retire from medical practice implied obligation not to return to practice after eighteen months); Ulrich v. Hull, 17 Wis. 424 (1863) (agreement to permit a dam to be taken down implied a covenant against rebuilding it); Harkinson v. Dry Placer Amalgamating Co., 6 Colo. 269 (1882) (engineer's salary, which was to be paid out of earnings of machines, could not be withheld because defendants did not put them to use); Creamer v. Metropolitan Securities Co., 105 N.Y.S. 28, 33 (App. Div. 1907) (value of the purchase of a railroad dependent on defendant's bringing litigation regarding the railroad's status, the obligation to bring such legislation was implied, with the court saying, "And such implication will always exist where equity and justice require the party to do the thing in question, even though it expressly

Attempts to Void the Contract for Lacking Mutuality or Definiteness

The second group of cases, where one party claims the contract was indefinite or lacked mutuality, are instances of the court saving the contract from one party's attempt to renege on its commitments by challenging the contract's validity, or at least its power to impose obligations. One example is the case of *Luther v. Bash*, where plaintiff was a real estate broker who claimed commission earned on a deal agreed to by defendant, but then never consummated.[64] Defendant tried to avoid liability by relying on the agreement's indefiniteness, because it mandated a commission of 2 percent, without specifying the price. The court held that since the exact price of the sale could not be known at the time of contracting between the parties, it could be "fairly inferred that the 2 per cent was to be calculated upon the amount appellant was to receive for the real estate." The court continued: "Whatever may be fairly implied from the terms or nature of an instrument is, in the judgment of law, contained in the instrument."[65] Here, the court prevents an opportunistic resort to a technical rule of indefiniteness and implies a term to achieve what it calls fairness, which could easily have been called good faith.[66]

---

appears that he never made the promise or agreement which by such implication the law attributes to him"); Millan v. Bartlett, 71 S.E. 13 (W. Va. 1911) (sublessee held to implied duty not to sell leases if this would put it out of his power to perform his covenants); Blake v. Scott, 121 S.W. 1054 (Ark. 1909) (reasonability required that defendant pay for the building of the curb, attached to the wall he requested); Booth v. Cleveland Rolling Mill Co., 74 N.Y. 15 (1878) (patent license for steel rails included implied covenant to use proper efforts and diligence in manufacture and sale of the rails); Wilson v. Marlow, 66 Ill. 385 (1872) (assignment of patent right included implied covenant to carry on the business); Martin v. Kippitz-Melcher Brewing Co., 96 N.E. 4, 6 (Ind. 1911) (a lease was dependent on acquisition of a license to operate a saloon, and though there was no explicit reference to the person making the application, the court held: "Good faith on the part of the appellee required that a qualified person make the application; otherwise the situation would be precisely as if no application had been made"); *Southern Railway Co. v. Franklin and Pittsylvania Railroad Co.* (good faith required lessee to continue operation of railway for entire term of the lease, though no express stipulation to continue operation was included in the language of the contract); Zell v. Dunkle, 27 A. 38 (Pa. 1893) (good faith and common fairness required that bailee exercise reasonable care and diligence in storing plaintiff's property).

64. 112 N.E. 110 (Ind. App. 1916).

65. Id. at 111.

66. For like cases, see, e.g., Hayes v. Clark, 111 A. 781 (Conn. 1920) (brokerage agreement held to imply good faith and reasonable efforts on the part of the broker in finding buyer, thus avoiding claim of lack of mutuality or illusory promise); Miller v. Leo, 55 N.Y.S. 165 (App. Div. 1898) (obligation to take requirements of bricks for construction of a building imposed in order to avoid lack of mutuality); Carns v. Bassick, 175 N.Y.S. 670, 673 (App. Div. 1919) (attempt to make a sale directly after having hired a broker to negotiate held breach of contract, with the court saying: "The law reads good faith into every

Raising Obstacles to Performance

The third group of cases are those where one party raises an obstacle to performance on the part of the other, making it impossible for the second party to perform, or to reap the benefits of the agreement. An instructive illustration is the case of *United States v. Peck*, where the government, through a military officer, contracted with Peck, who was to provide it with hay, with the understanding that the hay was to come from a particular source.[67] Fearing that Peck would be unable to fulfill the contract, the government allowed others to cut the hay and attempted to charge Peck for the increased cost, claiming that his nonperformance was not excused, since the contract did not expressly provide that the hay come from that source. The Court rejected the argument, holding that the government had prevented and hindered Peck from performing his part of the contract, saying that "he who prevents a thing being done shall not avail himself of the non-performance he has occasioned," and that "the conduct of one party to a contract which prevents the other from performing his part is an excuse for non-performance."[68]

---

contract. Reasonableness is the rule for construing contracts and determining their implications. To hold at one may employ another at an agreed compensation to do a specific thing, and yet may with impunity deliberately prevent the other from doing that thing, is so plainly violative of good faith and reasonableness as to preclude extending the rule in ordinary brokerage cases to such a case as this"); Page v. Cook, 41 N.E. 115 (Mass. 1895) (where literal terms of a note said it would be payable when parties agreed, court implies an agreement to agree within a reasonable time); Simon v. Etgen, 213 N.Y. 589 (1915) (in contract to make payment out of proceeds of a sale, court implies obligation that the sale will be made within a reasonable time); Chesapeake and Ohio Railway Co. v. Herringer, 164 S.W. 948 (Ky. 1914) (agreement to agree on placement of railroad crossing could not be withheld capriciously, arbitrarily, or in bad faith, and thus agreement was not illusory or lacking in mutuality); Wood v. Lucy, Lady Duff-Gordon, 222 N.Y. 88 (1917) (implying an obligation to use good faith efforts in sales agency contract); Swedish-American National Bank v. Merz, 179 N.Y.S. 600 (Sup. Ct. 1919) (reasonable terms implied in option contract for purchase of real estate to avoid indefiniteness); Cumming v. Nielson, 129 P. 619 (Utah, 1912) (implying good faith obligation in the exercise of a right of first refusal on sale of share of real estate); Burt v. Stringfellow, 143 P. 234 (Utah, 1914); St. Louis and Denver Land and Mining Co. v. Tierney, 5 Colo. 582, 587 (1881) (requirements contract for coal, where court said defendant had an implied obligation to "continue in good faith the business which constituted the basis of the contract"); Baker Transfer Co. v. Merchant's Refrigerating and Ice Manufacturing Co., 37 N.Y.S. 276 (App. Div. 1896) (implying good faith in a requirements contract for ice); Black v. Woodrow, 39 Md. 194 (1874); Lewis v. Atlas Mutual Life Insurance Co., 61 Mo. 534 (1876).

67. 102 U.S. 64 (1880).

68. Id. at 65. For additional cases decided on this principle, see Uhrig v. Williamsburg City Fire Insurance Co., 101 N.Y. 362 (1886) (insurer's bad faith in preventing successful arbitration of claim excused claimant from compliance with arbitration clause); Bates and Rogers v. Board of Commissioners of Cuyahoga County, Ohio, 274 F. 659 (N.D. Ohio, 1920) (defendant's delays in delivery of construction site within a reasonable time held good cause of action for breach and damages); Johnson v. City of New

Technical Defaults or Substantial Performance

The final group of cases are those where one party has performed his obligations under the contract, but has not performed those obligations completely or perfectly. The most common, though not exclusive, context for cases like this is construction contracts. An example is *Dodge v. Kimball*, where plaintiff was a builder hired to erect a large building for defendants, but left certain parts of the building incomplete.[69] The court explains that whereas the older rule would have prohibited recovery except for strict compliance with the contract,

> in most of the American states a more liberal doctrine has been established in favor of contractors for the construction of buildings, and it is generally held that if a contractor has attempted in good faith to perform his contract and has substantially performed it—although by inadvertence he has failed to perform it literally according to its terms—he may recover under the contract.[70]

The court adds that in Massachusetts, the rule is different, but still allows contractors to recover in *quantum meruit* if they have acted in good faith. In this case, plaintiff's failures were so serious as to constitute bad faith, and recovery was denied.[71] Other cases show an application of the principle, and are not limited to construction contracts.[72]

York, 181 N.Y.S. 137 (App. Div. 1920); Wheeling and L.E.R. Co. v. Carpenter, 218 F. 273 (6th Cir. 1914); Rioux v. Ryegate Brick Co., 47 A. 406 (Vt. 1900) (fair and just construction of the contract required that defendants carry out their implied duties to sell the bricks made by plaintiff in time to supply him with additional materials); Schlottman v. E.I. DuPont de Nemours Powder Co., 210 F. 356 (S.D.N.Y. 1913) (defendant's prevention of condition was a breach of implied duty to use reasonable diligence to ensure the fulfillment of the condition).

69. 89 N.E. 542 (Mass. 1909).

70. Id. at 543.

71. Id. at 544.

72. See, e.g., Flannagan v. Nasworthy, 20 S.W. 839 (Tex. Civ. App. 1892) (good faith as test for performance when rules of the land board "are not rigidly complied with" in order to avoid injustice and uncertainty under land purchase statute); Denton v. City of Atchison, 8 P. 750, 752 (Kans. 1885) ("equitable rule has been generally adopted which permits a recovery by one who in good faith attempts to perform his contract, and does so substantially"); Gill v. Bradley, 21 Minn. 15 (1874) (good faith and diligence on the part of a purchaser of land excuse late payment of purchase price for real estate); *Bradford v. Whitcomb* (builder attempting to comply in good faith with contract may recover despite slight defects); Austin v. Wacks, 15 N.W. 409 (Minn. 1883) (good faith reasonable efforts and diligence of plaintiffs warrant specific performance of contract to purchase land despite a technical default regarding time of performance).

SUMMARY

There is a wealth of case law from around the turn of the century in which courts prevent opportunistic behavior by the parties, and impose upon them norms of reasonability, or limit arbitrary or capricious action in order to complete or fill in gaps in the agreements the parties entered into. Often, they resort to a rhetoric of effectuating the intent of the parties, or of giving business efficacy to their contracts. The courts are in effect supplying a mechanism that assures that the business mores that generated agreements between parties would be those they adhere to during performance. In so doing, the courts are not trying to find some external code of morality to impose on the market. Instead, they begin from the notion that the market has its own morality (one closely linked to reasonability, and not far from that of general interaction, though not so strict as that between family members), and that their role is to ensure that that morality is not subverted by opportunistic behavior or sharp dealing. The fact that many of these cases are commercial cases from New York reinforces the idea that a market morality is that which is reinforced.[73] But the fact that the cases are numerous and drawn from jurisdictions ranging from Arkansas to South Dakota to Utah to West Virginia should put aside the thought that good faith was only marginally important.

While the leading classical thinkers did not carve out a central role for the doctrine of good faith in their articulation of contract, the importance of good faith was not completely lost on scholars of the period. Thus, on a general level, Sir Frederick Pollock could describe the law of contract as "the endeavor of the State, a more or less imperfect one by the nature of the case, to establish a positive sanction for the expectation of good faith which has grown up in the mutual dealings of men of average right mindedness."[74] And the reference to good faith was not limited to the general idea of contract, but extended specifically to the obligations of performance, with one treatise summing up the doctrine by noting that the law will "imply whatever the parties may reasonably be supposed to have

73. "If the good faith rules are accepted we have in place a coherent system of business morality . . ." Reziya Harrison, *Good Faith in Sales* 448 (1997). The view forwarded here, that good faith was used in the late nineteenth century to enforce market morality, is directly at odds with Pratt, "American Contract Law at the Turn of the Century," who argues that the development of good faith relied on antimarket values.

74. Sir Frederick Pollock, *Principles of Contract* 1 (6th ed., London, Stevens and Sons 1894).

meant, and what is essential to render the transaction fair and honest," and adding conclusively: "When the parties enter into a contract in terms, the law presumes each of them to be acting in good faith toward the other; and it binds each to the other, to whatever good faith requires."[75]

The case law of the classical period, examined in detail, reveals a deep structural flaw in the debates over incomplete contract. These debates rely on a fundamentally inaccurate historical assumption regarding the movement from formal, intent-based adjudication, to activist intervention in contractual terms. The prevalence of the flawed narrative on both sides of current debate challenges our thought about the role of legal history in imagining a regime of contract. I turn to that challenge in the following chapter.

75. Joel Prentiss Bishop, *The Doctrines of the Law of Contracts* 37–38 (St. Louis, Soule, Thomas and Wentworth 1878).

ELEVEN

Evaluating the Frame of Incompleteness Discourse

Thus far I have argued that the current academic debate over incompleteness is polarized, and that rivals in the debate rely upon opposing interpretations of a common historical narrative. The narrative, the content of which is a familiar story of the socialization of contract, is typically stated in general terms or in passing, rarely presented as a logically necessary part of the justification for a position within the debate. The narrative takes its starting point from the work of classical scholars, but in doing so it relies on an idealization of an idealization as an account of historical fact. Classical articulations of a system of contract law were first of all a normative program, a suggestion for the way contract ought to be. They aspired to a much higher degree of order and systematicness than the case law or the relationship of existing legislation to contracting practice and litigation ever evinced. And while classical articulations of contract law aspired to abstraction, in elaborating the detailed rules of contract they made quite a bit of room for specialized standard relationships. But the common historical narrative within the implication debates takes the idealized image presented in the classical program as evidence about social life. It uses an idealized individual as the starting point in depicting the core of contract as private lawmaking, from which twentieth-century developments are presented as deviations.[1]

Upon closer examination, however, the historical narrative turns out to be flawed. First of all, on the level of the conceptual basis of contract, it is one thing to recognize an element of voluntariness as the point of entry into contractual relations, and another thing altogether to claim that the only source of content for such obligations is the consent of the parties. In addition, perhaps the clearest evidence that the common narrative is flawed lies in the work of judges in implying contractual obligations, even at the height of the classical period. Implication based on community standards of fairness and justice was widespread both to generate obligation in the first place (quasi contracts), and even more so to elaborate particular duties within ongoing contractual relationships. The most important examples of such implication are the early cases that can be seen as developing a general requirement of good faith in performance, cases that have been ignored because of the power of the accepted historical frame of the debates on incompleteness.

It is important to note that the cases implying duties of reasonableness, fairness, or good faith were business cases: they were about making commercial relationships work. In other words, the implication of good faith was not an antimarket maneuver. By setting limits of market morality, good faith cases aimed primarily at protecting the market from the kind of opportunism, sharp practice, and simple bad behavior that erode a basis for market activity—a combination of reliance and trust. Now, the point of showing that there were implied duties of good faith even in the classical period is not to justify their use today by appeal to the authoritative force of precedent. That would simply mirror a romantic position that we should go back to some golden age, because it supposedly once existed. Instead,

---

1. Thus, the narrative that frames the debate is not neutral with respect to its outcome. A detailed exploration of the issue is beyond my scope here, but the crux of the argument would be as follows: By assuming that originally, contract was first and foremost about private consent, the entire debate becomes right-leaning. The burden of proof, as it were, for deviation from party determination of duties is on the party arguing for some other source of obligation. In other words, in the current framework of the debate, both sides agree that the core of contract is the parties' own determination of their duties: the debate is not over the meaning of contract, but rather over the question of whether certain public policy goals justify deviation from that meaning. However, the fact that the debate is tilted does not mean that the results are predictable. While the rhetoric of the ultimate value of the parties' consent predates the classical period by at least a century, until the classical period it seemed to coexist peacefully with the (seemingly contradictory) idea that the law is the source of most contractual obligations. While the latter idea has faded from view over the past century and a half, its implications for doctrine continue to shape the outcome of many cases.

the point is to weaken the justificatory force of an inadequate historical story, and to notice how the rhetorical frame sets up a particular and limited argument, polarized around a false choice. The false choice is one between accepting contract either as a facilitator of pure private ordering based solely on party consent or as a system of regulating economic behavior, a mechanism for encouraging cooperation, when in fact there is every reason to believe that these goals can be and are constantly pursued together.[2]

Having restated the argument about the frame of the debate, the question is what to make of the use of the narrative as common background material. It may be worthwhile to begin by reiterating what I do not want to do by suggesting a critique of the narrative. First, it is not my goal to replace the existing narrative with an alternative or "corrected" narrative while leaving the structure of justification in place. This would miss the point of the critique. It would allow the productive or constitutive work of the structure of the debate to recede again into the background, from which I have labored to extract it. Second, despite the fact that I do not view the effects of the framework as balanced, it would be a misunderstanding to apply my claims as a critique of one position in the debate without a concurrent critique of the other position. Both sides of the incompleteness debates are guilty of the same sin.

The critique of the common narrative sets the stage for the following claim: the effect of the framework is to grant the debate over incompleteness intelligibility in a broad cultural debate over the individual subject, including the relationship of the subject to the market. Any method of interpreting contracts or supplying terms must commit to some image of the contracting individual, even if it does not do so consistently across cases. In this sense, an imaginary construction of the individual contracting party is an inescapable element of contract law. In particular, when dealing with cases of contractual incompleteness, that imaginary individual seems to be

2. The idea that contract law is as much about regulating behavior as it is about facilitating the expression of independent individual wills was a theme for realist writers on contract and has been resuscitated as a central claim of critical scholars. For some key examples see Arthur L. Corbin, "Offer and Acceptance, and Some of the Resulting Legal Relations," 26 *Yale L.J.* 169 (1917); George K. Gardner, "An Inquiry into the Principles of the Law of Contracts," 46 *Harv. L. Rev.* 1 (1932); Morris R. Cohen, "The Basis of Contract," 46 *Harv. L. Rev.* 553 (1933); Robert W. Gordon, "Unfreezing Legal Reality: Critical Approaches to Law," 15 *Fla. St. U. L. Rev.* 195 (1987); Duncan Kennedy, "Form and Substance in Private Law Adjudication," 89 *Harv. L. Rev.* 1685 (1976). For the related argument that the enforcement of contracts cannot be separated from distribution and paternalism, see Anthony T. Kronman, "Paternalism and the Law of Contracts," 92 *Yale L.J.* 763 (1983); Anthony T. Kronman, "Contract Law and Distributive Justice," 89 *Yale L.J.* 472 (1980); Duncan Kennedy, "Distributive and Paternalist Motives in Contract and Tort Law, with Special Reference to Compulsory Terms and Unequal Bargaining Power," 41 *Md. L. Rev.* 563 (1982).

at the heart of the decision-making process, even if the work of imagining the individual has taken place elsewhere.[3] Constructing the image of the contracting individual is a key element of the rhetoric surrounding the law of formation, in particular the doctrine of consideration, while the effects of that construction are felt in disputes over the content of the obligations—here, disputes over incompleteness.

Importantly, constructing an image of the contracting individual need not imply that the creation of that image is a matter of conscious choice: an adjudicator, taking into account a set of policy objectives, does not simply choose among available images of the individual. While such voluntary choice may be a useful idealization of the judge and thus a convenient spotlight for necessary choices in adjudication, my current focus is on the more oblique effects of imagining the individual, effects that are less susceptible to conscious control or choice by judges or academics. In order to get at the more oblique effects, it pays to conduct a genealogical speculation on the common historical narrative.[4] To this end, two historical moments must be considered: first, the classical revolution in contract law; and second, the current debate.

CLASSICAL CONTRACT: CONCEPTION AND RULES

One of the main tasks of classical contracts scholars was to turn the repeated statements about the centrality of the intention of the parties (morphed into objective manifestations of intent) into the animating feature of a theory of contract that could generate technical rules at every level. The idea was the

---

3. One influential explanation of the necessity of an imagined individual concentrates on dimensions of generality and idealization. In order to reach a conclusion regarding interpretation or supplementation, a decision maker may investigate the understandings of the particular parties to the suit, or alternatively may construct a hypothetical bargain based on a generalization regarding all contracting parties (generality); similarly, the adjudicator may view the parties as hampered by their own particular limitations, or alternatively may treat the transaction as if it were conducted between sophisticated parties with access to unlimited information (idealization). Differing theories as to the proper level of generality and idealization will lead to different answers to interpretive questions. See David Charny, "Hypothetical Bargains: The Normative Structure of Contract Interpretation," 89 *Mich. L. Rev.* 1815 (1991).

4. I refer to genealogy as opposed to intellectual history. In other words, I am not interested in exactly how the common narrative became so established and popular, but rather in the differences between the narrative at its point of departure or emergence and its current use, and the effects of the use of the narrative. For this reason, I examine the emergence of the narrative as part of an existing conflict, one that has been transposed into a different, but current, conflict. For an analysis of genealogy as a historical method, see Michel Foucault, "Nietzsche, Genealogy, History," in *Language, Counter-Memory, Practice* 139, esp. 148–57 (Donald F. Bouchard ed., Donald F. Bouchard and Sherry Simon trans., 1977).

same as that employed by will theorists, with two modifications: first, that the will itself was subordinated to objective manifestations of intent, thus retaining the private lawmaking element, but elevating security of exchange by abandoning a search for idiosyncratic intention; second, whereas the original will theorists sought to explain existing contract rules by reference to various principles, first among them the will of the parties, classical theorists posited their first principles as sources from which to deduce the rules of contract. This was a revolutionary maneuver. Its most important effect was to generate a new framework for discussion of the importance of contract as a distinct realm of private ordering, and the revolution succeeded. Its success is not measured in the extent of acceptance of particular deductions, regarding which in any case the classics differed among themselves. Rather, the success is measured by the acceptance of the framework.

One of the best ways to measure acceptance of the framework is through the works of the period's critics, which took two different paths. One path was an internal critique, whose goal was to show that the concrete rules the classics argued for could not be deduced from the general propositions.[5] The more dominant strand of critique was external, claiming that freedom of contract was inappropriate to conditions of concentration of wealth and power.[6] The important aspect of this development is not the

---

5. There were two ways to understand the effects of this critique. On the one hand, the more sweeping and political interpretation would be to point out that only deduction from agreed-upon first principles had justified a conception of private law in which judges were not imposing ad hoc political judgments on the parties. In other words, if the procedure of deduction was rejected, private law adjudication was legislative, and public and private law could not be distinguished. See Cohen, "The Basis of Contract"; Robert L. Hale, "Coercion and Distribution in a Supposedly Non-Coercive State," 38 *Pol. Sci. Q.* 470 (1923). The other interpretation was limited to the procedural aspect, without directly considering its political implications. On this interpretation, deduction simply fails to provide coherent justifications for rules, and thus should be replaced by the balancing of a set of considerations, all of which should be drawn from the pool of legitimately contractual principles. For a discussion of both internal and external critique in contract, see Duncan Kennedy, "From the Will Theory to the Principle of Private Autonomy: Lon Fuller's 'Consideration and Form,'" 100 *Colum. L. Rev.* 94, 115–21, 126–32 (2000).

6. This aspect of the critique was led by figures such as Roscoe Pound in the legal academy, though it had a wider body of proponents, with an important contributor being Richard Ely. One of Pound's articulations of the principle of critique argues thus:

> Probably one may summarize this first point by saying that a gulf has grown up between social justice, which is the end men are seeking today, and legal justice; that the movement away from the puritan standpoint in our social and economic and political thought has not been followed by legal thought, and that we still adhere to the idealistic, or at least to the political interpretation of, legal science, although in kindred branches of learning the economic and social interpretation is now more and more accepted.

Roscoe Pound, "Law in Books and Law in Action," 44 *Am. L. Rev.* 12, 30 (1910). See also Roscoe Pound, "Liberty of Contract," 18 *Yale L.J.* 454 (1909); Richard T. Ely, *Property and Contract in Their Relations*

change in contract rules, which in any case proceeded far more chaotically than scholars would have hoped. Rather, the crucial issue is that this maneuver lent the discussion of contract rules intelligibility within a wider cultural debate over the big questions of the role of the individual in society. The external critique drew the battle lines between different visions of the economy and the self that were in play among politicians, social scientists, and cultural critics. Within the cultural debate, various issues revolved around the role of the individual. Subjectivity had become "an open question—even a political issue." Social activists on the one hand, and philosophers and cultural critics on the other, were actively involved in attempts to "redraw the boundary between self and society, reason and desire, mind and body, science and ideology." By claiming that rationality itself was built on the characteristics of particular communities and traditions, they "proposed to substitute the 'social self' for the 'man of reason.'"[7]

This is not to say that classical legal scholars stood together on one side of these debates. Being a classical scholar did not necessarily determine one's position on societal questions.[8] The reception and critique of classical legal thought, however, did insert private law theory into social debates in the particular form of an argument for private ordering. My contention here, then, is that classical contract theory was not the equivalent of a position in the social debate; rather, it was a way of thinking about law that could be intelligibly inserted into the wider social debates. Beyond any practical claims as to the desired state of the law of contracts (something in contention among classical scholars), classical contract provided an imaginary point of pure contract, derived from first principles, which was the logical counterpart of a system of pure private ordering, opposed to a system of societal regulation. At this imaginary endpoint, the role of the state was

---

to the Distribution of Wealth (1st ed. 1914); John R. Commons, *Legal Foundations of Capitalism* 288–98 (1924). The external critique and its progressive political counterpart were often associated with German social science; for an account of this complex relationship highlighting the crucial role of Richard Ely, see Daniel T. Rodgers, *Atlantic Crossings: Social Politics in a Progressive Age* 97–111 (1998). On some level, it may be artificial to distinguish sharply between internal and external critique, especially regarding Pound, who participated actively in both kinds, at times even in the same work; see Roscoe Pound, *An Introduction to the Philosophy of Law* 265–69 (external), 271–84 (internal) (1922).

7. James Livingston, *Pragmatism and the Political Economy of Cultural Revolution, 1850–1940*, pp. 80–81 (1994).

8. A poignant example is Williston's own critique of the sociopolitical positions associated with the slogan of freedom of contract. See Samuel Williston, "Freedom of Contract," 6 *Cornell L.Q.* 365 (1921).

merely to ensure enforcement of contracts according to their terms.[9] This imaginary endpoint of the thought experiment of classical legal science authorized the dichotomy between, say, contract and regulation, or between the free market and intervention.

CURRENT CONTRACT THEORY: THE SOCIALIZATION NARRATIVE AS RHETORICAL BRIDGE

Current contract theory has abandoned the half of the classical revolution that relied on the possibility of deducing contract doctrine from first principles.[10] However, the other half of the revolution that established the image of pure contract as obligation flowing solely from the consent of the parties has weathered many critiques and still animates mainstream contract theory. In theory, the abandonment of a model of deduction means that a general conception of contract should have little if any effect on the rules of contract doctrine, particularly on default rules or the mechanisms for dealing with contractual incompleteness.[11] This is because in the absence of deduction, one has to consider various justifications for each rule, and it is implausible that there would be one particular justification that could support every rule choice.[12] Conceptions of rights or entitlements, fairness, institutional considerations, and welfare or efficiency arguments have varying impacts, according to the rule in question and its likely points of application. The pluralism of justification takes hold even before the divisions within any particular style of justification, which is just another reason that the deductive model retains so little persuasive power. Thus, the elimination of the model of deduction severs the ties between arguments over contract rules and the wider cultural debates, ongoing though transformed, about the individual subject. Or so it would seem.

---

9. There are of course, a few additional marginal duties, like protecting infants and the insane from contractual obligation, and preventing fraud or the use of duress.

10. The widespread acknowledgment that the classics overestimated the power of deduction has sometimes been translated into the aphorism that "we are all realists now." See generally, Joseph Singer, "Legal Realism Now," 76 *Cal. L. Rev.* 465 (1988).

11. See Richard Craswell, "Contract Law, Default Rules, and the Philosophy of Promising," 88 *Mich. L. Rev.* 489 (1989).

12. See generally Robert A. Hillman, *The Richness of Contract: An Analysis and Critique of Contemporary Theories of Contract Law* (1997).

My contention is that the historical narrative, with its inherent polar distinction, provides the rhetorical bridge that reinstates a connection with the debate over the individual subject. In a sense, the historical narrative preserves (with modification) the function of deduction in the relationship between classical contract thinking and turn-of-the-century debates over the subject, but without committing current contract scholars to a moribund theory of legal reasoning. In other words, for classical contract theory, the idea that rules could be derived from first principles connected the debate over the rules to the debate over what was at stake in the articulation of the first principles themselves. For current contract theorists, this precise connection is unavailable, since we no longer believe that a commitment to any particular definition or concept of contract will provide, by logical deduction, a justification for a particular rule choice.[13] Instead, passing reference to the historical narrative, with its understandings of the distinctions between promarket and proregulation positions, is enough to grant intelligibility to arguments over technical rules within a framework of more general social issues.

COMPLETIONS

The previous parts of this book have shared a structure from which this part has diverged. In each, an area of contract law traditionally considered marginal (gifts, wagers) was examined; in both cases, I claimed that the framework of debate in this area of contract law actually reveals concerns that are central to understanding contract more generally. More importantly, in each area, core conflicts within particular areas of doctrine were explored, showing a wide range of possible outcomes, even on issues where specific doctrinal formulations (rules) were not challenged. Extensive academic and judicial energies are poured into these questions, but the results do not seem to affect the behavior of contracting parties. In other words, there is no

---

13. I refer here to rules on incompleteness, though I think the argument could pretty safely be generalized to include rules of formation. I do not mean to suggest that this account of contract theory is accepted across the board. A conceptual account of contract still may have direct consequences for rule choices, including the rules dealing with incompleteness. See, e.g., Randy E. Barnett, *The Structure of Liberty: Justice and the Rule of Law* (1998); Randy E. Barnett, "A Consent Theory of Contract," 86 *Colum. L. Rev.* 269 (1986). Peter Benson, "The Unity of Contract Law," in *The Theory of Contract Law* 118, 126–38 (Peter Benson ed., 2001).

overwhelming incentive effect to a change in the rules discussed in these areas. But this does not mean that the doctrinal discussions are devoid of meaning. Instead, I have suggested a two-tiered examination of the meaning of doctrinal conflict. First, doctrinal conflict is a site of contention that participates in a dynamic of cultural training, a battle over the nature of the individual who contracts. Classical contract theory takes up the task of inventing or at least promoting an image of the individual as calculating, and thus as calculable. It posits a rationality that can in its most important particulars be reduced to wealth maximization, limiting the importance of utility that cannot be easily measured in money. Current contract thinking revolves around this image of the individual, even when theorists are not committed to defending the image of the calculating subject. Second, the effects (in contract law) of the cultural battle over the nature of the individual are not felt directly in the place where they are conducted, that is, in the doctrinal conflicts over the validity of contracts, but rather are seen in distinct (though not unrelated) conflicts over the content of obligations.

This part has taken the next step in this argument, examining the conflicts over the content of obligations, with particular reference to incompleteness and the implication of contractual terms. I have offered a reading of current contract theory, of the recent history of contract, and an account of the uses (or misuses) of a narrative of the socialization of contract. It would be convenient if the combination were to yield a straightforward normative program, a way to rewrite contract law, or a way to rethink the subject. Too convenient, perhaps. But it is worthwhile trying to reiterate the achievement of this part, to the extent the argument has been convincing. First of all, I have extracted a legal debate and its underlying historical narrative from their role as passive background elements—like the air we breathe, taken for granted. In the process, I have attempted to expose the productive role that the framework plays, both in blinding the participants in the debate to history as evidenced in a large body of relevant cases, and in generating intelligibility for their political positions.

The point of accounting for the specific workings of this shared rhetorical structure is to reveal its limitations. The accepted narrative allows theorists and readers the easy intelligibility of battle lines drawn decades ago and familiarized by reductive restatement since then. One of the problems is that these discussions do little to clarify complex problems, and little to convince anybody but the already converted. Writing in 1937, Thurman Arnold warned of the limitations on thinking that resulted from relying on "polar words" such as "paternalism" and "rugged individualism," in discussions of social problems. Polarized argument could "never get anywhere in persuading the other side." While it might create enthusiasm on the public stage, its danger for the diagnostician or legal scientist was that it contained "traps which ruin his judgment." In the midst of the battles to impose fundamental reforms in the shape of the American economy, Arnold recognized that much of the argumentation over such reforms could be reduced to repetitive rhetorical thrusts. Reduced to their status as formal rhetorical maneuvers, the arguments on both sides of the debate lose their sheen; indeed, they may take on an air of the comic.[14]

More recently, Albert O. Hirschman has demonstrated that support for and opposition to reform are consistently based on such maneuvers. His study, *The Rhetoric of Reaction*, combines the kinds of insights presented by Arnold with a broad historical survey of the uses of such rhetoric. Exposing recurrent pairs of reactionary and progressive statements, he explains, "Once the existence of these pairs of arguments is demonstrated, the reactionary theses are downgraded, as it were: they, along with their progressive counterparts, become simply extreme statements in a series of imaginary, highly polarized debates. In this manner they stand effectively exposed as *limiting cases*, badly in need, under most circumstances, of being qualified, mitigated, or otherwise amended."[15]

The common historical narrative underlying the incompleteness debates allows their participants to plug into these accepted rhetorical modes, in just the way that Hirschman shows that the arguments themselves enjoy appeal "because they hitch onto powerful myths."[16] The work of this part of the book has been to show how the misuse of history leaves us in this same argumentative bind. The rhetoric that connects our contract theory and our conflicts over the individual and the market is inadequate; perhaps we can find better ways to make the connections. Perhaps a redrawing of the battle lines can displace a familiar, tired politics with another yet to be invented.

---

14. Thurman W. Arnold, *The Folklore of Capitalism* 169–74 (1937).

15. Albert O. Hirschman, *The Rhetoric of Reaction* 167 (1991); emphasis in original.

16. Id. at 166. Here I have in mind particularly the myth of liberal individualism and the myth of statelessness. For an account of the power of these myths (and others) in American historiography, see William J. Novak, *The People's Welfare: Law and Regulation in Nineteenth Century America* 1–8 (1996).

Conclusion
Undermining the Metaphysics of Contract

In *Shakespeare: The Invention of the Human*, Harold Bloom argued that our fundamental sense of the meaning of humanity, of the multiplicity and conflict within personality, are shaped and forever changed by Shakespeare's plays. Of course, there were human beings before the Bard's birth; but Shakespeare's portrayals of character changed our conception of humanity so fundamentally that it is difficult to imagine what came before, or how it could have been otherwise.[1] A similar dynamic is at stake in the relationship between contract and the individual.

Students of economic and political thought have long mused over the processes through which the West learned to imagine individuals as rational, autonomous, calculating, and finally, calculable. These processes have their roots as far back as the sixteenth century, and go hand in hand with an ever expanding vision of a market peculiarly hospitable to these abstract, calculating creatures.[2] Late nineteenth-century contract law took shape in

1. Harold Bloom, *Shakespeare: The Invention of the Human* 4–7, 12–17 (1998).

2. Two of the most provocative and enlightening accounts of these processes are Max Weber, *The Prot-*

the conflicts that were the culmination of this process of imagining the individual subject. That vision of contract, and that imagination of the subject, in turn govern the way Americans think about contract even today.

This formulation raises two questions: First, what is the content of this imagined subject? Second, how does the process of imagining the individual subject take place in the contractual arena?

The calculating subject is the individual with market consciousness, for whom most things can be reduced to market goods and their ultimate and ultimately abstracted measure, money. Writing at the turn of the twentieth century, Georg Simmel remarked that one could "characterize the intellectual functions that are used at present in coping with the world and in regulating both individual and social relations as *calculative* functions."[3] For Simmel, money is both the key to the process of becoming calculable, and the ultimate example of the kind of abstraction that cleanses objects of character. Importantly, the abstract form that represents the value of objects eventually

> reflects upon the objects themselves. . . . If it is true that the art of a period gradually determines the way we look at nature, and if the artist's spontaneous and subjective abstraction from reality forms the apparently immediate sensuous picture of nature in our consciousness, then so too will the superstructure of money relations erected above qualitative reality determine much more radically the inner image of reality according to its forms.[4]

The system of exchange prevalent in a developed money economy encourages recurring descriptions of objects in terms of their money value, and that in turn leads to their appreciation or understanding primarily as holders of such value, fungible in all senses. Money describes value, and objects increasingly correspond to its rationalization, precision, and calculation.

Contract at the turn of the twentieth century takes part in this same economy of generating calculability. The imagined individual of theoretical contract discourse begins as an abstraction describing the real-world persons, natural and corporate, who engage in contractual activity. But this image does not stop at description. Instead, it transforms the objects it pur-

---

estant Ethic and the Spirit of Capitalism (Talcott Parsons trans., 3d ed. 1985), and Albert O. Hirschman, *The Passions and the Interests* (1977).

3. Georg Simmel, *The Philosophy of Money* 444 (Tom Bottomore and David Frisby trans., David Frisby ed., 2d ed. 1990) (1900).

4. Id. at 445.

ports to describe. The "inner image of reality" is transformed as it sheds the characteristics of communal connection, passion, anxiety, beneficence, trust, in favor of precision and cold calculation.

Perhaps the leading contemporary ideologue of free contract summed up this vision: "In the United States more than anywhere else, the social structure is based on contract, and status is of the least importance. Contract, however, is rational—even rationalistic. It is also realistic, cold, and matter-of-fact. . . . In a state based on contract sentiment is out of place in any public or common affairs." The individual in such a state is an "isolated man," independent and sovereign; he has sloughed off ties to family, leaving himself relations that are "open and free, but . . . also loose." His personal independence has led him to the point where he has only a minimal need for government, no need of labor unions, and indeed he has reached "the point where personal liberty supplants the associative principle."[5]

Classical contract theory took its cues from such a vision of the individual, first by positing this idealization as a working assumption and then reinforcing the image by relying on it as a justification for particular rules. But the idealized image was never an accurate description; indeed, acknowledged as an abstraction, it never needed aspire to accuracy. The image constructed by contract discourse at once denied interdependence and highlighted autonomy.

One source of interdependence denied by contract discourse was the world of relational pairs, whose incidences were determined by law. Relational pairs—master-servant, landlord-tenant, bailor-bailee, principal-agent, even husband-wife—appeared to contract theorists as tainted by the concept of status, and indeed by a world where interdependence was dangerously close to dependence and subservience. With the institutions of slavery and coverture still fresh in their collective legal consciousness, the association of classical theorists between relational pairs and dependence was understandable.

And so, classical theorists developed a *general* theory of contract that in fact limited the scope of the contract idea. Labor and employment and bailment and marriage and a host of other relationships would be pushed out of what antebellum legal scholars had imagined as the realm of contract. More importantly for our purposes here, the image of the contracting

---

5. William Graham Sumner, *What Social Classes Owe to Each Other* 25, 39, 96 (photo. reprint 1972) (New York, Harper and Brothers 1883). See also Amy Dru Stanley, *From Bondage to Contract* 1–4 (1998).

individual changed the taken-for-granted background of contract discourse. For Parsons, writing at midcentury, contract ranged so broadly as to encompass even the duties of care between parent and infant. Such contractual obligation

> is implied by the cares of the past, which have perpetuated society from generation to generation; by that absolute necessity which makes the performance of these duties the condition of the preservation of human life; and by the implied obligation on the part of the unconscious object of this care, that when, by its means, they shall have grown into strength, and age has brought weakness upon those to whom they are thus indebted, they will acknowledge and repay the debt.[6]

Contract was "coordinate and commensurate with *duty*"; it was animated by "common principles which all are supposed to understand and acknowledge"; it connected all members of society in "the web and woof of actual life."[7] The distance between this antebellum individual subject and classical theory's "isolated man" is great indeed, not only at the level of imagery, but also at the level of legal rules. Could we even imagine a greater divide than that between Parsons's discussion of the obligation implied by the cares of the past and the steadfast statement of classical theorists that past consideration is no consideration?

But the image of interdependence rooted in the past was only half the problem for classical theory. Just as threatening was a new type of interdependence looming in the not-so-distant future in the shape of corporate capitalism, most pointedly in its managerial organization of work. The turn of the twentieth century saw a rise in economic concentration, and with it a limitation of "ruinous competition" and an accelerated shift in employment patterns: more and more Americans worked for a small number of (giant) corporations. And the workplace was increasingly managed not by skilled workers themselves serving as shop foremen with wide discretion over work practices, but rather by an army of management engineers, equipped with a scientific technique explicitly designed to rationalize the workplace.[8]

---

6. 1 Theophilus Parsons, *The Law of Contracts* 3–4 (1st ed., Boston, Little, Brown 1853).

7. Id. at 4.

8. See David Montgomery, *The Fall of the House of Labor: The Workplace, the State, and American Labor Activism, 1865–1925*, pp. 214–56 (1987); Naomi R. Lamoreaux, *The Great Merger Movement in American Business, 1895–1904*, pp. 1–13 (1985); Alfred D. Chandler, Jr., *The Visible Hand: The Managerial Revolution in American Business* 411–14, 484–93 (1977); John Fabian Witt, *The Accidental Republic: Crippled Work-*

Two aspects of this transformation bear emphasis. First, economic concentration under the corporate form had wide ranging *cultural* effects. It changed not only business practices, but also people's perceptions of the shape of the market, the social body, and its elements. Critics of economic concentration as well as its most ardent proponents were joined in understanding the rise of the corporation as entailing the decline of entrepreneurial capitalism and with it, the decline of the freeholder or small producer as the model of the modern subject. Journalist and cultural critic Walter Lippmann, for example, claimed that corporate concentration was "sucking the life out of private property," and that theories of autonomous personality based on older notions of property would have to be reexamined if not discarded altogether. John D. Rockefeller understood the significance of the new corporate order in even simpler terms: "The day of combination is here to stay. Individualism is gone, never to return."[9]

Second, just as the number of people working in large industrial concerns was mushrooming, scientific management was cutting away at the individuality and the autonomy of the worker. Frederick Winslow Taylor, one of the founders of scientific workplace management, claimed that scientific management involved "a great mental revolution," a revolution geared perhaps more toward managers than workers. With actual production processes broken down to the minutest details of physical movement, workers often felt like they were being reduced to parts in a machine, and new managers were encouraged to view laborers instrumentally. While some would rail against the mechanization of the worker's body as others would hail the advent of new levels of cooperation, one thing was clear: the individual was in decline. As Taylor testified before Congress in 1912, the new scientific management would be "entirely impossible with the independent individualism which characterizes the old type of management."[10]

Against this background, the legal arena was one more locus of cultural engagement over the shape of the individual. As John Witt has recently

---

ingmen, Destitute Widows, and the Remaking of American Law 103–9 (2004); James Livingston, *Origins of the Federal Reserve System: Money, Class, and Corporate Capitalism, 1890–1913*, pp. 55–57 (1986).

9. Walter Lippmann, *Drift and Mastery: An Attempt to Diagnose the Current Unrest* 45 (William E. Leuchtenburg ed., 1961) (1914); Rockefeller quoted in Alan Trachtenberg, *The Incorporation of America: Culture and Society in the Gilded Age* 86 (1982). See also James Livingston, *Pragmatism and the Political Economy of Cultural Revolution, 1850–1940*, pp. 66–77 (1994).

10. Frederick Winslow Taylor, "Taylor's Testimony Before the Special House Committee," in *Scientific Management* 30–31, 76 (1947). See also Livingston, *Pragmatism and Cultural Revolution*, 89–95.

shown, one of the key inroads that scientific management would make in transforming traditional individualism was through workmen's compensation programs. These programs enhanced managerial responsibility and with it managerial control; their working principle was that workplace accidents and consequently employees had to be managed in the aggregate, rather than as individuals. Lawyers were quick to understand that sanctioning workmen's compensation programs would erode at least the legal image of individualism and personal responsibility embedded in tort law. By about 1915, however, the battle over workmen's compensation had been fought, and the legitimacy of workmen's compensation statutes had been established.[11]

Classical contract theory was wary of interdependence in both these forms, but it reached out to both the past and the future in order to build an image of the contracting individual. The imagined individual subject of classical theory was in part an allusion to the republican tradition. This was the individual imagined as self-possessed property holder, sole entrepreneur, responsible and independent. Indeed, this aspect of the contracting subject is figured quite precisely in what historians refer to as free labor ideology.[12] The actual existence or prominence of such a contracting subject is secondary; the figure of such a subject was clearly salient, its image forming a clear point of identification in building a theory of contract.

The other aspect of classical theory's imagined individual was forward-looking, embodying a spirit of calculative rationality difficult to imagine prior to the classical period. Interestingly, the spirit of calculation is closely analogous to that evinced in scientific management itself. The cardinal feature of the calculative ideal is the ability to make decisions on the basis of functional equivalents, which requires that the decision-making agent be able to make accurate and precise comparisons among the elements of exchange. The structurally necessary condition for such calculation, as the founders of modern sociology have famously shown, is a developed money economy. But while money is a necessary condition, by itself it is not sufficient. In order for calculation to take hold, market actors must be able to view exchanges abstractly, paring away extraneous features that threaten to cloud the essence of exchanging values. In its purest form, calculation en-

11. See Witt, *Accidental Republic*, 109–22, 171–86.

12. See, e.g., Christopher L. Tomlins, *Law, Labor, and Ideology in the Early American Republic* 259–92 (1993); Robert J. Steinfeld, *The Invention of Free Labor* 147–56 (1991); Stanley, *From Bondage to Contract*, 1–10.

tails a leveling of all goods, services, assets, or utilities potentially available to an individual. For the calculating attitude to be complete, all qualitative differences are erased, and all things may be compared as values, endlessly interchangeable for one another.[13]

Classical contract assumed contractors who could calculate in this abstract manner, not as a matter of description, but as a matter of theory. The assumption of calculation is encapsulated in the theory of consideration, which at once strips the past of meaning (past consideration is no consideration) and at the same time assumes equivalence while denying the law's capacity for examining consideration's adequacy. The refusal to examine the adequacy of consideration is a statement of contract law's confidence that contracting parties always calculate and trade on the basis of constitutively equivalent values. What Ian Macneil has called "presentiation," or the bringing of future value to a present exchange, is an additional aspect of contract's commitment to the calculating attitude.[14]

Clearly, few human beings actually approach this calculative ideal. However, there is a contracting individual who more closely aspires to it: the corporation. The corporation, as disembodied individual subject, comes close to assuming the powers of abstraction and calculation that contract theory lays at its own foundations. The corporation ignores affective ties with impunity (and without pangs of conscience), indeed advancing as its virtue the seeking of profit for its shareholders. It can plausibly be characterized as single-minded. To adapt Karl Polanyi's phrase, it subordinates society to the market.[15] And thus, it is the corporation that becomes the model of contractual man. But if the corporation is the imagined individual of modern contract, and if, to turn a phrase on its head, contract would become the nexus of corporations, what place would autonomy hold in the vision of contract? Would justifications of contract that rely on autonomy have a place in a world of contract based on the corporation as the contracting subject?

---

13. See Simmel, *Philosophy of Money*, 443–46; 1 Max Weber, *Economy and Society* 80–94, 107–9 (Guenther Roth and Claus Wittich eds., 1978).

14. "Presentiation is a way of looking at things in which a person perceives the effect of the future on the present. . . . [T]he presentiation of a transaction involves restricting its expected future effects to those defined in the present, *i.e.*, at the inception of the transaction." Ian R. Macneil, "Contracts: Adjustment of Long-Term Economic Relations Under Classical, Neoclassical, and Relational Contract Law," 72 *Nw. U. L. Rev.* 854, 863 (1978). See generally Ian R. Macneil, *The New Social Contract* (1980).

15. See Karl Polanyi, *The Great Transformation* 68–76 (1944).

To sum up: The abstracted ideal subject of classical contract teetered on a precarious perch between two different forms of interdependence, one based in the past, the other in the future. The past was the interdependence of standardized relationships, of local communities, of a well-regulated society; the future would be the interdependence of large-scale industrialized society, of man in the organization. At the same time, the idealized subject reached out to two different images of independence and autonomy, one culled from the past and one in the process of becoming. From the past came the republican image of the self-possessed individual, the product of free labor ideology; from the future, the ultrarational calculator. The work of creating the individual subject in contract discourse may then be seen as double: on the one hand, a distancing from past and future (in short, from history); on the other, an appropriation of idealized elements of that same history. The case law is not the advancement of a position in these debates, but rather a locus of cultural conflict. It exhibits a working through, a negotiation, an endless series of reformulations of possibilities of the position of the subject, together working toward a mediation of conflicting visions.

I have concentrated on three realms in which the calculating subject was conjured and reinforced by the classical revolution in the conception of contract. By banishing gift promises from the kingdom of the enforceable, contract theory helped purge the complex entanglements of the past. Rationalizing consideration doctrine meant limiting the ways in which obligations based on family and friendship, rather than calculable economic interaction, could be recognized and integrated into legal duties. By internalizing the logic of speculation and insurance, contract provided for the taming of an uncertain present. Statistical calculation, based on the law of large numbers, of the chances of rise and fall in value or of life and death, fed the illusion of a world susceptible to scientific management. Finally, by positing the contracting parties as the sole source of obligations, a formal vision of contract put the individual in control of a future he may never have considered.

So how does this calculating subject become the individual of contract? As should be clear, it is not a question of a particular doctrinal rule being adopted or rejected. No rule of contract law could establish the image of the autonomous individual as the subject of contract. In that sense, there is no position within the discourse upon which the shape of the individual turns. This is because subjects are created by discourse itself, and not by a position within that discourse. It is not the articulation of any particular argument in the debates over contract rules that creates the individual, but rather the framework of the debate itself. And the framework, by its very ubiquity, becomes almost unseen, nearly invisible. In this sense, imagining the individual is an ideological project: the "individual" is a role in the drama of private ordering. That role is created by the balance of positions in a discourse, a discourse whose persuasive force hinges on its ability to veil its own constitutive power.

The work of the classical revolution in contract was to establish a new framework for the debate of contractual questions. This framework, in turn, at once relied on and established a new contractual subject: autonomous, calculating, and calculable. The success of the framework lay in establishing the parameters for argumentation. The framework was formal, then, in just the sense that formality is considered in the field of art, as Bloom and Simmel both tell us. It establishes the rules of relevance, the criteria of visibility. Validity of the contractual relation turns, within the new framework, on bargains that make up economic exchange. Personal loyalties, moral obligations, and familial connections are expunged. The fear of damnation is submerged into the mechanics of a rational coping with risk. The indeterminacy of the future is reduced to an all-encompassing exchange of entitlement at the moment of contract formation. We become interested only in the question of the presence of a formal bargain. Finally, we translate the idea of the formal bargain into an undertaking that can only be adopted by a willing free agent, and we label the undertaking a promise.

Thus, with contractual obligation having been engulfed by the classical framework, it is widely accepted, within legal academia and outside it, that contract law is about enforcing promises.[16] That acceptance is the first measure of the success of the classical revolution in contract thinking. More than positing a new definition of contract, the classical revolution was so sweeping as to generate a reinterpretation of the history of contract.[17] Based

16. One clear indication stems from definitions: Pollock's definition, discussed at length in Chapter 1, became the basis for the most traditional and widely accepted American definitions of contract. See *Restatement of Contracts* § 1 (1932) ("A contract is a promise or a set of promises for the breach of which the law gives a remedy, or the performance of which the law in some way recognizes as a duty"); *Restatement (Second) of Contracts* § 1 (1981) (same); 1 Samuel Williston, *The Law of Contracts* § 1 (1st ed. 1920) ("A contract is a promise, or set of promises, to which the law attaches legal obligation").

17. Grant Gilmore famously commented that classical scholars, primary among them Holmes, Langdell, and Williston, had to perform "major surgery" on the cases in order to arrive at their general theory of contract, and he offered competing readings of several leading cases to justify his viewpoint. See Grant

on an understanding instilled in every student of contract since the late nineteenth century, we have all been trained to read the history of contract backward, as the often misunderstood but finally perfected art of enforcing promises. It has become nearly impossible to read the history of contract without initially conceiving of contract as an issue of enforcing promises, whence the necessity of dividing promises into the enforceable and unenforceable kinds. In this sense, the classical thinkers established a metaphysics of contract, reasoning that earlier conceptions of contract were primitive, unperfected, incomplete, but that the real basis of contract was eternal.

My claim in this book has not been that all such views are based on a misunderstanding. Indeed, as much as it is a mode of economic regulation, contract is a conception, an intellectual construct: it is primarily what people believe it to be. The popular belief is not wrong. But there may be better beliefs available, if someone has the impulse to look. This book does not seek to establish an alternative metaphysics of contract. It does, however, suggest that it would be more useful to think about contract as a framework for cooperation, the central element of which is the set of relationships whose terms are potentially regulated by the state.[18] This conception is both a better account of judicial practice, and a way to improve on that practice by ridding it of those commitments that have the effect of limiting contract's fairness-promoting, or redistributive potential.[19] Contract is a conception, and thus, it may be reconceived, or reimagined. A prod to our imagination, and a reminder that the current conception is neither timeless nor transcendent, is the fact that only a century and a half ago, contract was conceived of quite differently. The transformation of contract is tied to complex economic and social changes, but its technical doctrinal manifestation is visible in the work of classical theorists. My claim here has been that what classical

---

Gilmore, *The Death of Contract* 24 (2d ed. 1995). Gilmore's history and theory have become objects of routine disparagement, but Gilmore's first calling was literary criticism, and his insights into the Nietzschean mode by which the classical interpretation of contract became dominant, and its violence in ousting previously popular interpretations of contract, remain salient. By subjecting the cases to a rereading, and by emphasizing how controversial the classical interpretations and classifications of the cases were when they appeared, Gilmore reminds us of the creative power of classical theorizing.

18. One of the important parts of such a view of contract would be some account of how potential regulation works, not only when the potential is exercised, but also when it remains in the shadows, since the refusal of the state to exercise power over a given relationship allows whoever wields power within the relationship to violate the relationship's norms with impunity.

19. At least one scholar has made the case that the best reading of the history of contract should place the fairness of distribution at its center, while retaining the focus on promise enforcement. See James Gordley, "Enforcing Promises," 83 *Cal. L. Rev.* 547, 548 (1995).

contract theory undertook piecemeal, it achieved wholesale. The rhetorical framework that made enforcing promises into the centerpiece of contract retains its power today, and perhaps is the major factor limiting contract's transformative potential.

Index

The authorized representative in the EU for product safety and compliance is:
Mare Nostrum Group
B.V Doelen 72
4831 GR Breda
The Netherlands

www.ingramcontent.com/pod-product-compliance
Lightning Source LLC
LaVergne TN
LVHW091516200926
848483LV00005B/428/J
* 9 7 8 0 8 0 4 7 5 3 9 8 2 *